FROM A BIOGRAPHY OF MYSELF

Books by Robert Henriques

NOVELS

No Arms, No Armour
Captain Smith and Company
The Journey Home
Through the Valley
A Stranger Here
Red over Green
The Commander

ESSAY

The Cotswolds

TRAVEL

Death by Moonlight

HISTORY

One Hundred Hours to Suez

BIOGRAPHY

Marcus Samuel, First Viscount Bearsted
Sir Robert Waley Cohen

From a biography of myself

a posthumous selection of the autobiographical
writings of

ROBERT HENRIQUES

LONDON · SECKER & WARBURG

First published in England 1969 by
Martin Secker & Warburg Limited
14 Carlisle Street, London W1V 6NN

© Veronica Gosling 1969

SBN 436 19304 3

Printed in Great Britain by
Western Printing Services Ltd, Bristol

Contents

Contents

Acknowledgment

I would like to acknowledge the massive editorial help given me in the preparation of this book by David Farrer who was at Rugby and Oxford with my father, and without whose assistance I would have been sorely at a loss, particularly in the central chapter of this book.

V.G.H. 1968

Foreword

Robert Henriques was born in London on 11 December 1905, to one of the oldest Jewish families in England. Like many of his ancestors for the preceding four or five generations, he entered the Regular Army at the conclusion of his education at Rugby School and New College, Oxford. After serving as an officer in the Royal Artillery for seven years he retired in 1933.

In 1937 he published his first book, *Death by Moonlight*, an account of one of his big-game hunting expeditions in Central Africa, and a treatise on the Arab tribes to be found in Western Sudan and on the borders of French Equatorial Africa. His first novel was published in England in November 1939, when it won the All-Nations Prize Novels competition. This book, *No Arms, No Armour*, was written at Le Trayas, Var, where Henriques lived with his wife and two children for the year preceding the war.

On his retirement from the Regular Army in 1933, Henriques had joined the Territorial Army as a Captain—the volunteer force which was immediately mobilised a few days before the declaration of war—and while at Le Trayas, he took by correspondence a course for Staff Officers which concluded with a few weeks study at the Staff College in July 1939. When this was over, Henriques wrote the short introduction to his novel which ended with the words: "I hope that I may be allowed to work out my three years in undistinguished obscurity and peace."

It was dated 15 August 1939.

In August 1940, Henriques was appointed Brigade Major, Royal Artillery—that is, Chief Divisional Artillery Staff Officer—to a Territorial division that was mobilising. He spent a few weeks in France, near Lille, in February, 1940, and then returned to England to prepare himself for an attachment to the French Army, which was due to start on 20 May. Unhappily this attachment was not possible.

In June 1940, after Dunkirk, Henriques sent his wife and two children to America. He was himself promoted to Major, but that same week there was a call for volunteers for the Commandos that were just being formed, and he chose to revert to his previous rank of Captain in order to raise and command his own Commando Troop, drawn entirely from cavalry and artillery units. He had completed his training, but had not yet had his baptism of fire in May 1941, when the eight Commando units that then existed in England were grouped together into the first Special Service Brigade under the command of Brigadier-General Haydon.

Henriques was almost at once appointed as Staff Captain to the Headquarters of this brigade, and all through the summer and autumn of 1941 was constantly engaged in planning minor operations and in embarking and disembarking in Scotland for operations which, on each occasion, had to be cancelled at the last moment. In November 1941 Henriques became Brigade Major—that is, Chief of Staff—to the Special Service Brigade, and during the next two months planned and took part in operations against German installations in Norway. The most successful of these was the famous Vaagso raid, in which Henriques was military chief of staff.

After the completion of the Norwegian operations, General Haydon and Henriques were transferred to Combined Operations Headquarters, where Admiral Lord Louis Mountbatten was in command. Here they were engaged in launching numerous raids across the Channel and in starting the long-drawn-out planning for the Second Front. It was, in fact, in February 1942 that Henriques was first engaged in examining the project for the liberation of the Cotentin Peninsula. At the same time he was partly responsible for the planning and organisation of the St Nazaire raid.

In the summer of 1942 Henriques was lent to General Eisenhower, who had then set up his headquarters in London; and since it was now apparent that major operations against the French coast were impossible that year, was employed on the planning of the North African landings. At the end of August, Henriques was attached to General Patton, went with him to Washington for the final planning of the Casablanca landings, and subsequently accompanied him on the campaign. He landed with the first American assault troops at Fedala and, for his part in the operation, was awarded the American Silver Star.

Before Henriques embarked with General Patton's forces for the Casablanca landings, he had left in America the manuscript of a book which he had written in spare moments during the previous two years. The famous American poet, the late Stephen Vincent Benet (author of *John Brown's Body*, etc.) agreed to edit this manuscript and to prepare it for American publication. It was published in that country under the title *The Voice of the Trumpet* early in February 1943, and in England under the title of *Captain Smith and Company* in May of that year. It was a compilation of prose and verse woven around the death of a Commando soldier in the sand dunes of the French coast, and the thoughts and emotions of the last few moments of his life.

Before this book was published in England Henriques had already left to rejoin General Patton in North Africa and was there employed planning the Sicilian assaults. Again he accompanied the American 7th Army on the actual operations and served throughout the campaign as General Patton's senior British Staff Officer, and as his personal Liaison Officer with General Montgomery. For his part in this campaign he was awarded the American Bronze Star.

At the conclusion of the Sicilian campaign Henriques returned to England and, until the following spring, was employed on the planning of the Normandy landings. During that summer and autumn he saw service in France, Belgium and Holland on various missions, one of which included a journey with Charles Morgan, first to Paris for the reopening of the Comédie française, and then to the fighting front in Holland where the two authors worked together in writing articles for the American press.

In the autumn of 1943, Henriques had been promoted to full Colonel and was chief military planner at Combined Operations Headquarters; but by the end of 1944, when it was apparent that no further amphibious operations would be necessary in Europe, the planning section was closed down and Henriques was lent to the Ministry of Information for the remainder of the war. In this capacity he was sent to America as the first British author in "speaking campaigns" and, during July and August 1945, served in Germany.

Henriques' novel, *The Journey Home*, was started in North

Africa in May 1943, was continued at odd moments throughout the Sicilian campaign, and was completed shortly before D-day in June 1944. It was published in England in December 1945, and was sold out on the day of publication.

After his demobilisation Henriques was engaged in writing a film script, an official treatise on planning for the War Office and a long novel published in 1950 under the title *Through the Valley*, which won the James Tait Black Memorial Prize.

His wife had returned from America in 1941 and they now had four children, two of whom were born during the war years. The family home was in Gloucestershire in the village where his wife and two sons still live and farm. There Henriques settled to the life of a writer, farmer and broadcaster, taking part frequently in The West of England programmes, *Any Questions*, under the questionmaster Freddy Grisewood, and publishing seven further books. One was a guide-book, *The Cotswolds*, there were two novels, *A Stranger Here* and *Red over Green*, and a posthumously published novel *The Commander*. There were also two biographies, *Marcus Samuel, First Viscount Bearsted* (who was his wife's grandfather) and *Sir Robert Waley Cohen*. He was invited to deliver the Cavendish Lecture in 1961 and chose as his subject "The Expression of Experience."

In 1956 he went to Israel and became involved in the country and the people, an attachment that was to intensify during the years leading up to his death. He wrote an account of the 1956 Sinai Campaign, *One Hundred Hours to Suez*, and also became President of a recently formed Anglo-Israeli Organisation called "The Bridge." He had previously taken interest in Anglo-Jewish affairs as President of the Anglo-Jewish Association, and on the committees and council respectively of the Anglo-Jewish Association, Association of Synagogues of Great Britain, and the Board of Deputies of British Jews. He always firmly denied any affiliation with the Zionist cause.

He had also contributed much to the local Gloucestershire country life; he was a member of the local Parish Council and was President of the Coln Valley cricket and football clubs, and was deputy Chairman, with the late John Moore, of the Cheltenham Literary Festival.

Those who knew him locally and those who worked for him found him surprisingly knowledgeable about country life. For two years he contributed a weekly somewhat controversial column to *The Field* entitled "Farmer's Ordinary."

After 1956 he made frequent returns to Israel and it was after one such spell, when he had been gathering material for a book, that he and his wife returned home suddenly, and he died in hospital a few days later.

> Let me be wanting rest
> At the time of the last touch
> Of human breath—
> Kind death
> Let me want you enough!

> Now I want sleep, oh I want sleep,
> But more, even more I want
> What must be done to-morrow,
> My promise to keep.

> Why must I do it, why *me*?
> Always will it be me?
> Even when death comes, he
> Will have to break me away
> From what I must do to-day.
> But perhaps, in my last bed,
> If I wanted to do it enough,
> Others will do it instead.

> Robert Henriques
> 16 January 1962

Introduction

Veronica Henriques

How, and where, after sixty years of versatile living can a man start to describe his own life? I echo my father's fumblings for such a beginning in my own efforts to make an introduction to the following writings of his.

In a confessed muddle I attempt to shake myself free of the countless thoughts that occur to me each time I begin, and of the many interpretations that tempt me to make a personal assessment of a man with whom I was far too closely involved in one way and from whom I was far too remote in another to be truly objective.

I know that my father, in assessing himself, was obsessed by the belief that he was really a coward. I know he suspected that half his acts, cited by others as deeds of bravery, were derived from motives of cowardice. I know that he intended to slant the narrative of his autobiography in such a way that it might, he hoped, disprove this theory.

Unfortunately he had reached no literary conclusion to this problem when he died early in 1967, at which time he found himself deeply immersed in the research for a comprehensive history of the Israeli Defence Forces, an account he was to stretch from Biblical times to the present day. He worked on this book till he literally could not sit for pain. He believed that only he could write the book on the levels he wanted it to be written, professional, personal, and emotional. Israel as a country was the embodiment of what he felt himself to be as a man. Israel as a country answered every personal need of his to be fully involved in every sphere of his interest. It was in Israel that he could function as a Jew, as a writer, as a soldier, as a social worker, as a farmer, and as a man who searched for a unifying sense of himself to set into a historical pattern. Israel, a small country, many of whose people had suffered as a minority elsewhere, fought for the survival, respect, love and efficiency for which my father fought in his own life; this fight he makes abundantly clear in the incomplete and unedited, yet very moving passages that form one of the final chapters of this book. Yet I don't believe this comparison of his personal life with the country he took to with such intensity and relief during the last ten years before he died ever occurred to him. He was never a Zionist, and he remained strongly committed to England; he loved his Gloucestershire home, where he found a complement to all his more restless and violent inner and outer experiences. All the same, in England, he no longer found an outlet for his talents and his passions.

Unhappily he left the Israeli History in note form only and it cannot be completed.

Of his own autobiography, two chapters, one a description of his schooldays, and the other his description of the 1942 landings in North Africa during the Second World War, were completed, and they are published here as he left them, virtually untouched. If there are inaccuracies it is because I am incompetent to correct them.

My father's intention, had he lived, was to compose his autobiography as a series which would include volumes of fiction, fact, poetry and drama, letters and fragments, and through these he meant to discover that from the ashes of a succession of personal failures had emerged an equal number of personal successes. This series he wished to call *The Phoenix Cycle. The Commander*, published posthumously in 1967, was the first of the intended series. His intention is partly realised in the publication here of the two passages he completed, in which he shows that from the awful debris of his schooldays he was able to construct a foundation upon which he built a sizable reputation in the adult world of men, which was one of the things he most desired. Nevertheless he despised himself for this most natural need. He hated himself for courting an approval without which he was to feel rejected.

In order to write of the very painful experience, and yet always important experience to him, that his schooldays were, my father decided to split his hero into two characters: that of Laurence Lamego, who is himself, and that of Laurence Lamego's cousin who is the "I" of the first chapter. In this way he felt free to write of himself more honestly without having to face an accusation of being overwhelmed by self-pity. My instinct was to omit the use of this device, but I am persuaded against my instinct by my father's friend and publisher, David Farrer, who tells me that the use of the first person by my father was quite deliberate and that he would not be dissuaded from this use.

My father, searching for an opening to his autobiography, a place at which to begin and a manner in which to begin it, writes:

> At various times, at various ages of my life, I have been so miserable a failure in several different spheres of endeavour, so sunk in the glutinous sin of self-pity and allowing myself to suffer so intolerably, that I cannot possibly write autobiographically of the constituent events. I must write as a novelist, who, myself, in the main dislikes my hero. I may therefore try and even hope to be both objective and accurate while not sparing myself the tears with which I have often refreshed my characters in their sadder encounters.

Maybe a novelist like my father, who uses his own experience so directly in work, in self-defence should not turn his insight towards himself and leave it there to fester. After all, his craft relies on the business of projection. I feel that my father's creative sensibility became a torturer's worst weapon when he pointed it back at himself; this he did when the impulse to explore, investigate and justify became cornered by his physical disability, and began to eat inwards, becoming cruel and destructive towards his personality. What emerges in much of my father's unprepared material is a portrait loaded against himself, both physically and intellectually; it is a castigation I find hard to bear. It is an intellectual suffering he seemed determined to administer to himself. He seemed intent in much of this writing on justifying the physical pain he was suffering in terms of self-analytical anguish.

A friend of his who has read some of the material in the latter chapter of this book said to me, "But this is not Robert as he was; you must describe the true Robert." He meant the intense, active, humorous man functioning to the point of exhausting those with whom he was; provocative, sometimes frightening for those near to him, but never dull, never still; he meant the man who in full health was constantly challenging the hierarchy whatever it was, who had to attack the status quo, and to undermine what he thought was the complacency with which the public would accept what he considered were intolerable conditions ("intolerable" was one of his favourite words), conditions which, in his terms of reference could relate to any kind of public inefficiency, from policies of agriculture to a telephone exchange which kept him waiting too long or even cut him off altogether.

To be cut off was what he most dreaded, and it was when illness severed him from the kind of hectic activity to which he was driven by nature that the despair, which his friend does not recognise in his work, ran riot. It was then that he delved into his past attempting to find in the sum of his experience a reassurance of achievement that had previously come from a public who listened to his broadcasts, read his books, or employed his brain in the defence of the country: this reassurance appears to have eluded him. His friends have said, "Robert was *not* an unhappy man."

I have by now been immersed in his unpublished writings, many very fragmentary and repetitive, for some time, and also during the last ten years of his life I had a full correspondence with him. I do not feel competent to say which is the true man.

What I do think is that the physical pain of my father's later years actively recalled to him his mental misery as a child, and even recreated for him the dread of being forgotten or rejected. He made it abundantly clear on many occasions what a miserable period that of his childhood had been and this even left him with such a deep dislike of young children that he used to physically recoil as they entered the room and even at the approaching sound of their voices.

I was once walking in the garden with him and he was expounding to me on the great pleasures of being a grandparent. At that moment one of his grandchildren came up to ask a question. "Oh, go away!" he said, flicking the interruption to his train of thought from his path, and continuing his dissertation.

Later, as inevitably the number of grandchildren increased, he managed to hide his instinctive reaction under a stream of anecdotes about these children, making humorous stories out of their various remarks and antics—incidentally enlivening them with considerable skill!

I think many people who were involved with my father might have asked of him the question he asks in this extract:

What is it that provokes this mad dashing about by Lamego from place to place, from one activity to another? What maintains the momentum? Behind the sense of urgency there must be a boiler-room, a stoke-hole, a fuel.

I think a lot of the fuel was provided by his desire and ability to be effective, his determination to eradicate and even justify by end results his early unhappiness and humiliation, and his genuine interest in a great many things.

He had never the temperament to work for long within a particular framework, to take up one activity and pursue it to its end. The pleasure to be gained from this kind of constancy was therefore not to be his. He began many things, but once they were begun, or he had mastered the principle, studied all there was to be studied, possibly become president of the relevant association, his interest would wane, and he delegated, or gave, to others; only his writing continued. His writing and his marriage lasted the years, and his affair with Israel was promising to be continually constructive when he died.

He himself considered that the military period of his life was his prime achievement, and it is this chapter which is by far the most complete of the writings he left, and from the documents and mementoes I have found, he obviously intended to write a good deal more, certainly a good section on his experiences of the Sicilian landings. In this military world of men and crisis he really felt fulfilled. He wrote:

There was just one period when Laurence Lamego was right by those standards of his which were such a burden and torment to him, and this was when he reached a peak of attainment which, in his own retrospective opinion, he will never again equal. Naturally this was during the war, when a soldier was relieved of many of his moral responsibilities as a human being, when mental competence, physical courage and endurance were all that were required of him and when to be expedient was the first Commandment, so that he could often see ahead the deliciously clear path of duty, of intelligent obedience and adequate command.

It was between the autumn of 1942 and the late summer of 1943, when Lamego was thirty-seven years old, that all his powers of spirit, mind and body seemed, in the military sense, to be fully mobilised and co-ordinated. As a person he became an effective force; he was dedicated to a purpose within his scope; and, most important of all, he was aware of this fulfilment.

Perhaps, after all the preliminary ordeals of training and preparation from infancy to that date, he then reached the summit of his capacities; if so, there is sense in his feeling today that all lesser summits are of no consequence to his private ambitions and there is not much point, even if it were possible, in repeating the same achievement. Nobody surely wants to climb up Everest twice?

And yet, I wonder if my father did not, in his relationship with Israel, catch a glimpse once more of the summit of his Everest? For in Israel he was a hero. Writing of the Suez War in 1956 he was in his element. Did his "other chance" lie in his relationship to Israel?

"To every man his Everest? That is the tremendous question which makes the middle-aged of the world go crying for another chance, another chance, just as they clutched at the angry skirts and gasped, screamed, sobbed in their earliest nursery, 'Please, please, give me another chance, just one more chance' . . ."

The following passage is dated 1957, one year after he had "found" Israel, ten years before his death. (I should explain that the origin of the nickname "Meego" for Laurence Lamego is to be described in the early chapter of the book.)

By Meego's private reckoning, his military life is the central theme of himself. At no time was this unhappy man so little unhappy as when he was first commissioned into the Royal Artillery from Oxford; and it was during the middle stretches of the war that he must have reached the peak of his powers and, more significant, of his importance. But this book shall not be allowed to become a memoir of his wartime experiences, salted with scandalous comments within the frame of a biographical note. His military life is interesting only in its relation to his other lives as a novelist and journalist, an unsuccessful businessman, a farmer of thirteen hundred acres, and, above all as a Jew, a member of one of the oldest Anglo-Jewish families who was a non-Zionist, until Israel summoned him at last.

My father was a very liberal Jew and although he considered it an important duty to participate himself in Anglo-Jewish life at one time and sit on various committees, he rarely went to synagogue or imposed a similar sense of obligation on his family. His sons were vaguely encouraged to learn Hebrew and there was the odd, amazing and somewhat hilarious emotional outburst about twice a year at his home deep in the Cotswold countryside, when candles were lit on a Friday night and dusty prayer books suddenly produced. Otherwise his family were brought up as any well-to-do unreligious English country children were brought up; we were sent to good conventional public schools and much encouraged to enjoy the pleasant but expensive country pursuits of hunting, shooting and fishing. We were encouraged to be loyal, ambitious, effective, honest and brave, the latter perhaps being of the most importance to my father. But he himself was always very aware of being a Jew, and his Jewishness became increasingly significant to him as he got older; he cared more about ancestry, and this was a fact which perhaps influenced his life, more than his family, by their upbringing, might have known.

He was very much a man who lived a life of emotional peaks and chasms, which meant that if he were not on a peak he must be in a chasm. Why did he have to be so high in order not to be so low? He was a man who only went to a lecture if he were the lecturer; he once told me that he had never bathed on a public beach or travelled by public transport.

Is some part of the explanation for this in the following paragraph?

> He [Lamego] wasted his powers in the pursuit of courage, in flight from cowardice, in trying to expunge shame which he was never really justified in feeling. He asked a lot. He wanted to be an ordinary but remarkable person, remarkable in the most ordinary way. Unable to bring himself to be extraordinary (in the literal and most modest sense of that word) he wanted to be like everyone else, but more so.

And what is more he wanted all his friends and his family to be like everyone else but more so! And whether they were or not he convinced himself that it was so; he exaggerated the qualities of his friends to his children, and those of his children to his friends. He was very much prone to the conversational pleasures of over-statement, although I think he often really believed what he was saying. Exaggeration was a feature of his talk, rather than his writing, and I often sat listening with others to his story of some hilarious adventure and it was not until I heard myself mentioned by name I realised that I too had been there!

He was a man who extracted great pleasure from his family, and especially out of his very fond and dependent relationship with his wife, "Your mother," he wrote in a letter to me, "Makes me laugh more than anyone I have ever known. Have you ever realised how much laughing at people contributes to attraction for them . . ." and writing of marriage on another occasion he wrote: "Do not believe people who say that understanding, deep affection, intellectual relationships or anything else can ever replace, or be as strong as, the inexpressible understanding of mutual physical love."

And yet, there is no direct mention amongst all the material he had gathered together for his autobiography of the domestic side of his life. There is no mention in this material that was supposed to add up to a factual image of the man of the pleasant home life which was in fact of extreme importance to him. By which I mean no mention of the physical pleasures in which he indulged, not only of love, but of walking round his land, of looking at his stock and his machinery, of strolling round his garden, to which he was constantly adding, planting another tree, another shrub, planning a pool. One might think, reading some of the unedited material that he was never free from the assault of nagging memory, humiliating incident and endless struggle. But this is not true. So, which man was he? The farmer discussing the genetics of his herd of cattle and which crop to put in which field, the country gentlemen presiding over the local cricket club or speaking at a meeting of the Rural District Council, the man gloating over his first editions of D. H. Lawrence and Hardy, the patron of the arts with the drawings he had just bought from an unknown but promising young artist, or the music lover, listening amazed (he was always rather amazed by musical beauty) to his large collection of the classics to which he responded emotionally, utterly unintellectually in this respect, or the host stimulating the conversation of his guests with carefully-chosen wines? Were all these aspects of the man only peripheral to the central core of his being?

Was he really forever the persecuted Jew, struggling in a hostile world, dogged by private standards of living to which he could not attain? He writes: "After saying so much, need I add the obvious—that Lamego is a Jew? That he still has a trace of Jewish self-pity, self-hatred and consequential arrogance which he has always despised and sought to escape from?"

Perhaps because he was a man of such diverse interests, he found it particularly difficult to decided on a beginning for his autobiography:

> Laurence Lamego had done a lot of very interesting things, all quite unrelated to each other, during the first fifty years of his life. As a rolling stone he had gathered so many different

kinds of moss that by now he is a relatively rare exhibit. But anyone can roll through life, and his revolutions have very little significance unless he has rolled to some purpose. Perhaps Meego has? This question is the excuse for this book. Was there any trail of cause and effect, any rhyme or design about his serpentine way?

Obviously in his search for the rhyme and design of his life my father, as a writer, wanted to make of his life a good book; in a way, to him, the value of experience was the recording of it; and yet from this very intention a highly misleading account of that life might have emerged, for, from the mass of notes and material he'd collected, he would have made cuts to this literary purpose rather than for the truer, and possibly less entertaining and saleable, one of self-exploration.

Nevertheless the exploration has value in itself for the quality of its writing as well as for the exposition of another dimension to a life ended prematurely by cancer.

My father left many odd paragraphs and whole long passages marked START HERE, and ANOTHER START? NO GOOD I THINK? and so on. I have no idea which one would have been the final choice, perhaps he would have begun it with the schoolboy chapter after all, although from this particular attempt it would seem unlikely.

> Where to begin the story of Laurence Lamego, the biography of a man who once was not unknown to the public and rated a success in most people's view but a failure in his own; as a person whose violent spasmodic efforts to live, rather than just exist have been original enough to be interesting.
> Where to begin his story?
> Almost anywhere except at the beginning. Because if there is a discernible pattern in a man's life and if you are trying to trace it, then the beginning of the story must be as significant as the middle or the end. But if you try to observe those scenes of infancy, childhood, schooldays and adolescence all through the lens significant to the whole you are bound to distort unduly which is what I want to avoid. I want to be accurate. I hope that if I first try to give a brief view of the whole pattern, then the incidents that I have to record may reveal their significance on their own account.

I think that in fact his unpolished work is as revealing of his kind of caring, of the things that really influenced many of his acts, as are his carefully prepared, finely written and conceived chapters.

I have therefore extracted as many of the fragments of his work as I could, and I have interfered as little as possible with them. Some consist of only a page or two, others are almost complete incidents in themselves which he certainly would have included almost as they are somewhere in his proposed series. I have included the "Oxford" passages in a slim section of their own as they are "finished" though not "complete." I have occasionally inserted a brief sentence of explanation where bits of his are either very repetitive or so muddled by his own notes and counter-notes that they are illegible or incoherent. Some passages I have included even though they repeat, but from another angle, what has already been said in another passage or in the finished chapters themselves. Some of the briefest extracts, attempts to grab a moment and swing from it, I have already quoted in this introduction.

I would like to say, in conclusion, that my father was always a man who responded magnificently to crisis: this was so during moments of personal danger during the war, and it was certainly so at the time of his death when his humour and love of battle kept him defying the authority up to the last moment.

I telephoned to him in his last hospital room and had to wait for a long time for a breathless answer: "Oh, it's you," he said, "I've been having a battle with the sister who insists it's good for a dying patient to be kept in a howling draught. I have had to climb up on a ledge to reach a tiny window kept open by an ingenious system of old rope and rusty hinges and I expect I've ruined any chance I had of survival in the effort, but the window is now shut and at least I shan't die in a draught!" He did not. He died surrounded by his children, with his wife sitting close to him in his room working on some tapestry. The day after he died there appeared his photograph and a long obituary in *The Times*. It is the sort of thing he would have loved, it was almost his ideal: a loving family, and public acknowledgment.

I believe this is what he longed for but did not dare to expect.

One of the things which we all miss most from my father's death are the immensely humorous times we all enjoyed with him. He loved people at whom he could laugh; his laughter was his kind of loving.

SCHOOLDAYS

I

Greenaways

Hillmorton Rd,
Rugby

Darling Mother,

The food is very bad now. Oswald has to say it is good in his letters because he says his mother would immediately write to Evers and he would never hear the last of it. We are keeping a list of the food we get to send you. We never go a day without their being some complaint about the food and quite often the meat or fish at BOTH breakfast and tea will be uneatable. For instance "lentil pie" is a sort of stodgy mess looking from outside like a fish cake. Then sort of compressed meat in slices all sodden, and pork pies, with goodness knows what meat inside and sausage rolls, with no meat at all. Then we got liver, which was also absolutely like leather and you couldn't bite at all. Lunches are good, I suppose because Evers has them with us and has to have the same as us. The porridge at breakfast though lumpy is quite good and the bread, milk and potatoes are all right, though the fish is usually unbearable and once the head of the house had to send it out because it was so bad. You won't write to Evers about it will you? I should never hear the last of it. Of course it may only be a bad spell because sometimes for several days we get quite good food, like once we got poached eggs and fishcakes on the same day . . .

In these days when Laurence Lamego was a schoolboy the inferiority complex was scarcely invented, or it would have been held responsible for Laurence Lamego's irritating, indeed infuriating, efforts to attract attention to himself when every shrinking instinct bade him succumb to his secret but intense shyness, his lack of confidence, his sense of insecurity (it would nowadays be detected and described) and to seek safety in ordinariness. I suspect that he used to pray to be ordinary; but rising from his prayers, he would forthwith behave in a manner which made him as extraordinary, and as unpleasantly extraordinary, as anyone could imagine.

From his earliest nursery days Laurence was always a nuisance. Being the eldest of a family of four in the charge of a series of old-

3

fashioned nannies, attended by harassed nursery-maids who were preoccupied with their own problems of adolescence and six flights of stairs from basement-kitchen to nursery-floor, Laurence, the nuisance, was intolerable in that nursery and attracted traditional retribution. His childhood became nothing much else but a succession of punishments administered automatically when any of the other four children misbehaved—all misbehaviour being certainly due to the bad influence and example of Master Laurence—and since a proportion of such punishments were in fact unjust, the sum effect was to convince him that the order of humanity was one of injustice.

At the age of eight, Laurence was taken from the last in succession of his exhausted and exasperated governesses and bustled off to a boarding school. The household had had enough of him. Moreover Laurence's father, the Doctor, who had long been a member of the Territorial Army, was due to go to France with the first London Territorial Division in the autumn of 1914. The paternal responsibility of selecting a suitable school was surrendered to the military necessities, and Laurence was packed off to Greenaways simply because a cousin had been there and found the place not unpleasant, while his youngest uncle [Basil L. Q. Henriques] had been there fifteen years earlier and had actually enjoyed it.

Those fifteen years had made a big difference to the school, because the headmaster, who was known to everyone as Bumpus, although his name was quite different, had slowly developed from a liberal-minded and sympathetic young hearty, who had been captain of England at both Rugby football and cricket, into an elderly blimp. In his earlier days Bumpus might have made a reasonable job of knocking Laurence into shape. In 1914, when he was just about to retire from his headmastership, but decided to carry on as his contribution to the war effort, he had forgotten that there was any other way of knocking a child into shape except knocking him about. When you knock a Lamego child about, no matter how undersized, grubby, repulsive, pimply and pasty-faced he may appear, his resilience is somehow summoned from his deepest inheritance and he responds by becoming even bloodier-minded than before. This is what happened at Greenaways. In fact, Laurence was doomed to misery at school from the moment when Bumpus welcomed the new boy with his customary speech: "All you need is to keep your eye on the ball, love God, do what you're told—and we'll make a man of you."

From the point of popularity with his fellow-pupils there was only one of these injunctions that mattered, and that was the first, and Lamego was totally unable to keep his eye on any ball. The fact that he was perhaps the only one of all the new boys who genuinely loved God, so far from helping him, caused his immediate downfall. On his very first Sunday he was scragged by all the other boys of the bottom form for being detected in school chapel singing "Onward Jewish Soldiers" during the concluding hymn.

I must make it clear that the school was not in the least anti-semitic in principle. One of the rules upon which old Bumpus insisted most firmly was that, as subjects of abuse between school-boys, neither parentage nor religion were permissible. This rule was generally accepted and obeyed. Neither Basil Henriques nor I had ever been subjected to anti-semitic persecution, although everyone knew perfectly well that we were Jews. Laurence was persecuted not because he was a Jew, but because he was a horrid little boy and needed persecuting, and since the process of perse-cuting anybody requires you to discover his most vulnerable point and keep on attacking it, Laurence's Jewishness was the obvious target.

To make it even worse for Laurence, it happened that his home was conducted with extreme priggishness. Whereas any other father would occasionally resort, in moments of intense irritation, to such expletives as "Damn it," or "Blast," such expressions would never be heard in the Lamego household, and indeed, if Laurence's mother had not been the first cousin of my father, and if our families had not known each other for a couple of centuries, Laurence would not have been allowed inside our house for fear of contamination from our rougher speech. It was I who, after my first term at Greenaways, played the familiar schoolboy trick on Laurence (I forget quite how it worked) of making him conjugate the verb—"I stink, thou stinketh, he stinks, etcetera."

This is not a digression but highly relevant to the whole process of Laurence's education.

During his second week at Greenaways he was sitting in the dining-hall, together with the rest of the younger boys, writing his evening prep under the distant eye of a junior master called Mr R. F. Sharpe, known not very originally as R.F.S. One of the

5

boys across the table from Laurence wrote him a friendly note. "Thou are not working, Lamego. R.F.S." Rather wittily, Laurence wrote under the master's initials: "Royal Field Stinkers." Those were the early days of the First World War when the names and titles of regiments and corps were on every schoolboy's lips and when everyone at school had a father and uncles in the Royal this or that, Royal Field Artillery, Royal Field Engineers... For a brief moment, in fact, when Laurence's words were read by the boys immediately around him and won their unqualified approval, he almost made good the calamity of his hymn-singing incident the previous Sunday. That night he was very nearly not unpopular.

This happy state lasted only until breakfast the next morning. Each day started with prayers in the school library, conducted by Bumpus often with a cricket bat in one hand and always with a Bible in the other. He would begin with a few hints on living the good life, such as: "You should spot a long-hop as soon as it leaves the bowler's arm, and at once begin to play forward to it with a straight bat by pointing your left elbow along the line of the ball. And Jesus said unto His disciples..." Thus from a portion of the Bible to a suitable collect and the Lord's prayer, after which the boys would proceed in an orderly manner to breakfast. Occasionally, however, when some particular awful crime had been committed, there would be an extra treat. This was one of those occasions. "There is a boy in this school," said Bumpus, "who has been using filthy and disgusting language. I am asking that boy to stand up."

This was tremendous fun. Above all, the boys wanted to know, not so much the name of the individual, as what disgusting language he had discovered that was unknown to the rest of them. They looked at each other in glee and excitement. It was fitting and proper for all to turn their heads and search the room for the criminal; and I well remember that when Laurence, who was sitting in front of me and to one side, caught my eye, I allowed myself to respond with the slightest suspicion of a smile, a courageous act on my part to anyone as unpopular as him, but justified by our life-long acquaintanceship and, even more, by his minor triumph of the previous night. Nobody had as yet stood up.

"I am giving that boy one more chance," said Bumpus. "The boy to whom I am referring scribbled a disgusting word on a

6

piece of paper and left it lying about in the dining-hall last night. If he owns up now, I may be lenient with him. Otherwise I shall not." The words were ominous enough to wipe the secret smiles from our minds. This had become serious. Nobody moved, and the library was very still. For perhaps a full twenty seconds we sat in suspense before Bumpus said softly: "Stand up Lamego." Laurence did so.

"Lamego, did you or did you not write a disgusting word on a piece of paper last night?"

"No, sir."

"Mr Sharpe has identified your handwriting. Do you deny that it is yours?"

"What word, sir?" Laurence asked. There was genuine puzzlement in his voice; in his own mind, at that moment, he was certainly innocent.

"If you make me repeat that filthy word in this room, Lamego, it will be the worse for you." Laurence remained silent. He was white and inward-turned, calling upon the kind of endurance, or perhaps even courage, with which his people have survived their centuries of persecution. He stood there, not just negatively silent, but positively and aggressively refusing to speak, as if the Roundheads were asking, "When did you last see your father?" He was plainly terrified, yet somehow aggressive and arrogant in his terror.

"The word to which I am referring," said Bumpus at last, "is that objectionable and disgusting term 'stinker'. Did you or did you not write it?"

"Yes, sir," Laurence said.

"Then why have you just denied doing so?" Laurence did not answer. No boy in the school could in fact have given an answer to that particular question in that context. "Very well," said Bumpus, "You have newly come to this school and, apparently, are not yet acquainted with its ordinary traditions of decency. You will have to learn them. I will not have new boys bringing into this school filthy and disgusting language of that sort. I cannot think, I do not care to think, where you can have picked it up."

In fact, the only place where Laurence could have picked up this particular word was in the Youth camp run for the East End boys by Basil Henriques whose Airedale dog had been christened

7

"Stinker" by Basil himself, a man already on the way to fame among the ex-pupils of Bumpus. However, Laurence had only once paid a visit to these summer camps with his father and it is probable that he had never heard the word until he had to come to Greenaways. Naturally he was unable to say so. He simply became more white, more mutinously silent and somehow more provocative than before. Bumpus broke the silence softly: "After prayers, you will go to my study ... Our Father which art in heaven ..."

When Laurence joined the rest at breakfast, they asked him the normal question: "How many?" and got the answer "Six" before they started on him. He sat down on the bench with an ostentatious bump which was typical of his bloody-mindedness that required him to show us that Bumpus's cane, operated with the expert wrist of one who had been the best bat in England, had not hurt him. There were no signs of tears, no expression on his face, which was anyway so pale that it could not show additional pallor.

"Where did you pick up that disgusting language, Lamego?" "Why do you bring disgusting language into this school, Lamego?" From somebody else: "Why can't you learn that you've come to a decent school, Lamego?" And so on during breakfast, during the rest of that day, the rest of that week, the rest of that month.

The whole school was genuinely affronted by Lamego's disgusting language. It did not matter that within the school the words "stink," "stinking" and "stinker" were more commonly used than any other and were certainly uttered by everybody not less than dozens of times daily. The actual word that Laurence had written was of course forgotten and irrelevant. What was remembered was the crime, specified and punished by Bumpus, of introducing disgusting ways, filthy manners, horrible habits from some awful place whence Laurence had come into a decent school. They hated the place themselves, but Laurence had no right to defile it. Consequently he was doomed to end his childhood as he had begun it, in a state of constant and bewildered oppression. It did not harm him in the least. He had been sent to school to be knocked into shape, and knocked he was. That the shape was not of the school's choosing, nor one which any schoolmaster could have consciously designed, but due to the Lamego blood, to two thousand years of regular persecution, to Sephardic snobbery, to in-breeding and line-breeding, to the prepotent Lamego characteristics, was a not unhappy chance of English upper-class education.

Henceforward Laurence suffered from active and intense unpopularity and, much worse, from his intolerable craving to be popular, to be liked, to be accepted. He was the only boy in the school who did not have a nickname and, above all he longed for one. More than a year after he first went to Greenaways, I was presented during the school holidays with an enquiry through family channels which were to me sacred and secret. My mother showed me a letter that had been written to Mrs Lamego by Laurence. The relevant passage read: "I am so happy, at last I have a nickname which everybody calls me. Everybody does, even Foster Major and Aird. They just started calling me by it the other day . . . Your ever loving son, Ikey."

I did not know what to say. I was not astute enough to guess that Laurence did not even know what Ikey meant, let alone that his secret craving had not allowed him to recognise that it was being used as a term of contempt and not of friendliness. In defence of old Bumpus I must admit that he forbade the practice of calling Laurence "Ikey" when at last it came to his notice. As it appeared to Laurence, this veto on the part of Bumpus was just one more instance of persecution on the part of a man who hated him.

2
Floreat, floreat, floreat Rugbaea . . .

Not much time need be wasted on the remainder of Laurence's schooldays which were spent at Rugby between 1918 and 1923. Many excellent novels (such as Alec Waugh's *Loom of Youth*) were written about the sort of system at public schools to which we were all subjected at that time. So far as Rugby itself is concerned, the conditions were not very different from those of *Tom Brown's Schooldays* (1857), except that the rigours and harshness of the nineteenth century would seem to be inspired with a certain compassion and even a savage nobility which was lacking fifty years later. This was perhaps due to a change in the social origins of the pupils. Whereas those of the years before 1914 were the sons of the humbler kinds of gentry, mostly professionals, those of our post-war time were too often the sons of pretentious would-be gentry, war profiteers who were in the process of consolidating their new fortunes by imprinting upon their offspring a style which they very reasonably coveted. Many of our fellow-pupils were being taught by their parents that they belonged to something distinctly higher than the middle class, to a kind of sub-aristocracy, while Doctor Lamego, who had been educated at Harrow and New College, Oxford, was insisting with strenuous pride that they were essentially a middle-class family and that any pretensions to be anything else or anything better were ill-bred and vulgar.

The House at Rugby to which Laurence was sent was a hideous and horrible building constructed in red brick around a central quadrangle of cobblestones which, owing to the Midland climate, were almost always wet, muddy and slippery, when not actually awash with rain and casual slops. This is the grim "Quad" which survives in the adult nightmares of many old Rugbeians who in childhood were puny or otherwise physically ineffectual. From the hideous street one entered the sinister Quad through a prison archway and fortress gates. Standing in the gateway you would see immediately ahead of you the block which contained the dining-hall with, above it, one of the three dormitories. The block on the right contained the other two dormitories on the first floor and, below them, the kitchen and servants' quarters which were protected from the quadrangle by a sort of cloisters. Opposite to it, that is to say on the left as you entered, there were three floors of minute rooms which were our studies, each being shared by two boys who were allowed to choose each other if they could. Since Laurence never could find himself a mate, he was always allotted as a partner one of the very few other boys who, like himself, were by nature friendless. To get to or from these studies boys climbed one of the two narrow, steep, stone staircases until they had reached their appropriate floor, where they turned either right or left along equally narrow and semi-derelict corridors into which their rooms opened.

These topographical details were of great importance owing to the system of "fag calls," harmless enough if exercised humanely or in moderation but, if abused, an undue torment for a skinny little rat of a boy like Laurence who was incapable of descending at speed a narrow stone staircase without falling down some part of it. In our House, at that time, the system of fag-calls was much abused.

It was, of course, the prerogative of only the topmost stratum of boys to stand in the quad and to call for a fag on a high, quavering note like an ill-sounded hunting horn—"Fa . . . a . . . a . . . g!" This was the summons which required every boy of the Lower School to quit his study and to race downwards into the Quad, the last arrival being charged with whatever trivial errand had been contrived by one of the sixth-form boys or games captains, who were privileged to exact this service. "You again, Lamego!" Crawford Major would say, as Lamego tumbled last into the quad: "Always you, Lamego . . . go round to Nickerson Minor and give him my compliments and say that I hope he is well this morning."

"Please, Crawford, what House is Nickerson Minor?"

Crawford Major, hands in his pockets as befitted his rank, looked long and warningly at Lamego. "I think I misheard you," he said at last, for he was a humane man who would give any wet little rodent a more than fair chance to escape chastisement.

11

As always Laurence failed to register the warning. "What House, please Crawford?" he asked for the second time, betraying yet again his sinful ignorance of essential knowledge. Nickerson Minor had just been awarded his first-XV colours and cap. Naturally a small boy was expected to know the House of every such personage.

"Lamego, Lamego," said Crawford sorrowfully, "yet again I shall have to have a word with you tonight after Lights Out."

Thus was initiated a perpetual cycle of chain reactions. It was always, "You again, Lamego," unless Laurence was already absent on somebody else's errand, because he had been allotted a study at the end of the corridor on the topmost floor and so was bound topographically to be last in responding to a fag call. And while there were ways and means of influencing the allotment of studies, Laurence was not the kind of boy who would ever discover them. Nowadays he would be described quite simply as a dope. At that time this useful word had not been invented.

Since Laurence spent the whole of his day, and all his days, being last at fag calls and running ridiculous errands contrived by his betters, he had no time for work. Hence he was always being punished for neglect of Latin prose or French translation with impositions that required him to write out fifty, a hundred or even five hundred times some particularly inappropriate and useless phrase, or else to be chastised at the end of the class with a cane which he would first have to fetch from the ex-Sergeant Major who held the office of School Marshal. Writing such impositions, answering fag calls and running errands, kept Lamego adequately occupied for such time as was not spent in playing compulsory games, at which Laurence was easily the worst boy in the whole school, or in going compulsory runs, when Laurence was invariably last, or actually attending lessons which Laurence, in a state of depressed inanity, seemed unable to assimilate. For this, again, he very properly suffered retribution. Just as it had been in the nursery, and also at Greenaways, Laurence's life at Rugby at once became reduced to a simple succession of crime and punishment.

I need write little about our school meals, since Laurence had none. For the sake of orderliness there had been devised in our House an excellent system whereby any boy who required an extra knife, fork or spoon, a plate, cup or saucer, more bread, margarine or jam, more salt, pepper or mustard, or a drink of water, would simply pass a message down the long table—"Bim Man, fetch more bread!" "Bim" meaning "bottom," this "Bim Man" or honorary lackey was one of the two boys who had drawn the seats nearest the door at the foot or bottom of the lowliest dining table. During his first term, out of the dozen new boys in our House, Laurence, a bim man by nature, invariably found himself at table in the bim man's place. He was too slow to get himself seated elsewhere and, if and when he did, he was too feeble to escape immediate dislodgement.

This system was more subtly punitive than I have yet been able to indicate, because I had forgotten about the "Bucks." According to his athletic prowess, or academic progress, or ultimately sheer longevity at school, a boy ceased to be a fag and, while not yet a fag-master, was promoted to a buck. In the dining-hall there were two long tables parallel to each other, seating respectively the bucks and the fags. Across the top of them was a third table for the housemaster and the boys in the sixth form or of equivalent athletic status. It was a rule that all fags remained standing at table until the last of the bucks was seated, and that no fag remained sitting at table after the first of the bucks had risen and departed. If a single buck was very late in coming to a meal, and another buck—and this concurrence of events was quite normal—ate swiftly and left the table early, the fags would have only a few minutes in which they might be seated for nourishment. And since a bim man would usually spend all of those few minutes in running the capricious errands of boys seated above him, he would quite simply starve. In consequence he became still slower at answering fag calls, still more obtuse at his lessons and still more ineffectual at the art of survival. Yet Laurence did in fact survive miraculously for some six weeks of his first term at Rugby before being taken off to the sanatorium with a sickness which the school doctor, whose qualifications for the appointment were largely that he had played wing-three-quarter for Rugby less than a decade earlier, was completely unable to diagnose. The boy had no temperature but seemed unable to remain upright.

13

The traditional cure, which he prescribed automatically for Laurence's obscure ailment—as always for any disease which had no obvious symptom such as a rash or swelling or uncontrollable cough—was very simple food and very little of it, a diet which usually persuaded a malingerer—and most sick boys were of course malingering—to declare himself recovered and to beg for return to school again as speedily as possible. Inexplicably, Laurence failed to respond to this treatment. After a few weeks even the school doctor became worried and wrote a note to the Housemaster, who wrote a letter to Doctor Lamego, who, in a few days' time, paid a personal visit to the sanatorium together with a consultant physician from Harley Street, very old and a very old friend of our families, Dr S. J. Phillips. It took them a couple of minutes to diagnose acute under-nourishment amounting almost to starvation.

Just as I had almost forgotten to mention school meals as a factor in Laurence's education, I find that I have equally omitted sleep. In that respect also, Laurence was a deprived adolescent. On two or three nights a week, and frequently more often, a sixth-form boy or a games captain would fulfil his sentence of "a word with Laurence after Lights Out." This meant a visitation with a shaded candle-lamp called a "tolley" for illumination and a rather ineffectual weapon called a blind-pole. The timing of the execution depended on the sadistic tendencies of the executioner. If he were kind-hearted he came as soon as lights were extinguished; otherwise he might keep the victim waiting for a lawful half-hour. If he came a second later than the striking of the House clock, his chance was lost, and the punishment had to be abandoned. A kindly sixth-form boy called Knebworth, or something like it, used deliberately to come too late. With a great show of irritation with himself he would arrive with the clock's echoes. He was known to hold that half an hour of waiting for punishment was punishment enough; but we fags said that truly he was so feeble that he knew he could not hurt us and wanted to conceal his disability. A good, robust sadist would wait for twenty-nine minutes—which was twenty-eight minutes after all the boys, bar the victim or victims were fast asleep. (These minor chastisements

14

were so common, were indeed so much the normal occurrence of an evening, that nobody stayed awake to observe them.) They were not spectacular, nor savage. The procedure was simple. The sixth-form boy (or gamesman), who was prosecutor, judge and executioner without reference to any higher authority, would enter the darkened dormitory. One of the beds nearest the door was occupied by the elder boy in charge of the dorm, himself privileged to keep a tolley burning for that crucial half-hour, and here the punishment took place. Together the two tolleys were tactically sited to illuminate the victim's bottom when it was duly presented. And when the tolleys had been carefully arranged the executioner, in brisk and cheerful tones would call: "Lamego— I want a word with you."

At this, Laurence in his pyjamas would rise, walk down the dormitory and bend himself over the end bed where punishment was inflicted. Only two strokes were permissible on these occasions, and the blind-pole—which was the flat piece of wood inserted at the bottom of any blind to give it weight, and which were sold by the score in various shops of the town for this specific purpose— might only be used flat-ways on, and not with the cutting edge. The weapon was regarded as expendable, and any prefect who could not break it on the bottom of a small boy in a single chastisement would incur the contempt of the House. The art, therefore was to administer the first stroke with just sufficient restraint to leave the blind-pole intact, so that everything could be put into the second. This could hurt. But Laurence who, even at the beginning would never give his executioner the satisfaction of detecting the least sign of suffering, soon grew quite impervious to this particular pain. He simply did not mind having sore buttocks; and in this he was quite unique, because while every other small boy had to suffer on frequent occasions the same punishment, Laurence got it ten times more than most. In the thirty-six scholastic weeks of his first year at Rugby he was thus chastised— apart from more serious punishments administered by masters— one hundred and twelve times, which was how he ever afterwards remembered the constitution of a hundredweight. All it otherwise meant was that he lay for long hours in bed smarting not from his bruises but from his sense of injustice.

In this he was wrong-headed and irrational. Very few of his punishments were in fact unjust but, according to the complexity of rules and traditions which governed our lives, were fairly merited. For Laurence was incapable of mastering these regulations and, apart from such obvious sins of omission as not knowing the House of Nickerson Minor, was for ever committing offences which, if allowed to become prevalent, would threaten the whole structure of the school's community—putting a hand into his trouser pocket before he had been at school for a year, or carrying a book under his arm before he had been there four terms, or walking down the street with his collar rucked up when it might not be upturned, no matter the weather, before his third year. In this way and that, of more than a score of such ways in which no right-minded boy would overtly transgress, Laurence was consequently earning his punishments. Habitually he pleaded forgetfulness. Perhaps, unconsciously at least, he sinned on purpose, perhaps even intending to incur the inevitable retribution which, in his mind befogged by the recollections of nursery injustice, would give him concrete cause for his inescapable resentment.

Through much of the night Laurence would be awake enjoying his grievances. He would plan and envisage in valiant detail his ultimate revenge when the wicket would tumble and the oppressors be as dust. He schemed in biblical language and imagery. The night hours passed in half-sleep and broken visions of Israel triumphant. Towards dawn he would fall deeply asleep. This was the moment when, at six o'clock of a winter's morning, one of the junior servants, a houseboy called a "blog," would bring a hockey stick to batter on the dormitory door with all the protest of his social status against the privileged young gentlemen. It was a nasty kind of awakening. Rising then, at the thunderous and malevolent clatter of the blog, we would proceed, as ordered, to throw off pyjamas, seize towels from the central wash-stands and run naked along the dormitory, down a short flight of stone stairs, up another flight and into the bathroom where several circular tubs had been filled with cold water the previous night. Since the bathroom windows were always open, there was often ice to be broken as we plunged in, seating ourselves in a tub and sluicing the water over our limbs—(the taps were kept running)—and, to comply with the law of immersion, thoroughly wetting every part of ourselves except our heads, legally exempt, after which we would run back into the dormitory, dry ourselves and hurriedly dress. Within forty minutes of being woken we would have gulped a cup of thick, tepid cocoa, if there was any left, would have walked or run the half mile to the school chapel, and the Lord would have opened our lips that our mouths might shew forth His praise. When our prayers had been capped with a blessing from one of the several masters in holy orders, we would proceed to a classroom for the first lesson of the day, another forty-five minutes on empty stomachs, and thence to breakfast, and thence to queue in the roofless alley which gave access to the row of doorless lavatories. Again the bucks were naturally privileged and, apart from having half the closets reserved for their use, could displace a fag in the queue for any of the others. This was really the social occasion of the day when those defecating and those waiting to do so would exchange news, plans, instructions and idle pleasantries. For some reason or other, Laurence never got used to sitting on a lavatory in public: and his ridiculous embarrassment, which none of the rest of us shared, during his early days at Rugby seemed to survive for the next forty years, so that even during the war, when Laurence was really a quite adequate soldier, his professional usefulness could occasionally be impaired by an irrational reluctance to visit the latrines at the most appropriate moment.

Far worse, for Laurence, than these morning visitations were the occasions, four times a week, when we returned from compulsory games or cross-country runs and were required to clean off the mud and to change from our games clothes back into the school uniforms of grey flannel trousers with black coat and waistcoat. For these purposes the changing-room and adjoining bathroom were quite inadequate. A dozen boys would have found them cramped quarters and with the three or four dozen who had in fact to use them simultaneously (since to be late after changing was no less a sin than to be late at any other time) the place constituted for the puny boy a small corner of hell and a very suitable preparation and introduction for the worst that was likely to befall him in adult life. There was no ordeal for those who came and went quickly, since the elder boys, including of course the bucks, had three-quarters of the accommodation reserved for themselves and had thus no need to hurry. But the small boy who was unpopular needed to hasten: and at this stage of his life Laurence hastened more slowly than anybody else.

17

In the changing-room we threw off our shorts and vests before proceeding naked into the bathroom. This was a long and narrow chamber lit by a skylight, and containing a row of circular tubs similar to those in which we immersed ourselves every morning. The important feature of this room, so far as Laurence was concerned, was the constitution of its floor. This was of a kind of concrete which rapidly became slimy when awash with water, soap and mud, and on which it was verily quite difficult, after a while each winter evening, to remain upright and retain one's footing. Naturally Laurence did not. Only the two tubs furthest from the door might be used by the fags, which meant that ten or twelve small boys in succession would have to use each of these two particular tubs; and the order of precedence was not of the civilian queue but of the animal kingdom, strongest first, weakest last. Laurence was never not last during his first year at Rugby.

Laurence would arrive mud-stained from the football field. Quite a few of us were too decent to be positively beastly to him: but since we could not in any way help him, our most generous course was to pretend unawareness of the imminent situation and to make best speed to be out of the place and away to the tuck shop for a quick chocolate fudge or mallow before Laurence, naked, skinny, sallow all over except for the mud, was standing in the doorway to the bathroom whence came the familiar and inevitable voice: "Where have you been, Jew? Why have you kept us waiting, Jew? Why, Jew?" The questions were asked quite softly and patiently, with a long pause after each of them to give Laurence plenty of time to answer. "Why are you such a dirty Jew, Lamego? You are a dirty Jew, aren't you . . . aren't you . . . aren't you? No? But you *are* a Jew, Lamego? Yes? And you *are* dirty? Yes? No? Were you or were you not sent home by Blinkers for dirt behind the ears? You were! So you *are* dirty and you *are* a Jew. . . . So aren't you a dirty Jew, aren't you? Q.E.D., dirty Jew. . . ." Sometimes we might hear the first crack of a wet towel on Laurence's flesh before we cleared out of it.

Now, although any one of us—except perhaps Laurence who never had the chance to try—had learnt to draw blood with an expert flip of a wet towel-tip, it does not do to exaggerate the harshness of this pleasantry. There were certain rules governing the sport which, in Laurence's case, was called "Jew-baiting" on account of an illustration in one of the School's history text books:

a picture which, I should add, had been calculated to inspire hatred of persecution and compassion for its victims, but which naturally had the contrary effect. The first rule dictated the target area, which was confined to the buttocks with a certain licence regarding the upper thighs and the lower back. To flick any other part of Laurence's person, let alone draw blood from it, was adjudged not only bad marksmanship, but lack of sportsmanship which would incur the severe displeasure of Connelly, a boy who never failed to consolidate his displeasure with physical retribution. In this sport, as well as in several others, Connelly was principal exponent, referee and linesman all in one.

Connelly* led the scrum in the School Fifteen. His father, born Cohen and trading in Finsbury under the style of Sanderson and McKay Ltd, had made a fortune during the war in, I think, buttons for Service uniforms, or it may have been thread for sewing them on, or perhaps it was knitting wool or socks. Whether or not the father had been baptised on changing his name, the son had certainly been confirmed, and it is said that his rapt expression on that occasion, his momentary transfiguration, was of a genuine religious conviction. Incidentally, no one discovered until long afterwards that Connelly's father had changed his name; nor of course that Connelly was born a Jew.

Nor would Lamego criticise anyone who chooses to change his name or who thinks it right to change his faith. One of his own uncles became a Christian and was baptised accordingly; and it is always said of his maternal great-grandfather, who was born in 1825 as Hyam Leopold Moses (the son of Henry Moses who was born in 1791 and lived in Regents Park), that, on the morning when he changed his name by deed poll, the Stock Exchange, of which he was a well-liked member, carried a great banner reading affectionately: "AND THE LORD SAID UNTO MOSES 'GOOD MORNING, BEDDINGTON.'" In his own youth he often heard it said of his mother's family, the Beddingtons, some of whom have been quite distinguished, particularly as cavalry officers, that "They changed their name from Moses but they cannot change their noses."

* These minor events are strictly true, with only slight under-statement to make them easily credible. The name of the ring-leader was certainly not Connelly nor anything like it. But the boy in question was in fact the son of Jewish parents who had changed their name together with their religion. The firm of Sanderson & McKay is likewise pure invention.

19

Therefore Lamego has nothing against Connelly for changing anything, and is not even sure that he deserved censure for his methods in the changing rooms. On account of his great prowess at football, his useful capacity for almost every other game and athletic activity and, moreover, a very adequate brain that had got him slightly higher up the school than was normal for his age, he was invested with prefectorial authority requiring him to keep order, to prevent bullying and to correct any unseemly attitude in his juniors. All these duties he discharged conscientiously. When he was around there was never disorder; when he turned a corner to find a cluster of small boys engaged in tormenting one amongst them, they dispersed instantly and in terror, but were rarely quick enough to escape identification and a consequent assignment—the whole lot of them in succession—with Connelly after Lights Out; and in correcting unseemly attitudes, Connelly showed perspicacity by selecting Laurence for his concentrated efforts, since undoubtedly Laurence was more in need of correction than anybody else.

"You admit you are a Jew, Lamego. You are filthy, Lamego, as we can all see for ourselves. Therefore, Lamego, you are a filthy Jew, Q.E.D. Do you agree?"

The low room would be thick with steam, the unshaded lights blurred like lamps in a city fog, the atmosphere heavy with sweat, the tiled floor slippery and awash. Laurence's naked and undersized, under-developed body which showed no signs of adolescence at that time, although he was well past his fourteenth birthday, was certainly an unpleasant sight. He stood in a kind of trance, his eyes fixed on Connelly's pubic hair and all his senses suffocated in a kind of nausea evoked by the puberty of all the older boys who still remained in the bathroom. He would not, or could not, speak. On these and similar occasions elsewhere he never spoke.

"Do you agree, Lamego? Do you? So he . . . he won't talk. . . Tickle him up, somebody."

Bartlett or Fowler, Lambert, Moore, Jackson, Freeman or Barker would draw out his towel, stretch it, wet the end of it on the floor and flick it like a stock-whip against Laurence's backside. "Rotten shot! Somebody else!" The others would take their turn. When it was necessary, somebody would spin Laurence round with his foot in order to present the target area in the right direction. "Christ, you're a useless lot! Jesus, what a bore! I shall have

20

to see to it myself. Give me a towel, somebody." By then Laurence
would be blubbing, probably sobbing and gasping for breath.
Jackson might say "I think he does agree, Connelly." And Connelly might answer "We'll take it he does. Now, Lamego, why do
you cheat? You do cheat, don't you, don't you, don't you? You
must cheat because you're a Jew, mustn't you? You don't deny
that, Lamego? You can't, can you? Didn't I tell you on Thursday
to look up 'Jew' in the Oxford Dictionary? Didn't I? You know
there's one in the House Library? Have you ever taken it off the
shelf? Do you take the least notice of anything I tell you? Didn't
I tell you that the Oxford Dictionary says in black and white that
to Jew is to cheat. So you must cheat, mustn't you? Why, why,
Lamego, do you cheat? Oh for Christ's sake tickle the bugger up;
he makes me sick. . ." Sometimes when Meego was down on the
floor, they would sling him from one to the other, and he would
slide as smoothly and true on the tiles as a puck on the ice in a
curling match.

Despite all these efforts on the part of Connelly and the other
senior boys, Laurence failed to show any signs of correction.
Indeed he got worse and worse. He wasted much of his energy in
prayer when it could have been better directed to cleaning his
grubby ears and generally trying to smarten himself up or even
improve his physique. In and out of school Chapel he used to
pray with passion: "Lord God of Israel help Thou thy people and
me in particular to vanquish mine enemies and Connelly in
particular. Let the wicked not flourish." And when this proved
fruitless he even tried: "O gentle Jesus, if thou really art the Lamb
of God, strike Connelly dead!" But Jesus never did. Nor indeed
did any of His advocates, pupil or master—many of the latter
having taken Holy Orders and wearing their collars the wrong
way round—show the least interest in Laurence's soul, than which
nothing could have been riper for conversion to almost any faith
that would have offered him any kind of strength or consolation.
Thus Laurence, who had to persist in seeking divine aid, since
none other seemed available, reverted to the God of his fathers—
for it was easier to believe in a single divinity who declined help
than in a Trinity who all turned their backs—and to a small black
book in which Mrs Lamego had written a number of suitable
prayers from the Jewish liturgy.

Jehovah seemed a much more suitable patron for Laurence

21

than Jesus. In the first place, He was not there, but was away in a Synagogue in London, while Jesus was presented to Laurence daily at morning prayers, and twice on Sundays, with a character of meekness and gentleness which seemed scarcely appropriate to Laurence's circumstance. And in the second place, nobody could have accused Jehovah of being meek, gentle or mild, of being long-suffering, all-forgiving, having infinite compassion, or of doing anything so silly as to turn the other cheek. Although Laurence had never actually turned the other cheek himself, it had frequently been turned for him and had invariably been slapped. So that Laurence had not been many weeks at Rugby before Jesus and Connelly were identified in the boy's mind, while Jehovah remained aloof as a potential ally who, if only He would listen, as He had listened to the Hebrew Prophets, could put to confusion all Laurence's enemies in one awful stroke. And one day He did.

It was shortly before Laurence's fifteenth birthday when Jackson, in the bathroom, took a grip on Laurence's shoulders in order to slide him across the floor via Lambert, Bartlett, Fowler and Freeman to Connelly's embrace, that there entered into Laurence's heart a sudden gust of rage, not the nursery temper of impotence which was his usual state in these circumstances, but a breath of wrath which caused him to twist himself round with sudden violence and, shutting his eyes, clenching his fist, to strike Jackson across the bridge of his nose. It was the first time that Laurence had ever really hit anyone in his life. There could not possibly have been much strength behind the blow, because Laurence had none to mobilise for this effort. But by some freak of dynamics so improbable that it seemed the answer to a prayer, the balance of the two boys brought them into the maximum possible collision so that a stream of blood spurted out of Jackson's nose, and Jackson's eye was so severely bruised that it was scarlet within an hour, yellow by Lights Out and purple for a fortnight afterwards. From this incident Laurence gained no visible respect or affection from anyone, but forthwith the physical persecution in the bathroom was stopped.

Laurence's Housemaster, Mr Parsons,* heard of the affair. And although nobody will ever persuade Laurence that Parsons was

* There was no master by the name of Parsons at Rugby when Lamego was there.

in the least concerned over Laurence's spiritual and physical welfare, it was at this juncture that he decreed compulsory house boxing, to be held in the dining-room regularly each month.

Laurence was matched with a rather nice boy called Meadows who possessed both intellect and speed of foot which were rewarded with privileges, indulgences and popularity. He had never been particularly nasty to Laurence, nor had he ever been nice. Probably he served unwittingly, unconsciously to represent the hostile world; enough to inspire Laurence to the new experience of real physical effort. He had never before wholly exerted himself: his regular chastisements for slacking at games were all justified, for he invariably did slack: he did not know how to do otherwise. He had never felt in his heart the least desire to achieve the specific objects of football, cricket and athletics; he desired only to escape getting hurt; and facing Meadows before the start of the contest was the first occasion that Laurence wanted anything more than immunity from damage to himself. Suddenly he did not mind how much he was damaged provided he could make his mark on his opponent. At the striking of the bell he went forth insanely like a warrior of the Lord, touched gloves with Meadows and then smote Meadows with all his force in the stomach. In astonished pain Meadows clasped his stomach with both hands, and Laurence smote him full in the face. Laurence was dancing up and down like a vicious lunatic, repeating the same effective exercise—stomach, face, stomach... The previous contests had all been fairly decorous bouts between friends with smiles, good humour, good sportsmanship, give and take, and quite without enmity, nobody really hurt. Laurence went in to kill. And suddenly he had his first taste of maximum exertion, engendered by some flick of the mind and spirit in conjunction putting the body into over-drive, a supra-top gear, known to every athlete of any distinction, likewise to explorers, soldiers, sailors, escapers, etcetera, whereby the physical feat of an individual exceeds by far his imagined capacity. In the realm of physical effort it is perhaps the counterpart of the unconscious mind in creative or inventive adventures. It is surely a generic part of what is called "the unconscious," in so far as it operates without or beyond the orders issued by the mind. Anyway it is a faculty which some people, perhaps most people, are never able to find in themselves, or never want to find, and one which Laurence was

23

able to find and use on only a very few occasions throughout his life. He discovered it for the first time at the expense of poor Meadows who was quite severely hurt before somebody stopped the fight after ninety seconds. In that short space of time Laurence had explored the trance-like state in which he could be damaged but could feel no pain until later, and could meanwhile exercise strength and skill which were not normally his to command.

From that time onwards Laurence took up boxing. It was unfortunate for him that boxing at Rugby, in those days, was not an activity to which anyone attached much importance; it was the one schoolboy sport at which Rugby did not compete with other schools, so that neither prestige nor school colours—a piece of coveted braid around the cap which Laurence used literally to dream about—accrued to anyone who was good at it. This was a great pity. Most boys won some kind of distinction at Rugby, a braided cap which drew the eye being also an endowment of authority and all sorts of privileges. Probably it is good for boys to win this kind of success during at least some stage of adolescence. It may be equally good for them to fail to win it. Certainly this adolescent failure was a factor of considerable weight in Laurence's life. He had to wait for a distinctive cap until the war provided a chance to get himself promoted to the red-flannel ranks.

During the year following Laurence's fifteenth birthday, he enjoyed two other minor successes. The first was in the Arts Class, at which Laurence had never before shown the least aptitude. It was not altogether unseemly to enjoy the arts classes which were the recognised opportunity to idle but not to misbehave or rag the Art Master, old Morgan, a kind, sad, drooping, elderly man whose gentle disposition unsuited him to the control of savage adolescents. Uncontrolled they roamed, but quietly, the large bright studio known as the Art School, chatting, exchanging gossip, but not here resorting to brutality, and generally enjoying themselves for the hour a week during which they had to produce marks on a sheet of paper purporting to represent a still life or one of the various busts and statues which stood about the place. If a boy enjoyed drawing and was any good at it, he was usually

24

allowed, without subsequent retribution, to get on with the set job uninterruptedly and to win praise for it. It depended on the constitution of the form or class, of course; but generally at Rugby the form had no corporate spirit, nor was it drastically split into cliques. Boys were promoted from one form to the next semi-automatically but also according to the progress they showed in examinations at the end of each term; a form was therefore a constantly changing unit; it contained boys from every House; it was the House, not the form, which developed its own very marked and individual characteristics, impressing themselves in one way or another on all its members; and the blend of House characteristics which was found in any form had no time to solidify or to become an organic entity. True, a form in the Lower School moved as a whole throughout the day from master to master for every different subject, but it was a pliable creature in the hands of a schoolmaster with either personality or enough bloody-mindedness to keep order. In the Lower School which contained the youngest and also the least intelligent boys, consisting of three forms of nitwits or slow developers—(a boy *could* pass straight into the Upper School when entering Rugby, whereas Laurence passed into the Lowest Form of the Lower School)—the teacher with a vocation for teaching or a love of his subject was likely to be defeated. Although he might inspire those very few boys who were desperately unhappy and therefore receptive to the least sympathy, or the very rare boy who was passionately anxious to be educated, or the still rarer specimen who had real embryonic talent in a particular subject, he could not keep the majority quiet. They would rag him and rag or savage each other, and he would soon resign in despair and go to a Grammar School where the boys, not being the sons of gentlemen nor even pretending to be, took education as a serious business and applied themselves with diligence to the lessons of any competent teacher. The Lower School of Rugby was in those days no place for a master who was not a disciplinarian first and a teacher second.

A notable exception was old Morgan. He made no attempt to keep order. He did not care a rap—literally, for he never could have used a cane—whether a boy worked or not. If a boy became noisy, he was simply turned out of the class and told quite gently to go away, whereupon he found himself the most naked, defenceless and vulnerable of all creatures, a Lower School boy to be seen in the streets at an hour when all authority knew he ought to have been in class. Somebody in authority—a master, a master's wife or an elder boy whose timetable was different—would certainly detect the culprit and ask for an explanation. Since the penalty for falsehood was immeasurably more severe than that for misconduct, a boy so caught would usually confess the truth; and with the inevitability of police proceedings the confession would be transmitted to someone with powers of execution. Hence the boy turned out of class would ultimately get his thrashing, not severe but certainly more painful than anything the elderly Morgan could have administered himself; and hence it was generally accepted that misbehaviour in the Art classes was an unrewarding diversion; and hence, finally, it was in the Art School that Laurence, left alone and temporarily unafraid, did his best work.

In his second and unhappiest term at Rugby, Laurence had elected to spend several successive weeks on drawing a monstrous plaster head which could have been Sampson by Michelangelo. Perhaps from his desperate yearning for some of Sampson's bellicose qualities he began instinctively, unconsciously, to instil the head with life, to give it movement. Without the least contrivance or forethought he had started with pencil and a huge sheet of paper and then, a couple of weeks later, changed to charcoal. The result in Laurence's mind was a kind of self-hypnosis, a state which became familiar long afterwards whenever he was wholly engaged in inventive work and found himself isolated and insulated from exterior circumstance. And the result on paper was not half bad.

Mr Morgan was in peculiar ways a remarkable man at his job. Incapable though he was of inspiring the average Rugby schoolboy with the least interest in art, he had the gift of coincidence. Somehow or other he always happened to be at a particular point in a large class at the moment when a ray of light burst momentarily through the dull cloudscape of indifference to reveal a hidden talent. During the course of each year he would discover one or perhaps two boys who possessed, if not a real gift for the graphic art, an unconscious yearning to express themselves with pencil or paint. He was not a very good teacher. Starting at the front of his class, he would sit down beside a boy, take his

26

drawing-board from him and, confronted by a tangle of lines which showed not only no resemblance to the subject, but not the least effort to achieve one, would put the thing laboriously to rights. This done, he would proceed to the next boy and then the next. He would perhaps interest himself with half-a-dozen boys, at most, during the course of a period; and since the boys usually sat in the same order, with Laurence, as always, in a prepared defensive position, right at the back, it is probable that he had never before cast an eye on Laurence's work. Yet on this particular day some impulse made him abandon his usual routine and walk down the length of the class.

For some time, perhaps for several minutes, Laurence, who had been in his state of self-hypnosis over his drawing, was quite unaware that Morgan was standing behind him; but Morgan for his part was perfectly aware of his pupil's state. He waited quietly until the stick of charcoal came to rest before laying a hand on Laurence's shoulders and saying—"That is a remarkable picture; and really quite good." Laurence burst into tears forthwith. The shock of such unaccustomed sympathy and praise was too much for his emotional continence.

In defiance of every tradition of the school, Morgan put his arm round the boy's shoulders and led him as unobtrusively as possible out of the door which was immediately behind them. It happened that nobody noticed their exit. Outside the door, a short flight of stairs led to Morgan's private apartment which he shared with his wife, a woman who was herself an artist and who exhibited under the name of Gertrude Hayes. She was quite well known for her etchings.

What happened during the rest of that morning has completely vanished from Laurence's memory; but it is quite obvious that Morgan, who was normally the most timid of men, reluctant to set foot outside his Arts School except to lead a sketching expedition and still more reluctant to intervene in any matter that was not exclusively his own concern, must have had a long talk with our housemaster. As a result, no mention was ever made of Laurence's absence from the remainder of his classes that morning, and indeed he was instructed to let it be known that he had suffered from a sudden toothache and had gone to the school dentist. What really mattered was that Laurence was given the unique privilege of a key to the Arts School, was allowed to hide himself

27

there whenever he liked, and was even excused games on a day a week for this purpose. Shortly afterwards Mrs Morgan took him in hand and taught him etching.

A few weeks after this first incident which greatly affected Laurence, there occurred the second. It was the occasion of a school field day when the Rugby Officers Training Corps, membership of which was compulsory, paraded in uniform to march behind the band as far as the station, to entrain for some such destination as Aynho or Blenheim, and there to spend the day in tactical frivolities with the O.T.C. of some other school. It was all great fun for the masters, who comprised the officers and who thus had the privilege of deploying and advancing their troops, seizing and consolidating positions and carrying out an orderly withdrawal at a predetermined time when the special train was due to return to school; and it was not unamusing for the boys to have a day with sausage rolls and sandwiches, a large slice of currant cake, a stick of chocolate and an apple, away from school and in pleasant company. But for a small boy, who was carrying a rifle, a few rounds of blank ammunition, a haversack and a rolled-up groundsheet, it was usually a fatiguing occasion. By the end of it the very small boys, such as Laurence, would be all but asleep. Usually they would be excused evening prep, or would be given some nominal task requiring no skill and little effort. On this particular occasion, the prep which would normally have been assigned to Laurence's class was English composition.

The English Master who had the misfortune to deal with Laurence's class was another misfit as a Rugby schoolmaster. He was a large, plump, young man with a white face and thick spectacles, and his name was Mr Simpson: he was quite incapable of keeping order and not much interested in attempting to do so. The vast majority of the boys in his classes were unconcerned with the English language. They played their games, carved their names on desks, made and flew paper aeroplanes and slung ink pellets while Simpson, apparently oblivious of what was going on, spent the entire period reading aloud extracts from English prose and poetry which he thought might reasonably arouse some vague twitch of appreciation from someone in his audience. This someone was Laurence. And since the poet who had been "set" for that term was Tennyson, Laurence became imbued and even inspired with the sonorous, mellifluous imagery and rhythm of

Tennysonian verse. He was also, at these same classes, for some reason which he cannot now recall, presented with the myth of Eos and Tithonus which unaccountably seems to have excited him.

For those who have not had the benefit of Laurence's education, I should perhaps explain that, according to Homer, Tithonus, the son of Laomedon, King of Troy, was the lover of Eos, alias Aurora, who is the Goddess of Dawn. This lady, it seems, apart from bearing Tithonus a son, Memnon, did him the further favour of persuading the Gods to grant him immortal life. This they did; but since Eos and Tithonus between them had forgotten to ask for eternal youth, the Goddess found herself rising each morning at dawn from a couch shared with a lover who grew ever older and older, and presumably of less and less use to her. In course of time the situation became so intolerable that Tithonus begged for death. To his prayers, Eos had to reply that the Gods themselves cannot recall their gifts. In actual fact, after a lot of haggling, it was ultimately agreed that Tithonus should be transformed into a grasshopper; but Laurence had not pursued the myth to this extent by the time, on the evening preceding the school field day, Mr Simpson announced to his class: "Since you may be a little tired after your military exertions tomorrow, there will be no compulsory prep. But if any boy feels disposed to write a few lines of Tennysonian verse on the subject of Eos's reply to Tithonus, I shall take it as a personal compliment." Only the most sycophantic of boys would have responded to this invitation by serving up any prep at all for Mr Simpson; and Laurence, whatever else he was or was not, has never been a sycophant. Yet somehow he wrote his verse.

On the evening after the field day, he was so utterly exhausted that he could scarcely unwind his puttees and unlace his boots. He lay in the broken wicker chair, in the study which he shared with a boy called Blacker. This partnership had been arranged not by design or mutual choice, but by the fact that Blacker had been ill at the start of term, had returned late and had in consequence found himself saddled with Laurence in the least desirable of rooms at the furthest end of the topmost corridor. At heart a really nice chap, Blacker did his best to tolerate Laurence's company and, even if he was incapable of showing much positive sympathy, provided at least a negative anchorage where Laurence was fairly safe. Although he has not seen Laurence for some thirty years, I met him recently myself when I found that he recalls and confirms the strange story of Laurence's verses.

Normally the Lower schoolboys went to bed at nine o'clock; but after a school field day they could go to the dormitories, if they wished, half-an-hour earlier. At half past eight, Blacker, who was in the same form as Laurence, decided to decline Simpson's poetic invitation and to go to bed at once. This he did. Laurence had said that, as soon as he had got off his boots and puttees, he would do the same; and it is quite certain he was in fact in the dormitory by nine o'clock. Somehow or other the half-hour between Blacker's withdrawal to the dormitory and Laurence's arrival there had been entirely lost. Because of what followed, Blacker remembers quite clearly that he said to Laurence: "You took a long time getting off your boots," and that Laurence agreed he had. The latter seemed his usual cheerless, disinterested, dopey self, and was very nearly asleep.

The next morning, when both boys went to the study after breakfast, they found on Laurence's desk a sheet of foolscap which he still has in his possession. The handwriting was clearly Laurence's, rounded and childish. The name "L. Lamego" is written in the top right-hand corner, in the statutory position. The title is "Eos replies to Tithonus" and the verses which follow cover one side of the sheet and three-quarters of its back. The thirty-seven lines of verse were obviously written straight off, and must have been composed without the least hesitation, since a schoolboy could scarcely have copied them out in those thirty minutes. There are no corrections, except that the possessive adjective "your" has in two places been changed to "thine" and "thy" respectively.

Not only had Laurence no recollection whatever of writing the verses, but he was perfectly certain that he had never done so. At a quick glance they seemed to him quite readable and, since he was disinclined, even at that stage of his writing life, to let work go to waste, he duly showed them up to Mr Simpson at the English class that morning. The next day Simpson sent for him and questioned him about the work. It seemed probable that at least certain of the passages had been extracted, consciously or subconsciously, from the work of somebody else. Laurence neither admitted it nor denied it. Although of course he could

30

not bring himself to tell a master the whole story of how the verses had been found, he was capable of shaking his head when accused of plagiarism and of remaining dumb in face of flattering comments. Mr Simpson said: "But I am not accusing you of anything, Lamego, I am not even blaming you." But Laurence had too much experience of life to believe such an implausible statement or to regard it as anything but another trap. His natural response was to put on a blank expression, lower his head, withdraw into himself and remain stubbornly silent. He was told to take the verses to the Headmaster, the Reverend A. A. David, subsequently Bishop of Liverpool. Dr David, having read the work, asked questions almost identical with those of Mr Simpson. Then, retaining the sheet of foolscap, he dismissed Laurence with reassurances that were no more reassuring than those of the English Master. A few days later, when several members of the school staff had been consulted and had all failed to discover any source from which Laurence might have been quoting, the boy was recalled to the Headmaster's study. The poem was given back to him. At the top of the sheet, in red ink, there is written the mystical letter "C," enclosed in a circle, followed by the Headmaster's initials.

I should explain that when any boy served up a piece of work—an essay, a Latin prose or a Greek translation—he would be sent with it to the Headmaster for special commendation. A Lower School boy, such as Laurence and myself at that time, would normally be rewarded with a "D" written at the head of his work, standing for "Distinction." An Upper School boy might be, but was very rarely, awarded a "C"—which was worth no less than ten "Distinctions." When a boy had secured one "C" or ten "Distinctions," he was entitled to a prize of a guinea to be spent at the school bookshop on the Headmaster's account. This was the first occasion in the history of Rugby that a boy of the Lower School had won a "C" and the guinea prize outright. Laurence spent it on copies of Kipling's *Jungle Book* and *The Day's Work*, all three emblazoned with the school crest. In return he was required to make a copy of his poem and present it to the Headmaster.

On the normal standards of what is expected from child prodigies I cannot agree that this poem is of much merit. It begins:

I gave the wind her whisper in the dawn
That greets me as I rise up from the East ...

And it ends with Eos's conclusion:

But gifts that once from out my hand have gone
Can never be recalled whate'er may come.
Old age is thine, with it immortal life.
Most I would not have back, but there are some,
Like yours, which though I am thy wedded wife,
Must stay for ever till the end of all,
Until it pleases Zeus the world to rift,
To make the rivers break and mountains fall,
A God himself cannot recall his gift.

Notwithstanding their lack of any real distinction, even from the pen of a boy of fifteen, and even remembering that the whole poem was thirty-seven lines long and was written within half-an-hour, the circumstances of their composition were very strange. On Laurence the effect was momentous. He became aware of some totally unknown factor in himself, which might be called the sub-conscious brain, which had clearly been responsible for his earlier drawing of Michelangelo's head of Samson, and which he put to great use during the early part of his life. He soon discovered that, when he was required to learn a sonnet and have to repeat it the next morning, he need only read it through twice before going to sleep in order to be word perfect when he awoke. And later, when he started producing novels, he found that provided he set himself to write immediately on rising from his bed, and before he was properly awake, the words that appeared on paper were not only better than those of his normal work, but so strange to himself that he could never really believe them to be his own.

At the same time as Laurence found himself painting pictures and writing verses from some source, inside himself, with which he was quite unacquainted, and with a facility which seemed so strange, so unlikely, that he did not dare acknowledge it, he acquired also and quite suddenly a passion for music. Without the least musical talent or ear, he learnt nothing more than the ecstasy of plunging emotionally into music, of letting its tides sweep over him and of surrendering himself to its pluck and thrust. This was enough. Music became for him the same kind of escape as an engrossing book or the drawing school, into either of which he could lock himself up alone. Losing himself in music became a secret translation of himself as sharp as birth.

Something of the sort happened to many other boys. But for someone like Laurence who needed it so sorely it seemed a sanctuary of divine origin, although in fact it was very simply contrived by the senior music master, a bald, scarlet-faced, irascible, elderly little man called Mr Peppin. What old Pepper-john did was this. He staged an orchestral concert at the end of each term and prepared us for it with a series of weekly lectures. Although these lectures were voluntary, about a fifth of the whole school, perhaps a hundred and twenty boys, would attend them on Saturday evenings to hear Peppin take a symphony to bits and play us the parts on a skeleton orchestra, forcing the tunes into our memories, and a fragment of their meaning into our souls, by the violence of his own passion.

"Listen to this, you horrid little beasts! Do you know a horn when you hear one? Of course you don't! Give them a taste of it, Mr Palmer!" Mr Palmer, a local amateur, was not very good on the horn and, when he had played a few notes, Mr Peppin would silence him. "No, no, no, Mr Palmer! Oh dear me, no! What a terrible noise! Let's try another little tune. We'll play them the twenty-sixth bar, Mr Palmer, if you can find it." The horn would play the theme; old Pepperjohn would sing it in a voice which often cracked and went falsetto; he would leap for the piano and hammer the tune until the instrument quaked. "Sing, sing!" he would shout at us. Somehow we would all be singing—a theme from a symphony. "Shut up, shut up!" he would yell. "That's quite enough of that! Now listen, if you please; flap your ears and listen! Now we shall hear it, if you please, on the cello; we shall hear it the same theme but different... If you please, Miss Luke..." Miss Luke did her best while Peppin listened with an expression of anguish which enchanted his listeners. When the lady had done, there would be a long pause before Peppin had composed himself enough to say—"Never mind, Miss Luke... Thank you very much, Miss Luke. I'm sure we all know what you meant." He would swing round on us. "And now, you little beasts... Please listen to it on the flute, different again on the flute, but again the same if you will kindly give it your attention, not your *intelligent* attention ... just a little *rapt* attention, if you can manage it. On the flute, please, Mr Bates!"

His clowning left us ecstatically humming for a week. And by the twelfth week, when the evening came for a full orchestra to confront us in stiff shirts and dinner jackets, old Pepperjohn had got us ready for the ritual of re-birth. Laurence, even to this day, can never hear an orchestra tuning up without surrendering to a rich excitement below the ribs. When the conductor turns his back and lifts his elbows, and the silence slides over him, and is prolonged while somebody gives a last cough, before it becomes climactic, Laurence can still get a feeling of escape: He is free from that moment, even before the music starts. And the effect of it all on Laurence in those distant days of his captivity was tempestuous. When, after those twelve weeks of preparation, the pieces of the Pastoral Symphony were put together, and all the songs made one, and the cage was opened and the chains loosed, and the soul in its seismic liberation took to the air on strings, and Laurence for the first time knew himself embarked in an orchestra under full sail, he who had often wept with adequate cause now wept for happiness. There was, after all, a God.

By the time Laurence was fifteen-and-a-half, and had been at Rugby for two years, the school had, in its own ferocious way, done quite a bit of good to him. It had equipped him with a passion for music, with a subconscious brain which could be consciously set to work, with a very minor talent for boxing and with the key of the Arts School: all of them gifts whose subtleties were never to be revoked. Without the preceding period of discomfiture Laurence would not have been in a state to use such gifts or even to accept them. It was only after seven years of knocking about at Greenaways and Rugby that he was knocked into enough shape to start his education. By now the stunted plant was making normal growth. Taller, slightly broader although still very skinny, and perceptibly stronger although still pretty feeble, Laurence could now make some show of looking after himself. He was never popular but he was at least left alone; he fell into a few short-term friendships, and most important of all to his unconscious desires, he got at last a nickname.

It was won shamefully, a few months after his fifteenth birthday when his only real friend in the House was a boy called Enna. Of Latin extraction and appearance, Enna was almost as much despised as Laurence himself. He had the same pallid, dopey face, with blue shadows beneath his eyes, the same sallow skin that looked dirty even when it was clean, the same skinny and fragile body, and the same hunted expression which invited everyone to hunt him. Apart from his ineptitude at everything and his unpopularity with everyone, I doubt if he and Laurence had much in common; but since solitude at a boarding school, meaning isolation, is insupportable in conditions that do not allow boys to live within themselves, off their own resources, even if they are capable of such independence, these two preferred each other's company to none at all. Since to walk down a street alone was to attract unfavourable attention, they walked together. They went everywhere together until usage had turned this companionship into the only friendship ever enjoyed by either of them. Laurence betrayed it.

Enna's sister was getting married in London. It was a great escape for any boy when there was a wedding or a funeral in the family and he had a day and even perhaps a night away from school in order to attend it. The escape was more exciting, more complete a transformation (by reason of its fame) than even the end of term and the start of holidays. On these excursions, there was the thrill of the exotic: the same strange and brilliant liberation, almost a levitation, as Laurence got in those days when the curtain went up at a theatre and suddenly he had left himself behind and become airborne, as with music, and buoyant and inexpressibly free. When any near relative died or got married, the lucky boy who was thus bereaved or supplemented would enjoy a few hours of this particularly intense kind of liberty. He would leave behind his school clothes—black coat, grey trousers, white shirt, black tie and striped or chequered House-cap—and put on his "home suit" in which he had arrived at the beginning of term and would leave at the end of it. These "home suits" were mostly sober or drab, either a good deal too large so that we could grow into them or a little too small because we had just grown out of them. Naturally they were never meant to be becoming; they never fitted; it was bad form to be smart.

Enna, who was motherless, and whose father was yacht-bound and a professional, if dubious, aristocrat consorting with the ex-royalty that, even then, were beginning to gather on the Riviera, and disliking his son no less intensely than did everyone else, got his boy's clothes at a distance and indirectly by asking a female relative to take the boy to his own tailor. In consequence Enna had the grave misfortune for a Rugby schoolboy of a suit that fitted him and was of fashionable cut, built for him by Anderson and Sheppard of Savile Row. This the boys had dutifully discovered before Enna had been back at school ten minutes. Inside the pocket was a tab bearing the name of the tailors in print and, in script—"The Hon. Archibald Enna." He was the only Hon in the House: disgrace upon disgrace. Why had the father, the dubious peer, not had the little kindliness to send his rat to Eton where, relatively unobserved, he would not have been very much hurt?

"You are Anderson," said Connelly to Ridgeway; "and you, Shorter, are Sheppard. Give me the chalk!" He punted Enna across the dorm and laid him flat on his face, deployed to be fitted.

So Enna could now put on this suit—which had been cleaned and repaired since Connelly had dealt with it—and to attend his sister's wedding, could escape for the day and night to London. If he had had the least gumption, he would have been clear of the House, and en route for the station, before the others got back from early school. Instead, he let them catch him in the Quad.

By the time that Laurence, late as usual, returned for breakfast, a score of boys had bayed Enna who had got himself cornered on the cloister side of the Quad, reserved for the staff and the blogs, and out of bounds to the boys. For this trespass he could, of course, be beaten after lights-out when he got back from his outing to town. Meanwhile he stood white-faced, trembling with futile rage rather than fear, his long and skinny fingers intertwined, his mouth open in a kind of snarl. As Laurence arrived, somebody threw a broomstick at Enna which missed. Our cry rose in a concord of jeers and abuse. The spectacle of that ridiculous, double-breasted, dark blue suit, the long-pointed collar and scintillating tie, provoked us exquisitely. That white, hunted face

36

and those quivering legs united us in the companionage of the chase. Somebody threw a bucket left at large by a blog. Like the broomstick it missed.

It was raining, as always at Rugby, and the cobblestones of the Quad held puddles in one of which lay a string rag or cleaning cloth. Laurence, who had never in his life thrown or hit a ball with the least accuracy at even the shortest range, picked up this mud-sodden rag and flung it at his friend, the full length of the Quad. It hit Enna full in the face, full in the snarling mouth—a magnificent, impossible shot; the filthy water streamed down his collar and over his absurd clothes. His wedding appearance was ruined. The wretched jaws twitched sideways in a sort of convulsion—and Enna burst into tears. Then, inspired by desperation, he bolted and ran the gauntlet right through us. Connelly caught him on the bum with a glorious kick. Enna's arms windmilled as his feet skidded and he fell on his back in the slush. He did a kind of angular somersault, everything flapping and scrabbling, and got somehow to his feet. Mudsplashed, smeared all over, sobbing, gasping on a high, shrill note, he vanished and never, never came back. So he never got beaten for trespassing on the territory of the blogs. And Laurence, losing his only friend, had won his nickname. "By Christ, Meego," cried Connelly, "that was a sodding good shot!"

Meego was extolled with praise; he was Meego henceforward; and Laurence has spent the rest of his life in flight from that act of inspired cowardice and in pursuit of a courage that will allow him, one day, to throw a wet rag at a Connelly.

OXFORD

3

Getting into the College was easy. When Lamego arrived for the Entrance Examination, he came from the horrors and rigours of Rugby School in winter. As the train approached Oxford station at four o'clock of a frozen afternoon, the spires were invisibly dreaming in the bitter mists of dusk. All the clocks, if inaudible, were obviously chiming somewhere aloft in the fog. Eager for enchantment, Lamego was instantly enchanted; and with only a light suitcase he walked the mile from the station. As darkness grew, the architectural patterns of the Colleges produced glints, chunks and frames of light, and the odd finger of light thrusting high overhead, to punctuate oddly the massed and unexplained areas of shadow. An exciting, an enchanting and enchanted place! But a hostile place to all who neither had the right of entry nor were knocking on the door to be let in; and for the latter, it was by no means inviting but just intolerably desirable. Lamego was hammering on its gates until the knuckles of his soul were bleeding.

His father's old scout awaited Lamego's arrival in the rooms allotted to him. That wrinkled hand itched for the tip from a young gentleman with the hereditary *savoir faire* and not too indigent to be absurdly generous at the end of his visit. "The bed, sir, is well aired." It was in fact very damp. "I have closed the window, sir, and would advise you to leave it alone. It sometimes sticks." The window at that moment fell sharply open, completing the farce. "So I'll say good night, sir, good night." Alone for the night, Lamego went to the window.

Across the narrow street, in another window immediately opposite, a girl undressed and took a hip bath, only a few yards distant. She was the first naked woman that Lamego had ever seen. How to communicate with her? (He never solved the problem, although he had these rooms afterwards, and the girl continued this practice and was evidently aware of her audience.) By God this was Oxford and academic liberty! Hall, chapel, sublime

41

cloisters, quad and gardens, wine and cigars, the weightlessness of schoolboys ejected into the climatic liberties of Oxford: all was so exactly what had been told and anticipated, and the sum of it all was so scarcely different—indeed as if there had been no change but gravity suspended—that nothing came truly alive and was ever real at the time or afterwards in recollection.

The examination was easy enough although, even in those days, there were four or five candidates for every vacancy. For the average schoolboy of university standard the odds against his getting into this College were even larger than might be thought, because a number of places were naturally given, regardless of examination results, on the impressions of an interview where the right sort of would-be undergraduates were disentangled from the wrong. It must have been evident to anyone that Lamego was the wrong sort, as he was indeed to prove. But even in retrospect he was, and is seen, as the right sort of wrong sort. With the perspicacity of those who breed pedigree stock, or buy it to rear, the College authorities chose Lamego, and afterwards condoned his misadventures, because he was following the trail of his father with whom he could never be companionable, his uncles whom he had never really known and his great-uncles of whom he had scarcely even heard. But blood being thicker than ink, it did not matter that Lamego inadvertently missed his essential Latin paper. Only a tiresome and Germanic but relatively junior don perversely insisted on reverting to the question of that anachronistic Latin paper. In the middle twenties, before Hitler, the guttural accent was very rare. "As for your Latin paper, Mr Lamego . . ."

"And how is your father?" The question, asked by the remarkable Warden, revered as a personality and renowned as the perpetrator of a kind of Freudian lapse named after himself, might have come from any of the five octogenarian senators, guardians of the College spirit who sat at the broad table. Each was to repeat the question or ask something very similar, for all were very deaf, rather blind and somewhat mentally adrift. Their trembling hands on the College helm, steering by celestial navigation a course of blood-lines and inappropriate tradition, they kept this College among the foremost of the world's centres of learning. All five old men were shrunk very small into very large and splendid chairs; but in the largest and most splendid and of course the central chair sat the great, the incomparable Warden:

"Did you much enjoy Harrow?" he asked. For centuries they had successfully fought the woodworm in these limbs of the high ceiling and this deep panelling. Through Tudor windows the sun would have slanted across the table, but for a skirmish of undetermined wind, snow and sleet with what had been the makings of a bright day. "Harrow must be somewhat changed?" The old gentlemen would nearly all be Wykehamists, with perhaps one Etonian or Harrovian accidentally enlisted.

"I am at Rugby," Lamego said.

"He must be mistaken," said a senator. "The Lamegos all went to Harrow."

"My father sent me to Rugby. He thought Harrow was going through a bad patch."

"What a thing, what a thing to have to say!" The old gentlemen nodded and shook their heads, clicked their tongues like nannies gathered in the Park and generally expressed distress on account of bad patches.

"How did you say was your father?"

"In great heart, sir."

"In what?"

"Great heart, sir."

They clung to the word *heart*. "I'm very sorry to hear of it..." And from another: "It comes to so many of us these days. It's the bread." From the third: "He wasn't ever a heavy smoker."

Their Germanic obstructionist waiting for an opening thought he had slipped his foot in the door: "The Latin paper... If Mr Lamego would explain how he came to..."

"How is your father?"

"How is your Uncle Monty?"

"You mean his Uncle Manny."

"Poor Manny was at Oriel."

"On the contrary, we were on the same staircase."

"Mr Lamego, doubtless you can explain why you neglected to sit for your Latin paper?"

"He said his father was well?"

"Poorly, I rather gathered."

"His heart..."

"More's the pity."

"Manny is well enough?"

"At Oriel."

"Great-Uncle Manny is long dead," said Lamego sadly.

A few seconds of shocked silence through which the importunate question struggled: "Your Latin paper, Mr Lamego..."

"I saw Manny at the Eton and Harrow, the year before the War, or I daresay 1912..."

"At Oriel and dead. It was his heart. The bread, you know; it's getting them all."

"I was at Harrow with him."

"Eton."

"Permit me to know where I was at school."

"So you like Harrow, Mr Lamego?"

"That Latin paper, Mr Lamego, I really think we are entitled to be told..."

"I saw Monty at the last but one Gaudy—remarkably fit."

"Uncle Monty, Great-Uncle Monty," said Lamego, "died before I was born."

"A very great mistake... Last year when we met at his house in Haslemere I told him..."

"I don't think my Uncle Monty ever lived at Haslemere, sir."

"But I was there, my boy, I was."

"He means Manny."

"Manny was at Univ. Manny was never a member of this College."

"I must beg leave to disagree. Manny was a personal friend and we last met in the Athenaeum."

They no longer bothered much about Lamego himself, but revelled in dispute about his forebears. And of course—"You missed the Latin paper, I take it, on account of..."

"I am sorry to hear of your father," the Warden concluded. "We must hope for better news. Harrow may not be the best of schools these days but we hope..."

"The Latin paper."

"We hope you will be happy here."

Four other young men whose various ancestors had preceded them were, like Lamego, forthwith admitted to the College. The remaining many hundreds were told to await the results in six week's time. "I'll write to your father this evening," said the Warden to Lamego, "saying that we hope you'll like it here... Remind me, Dr Bruck."

"His Latin papers, Warden..."

44

"Remind me Bruck. I must tell him I'm sorry about the bread."

Lamego was so enchanted and imbued with the academic or mediaeval climate that he almost took the train back to Harrow instead of Rugby. A week later, arriving home for the Christmas holidays—or could he now say "vacation"—it was almost a surprise to find his father returning from a game of golf in his usual excellent health. "The Warden has written nicely about you," the elder Lamego told his son. "You seem to have made a good impression. We must discuss your allowance, and you should write about your rooms in College . . . What on earth made you tell him that I had a weak heart? He sent me a College loaf. You can't get bread like it in London, not these days." That was in 1924.

The chemistry course at Oxford took four years, the first of which was spent passing preliminary examinations in both chemistry and physics. If a schoolboy was sufficiently advanced, he could save a year by taking these "Prelims" before he went up to the University. Meego made the attempt, mainly for the sake of a jaunt to Oxford for the occasion. It was thought by his teachers at Rugby that he might possibly pass in chemistry but had no hope at all of doing so in physics. He passed in physics and would have done the same in chemistry if his papers had not been torn up on account of his first act of chivalry performed in aid of a girl, a very pretty girl, the first girl to whose attractions Meego had surrendered.

She was placed next door to Meego at the laboratory bench during the practical part of the examination. Candidates had to identify chemical compounds "A," "B" and "C" and, as proof that it was not mere guesswork, to record their methods of analysis. The tests were easy. Meego finished them with confidence in a short while, after which he looked at his neighbour who was quietly weeping. "What's the matter?" Meego asked. Walden, the invigilator, was at the far end of the laboratory. The girl said: "I don't know 'A.'"

"Copper Sulphate."

After a while the girl was again in tears.

"What's the matter now?"

"I don't know 'B' or 'C.'"

45

"Ferrous Oxide and Calcium Nitrate."

After a very short while the weeping was resumed.

"How do you tell?" asked the beautiful girl.

"Don't you know any of the tests?"

"Not exactly. Isn't it dreadful of me?"

"Yes," Meego said smugly. He slid his papers towards her along the bench. "But don't copy them out exactly, in case they're wrong." There was quiet for a while, but the girl was insatiable. "Can't you read my writing?" Meego asked. His calligraphy was shocking.

"Not very well."

"You put the copper sulphate with . . . etc."

It was then that Walden stamped down the laboratory. "Mr Lamego," he said, "you must not communicate with your neighbour, even if your neighbour is very pretty. Mr Lamego, I make enough noise clattering about the place for you to show the circumspection and the respect which are due to me. Mr Lamego, I shall have to take your papers and tear them into little pieces. [More in sorrow than in anger (in Latin.)]" Walden did so. Meego failed automatically. The girl passed. Meego never saw her again.

SEX AND PRAYER

It was to Walden, his tutor, that he said one evening, during his first summer at Oxford, that he thought he'd go into the Army. Walden did not ask why. On principle he never asked young men why they proposed to do anything, because, if they had a reason at all, it would not be a good one. On this occasion he simply said: "All armies have always been much-maligned communities. Have you ever considered the astonishing lack of excesses on the part of our troops in the Napoleonic campaigns? Rape, for instance. Rape is a remarkably interesting subject . . ."

Rape was an interesting subject to any adolescent, especially to one like Meego who knew literally nothing at all about sex. He had never been in the same room as a girl undressed, except a model in a "life class"; he had never kissed a girl, except his sister and cousins, not even on the cheek; most remarkable of all, for a boy from a Public School, he was not even aware that

46

homosexuality existed. Despite his studies of biology, and all the hours spent at Rugby dissecting frogs and occasionally a pigeon and one female rat, he knew so little about human physiology and was so ignorant of the elementary mechanics of sex that his erotic images and evil imaginings were most oddly aslant the realities of intercourse. Yet they were very insistent, and Meego, in his innocence and ignorance, believed them to be not only wicked but unnatural and abnormal, if not satanically unique. They added enormously to his sense of guilt. To quell them he called in God again.

This recourse was advocated, sponsored and actively directed by Meego's newest and closest friend of that era, E. F. M. Durbin, who felt himself just then to be particularly intimate with God. Evan Durbin was a scholar and the son of a notable Baptist minister, hence an hereditary evangelist, an enthusiastic amateur whose evangelism got greedily to work on Meego.

"Let us pray," said Evan to Meego. And uncomfortably but strangely unembarrassed the two men knelt before the window of Evan's rooms in College opening on to the garden and the ancient city wall. "Almighty Father who seest into the darkest corners . . ."

They prayed for spiritual strength that Meego might be saved from the tyranny of lust.

They might pray for spiritual victory over physical desire, but in fact the issue was opportunity versus ignorance. For once, the odds were on the side of the angels. Short of confrontation with a prostitute with enough professional pride to earn rather than acquire her fee—of which there was small chance in Oxford, except for the small clique of athletes who knew the fairly inno-cent underground—neither Evan nor Meego stood much chance of finding the temptation which so fervently they prayed to resist. Nor, having found her, would they have found their way round and through the buttons and elastic which preceded zip fasteners in feminine clothing. Indeed, but for Archie, the efficacy of prayer would not have been in doubt.

A friend from Brasenose College or B.N.C. and consequently a Rugby footballer of extreme promise and near-Blue achievement, Archie was severely troubled. His anxiety about his landlady's daughter, a lovely little girl called Pegs who believed herself pregnant, was quite destroying Archie's sure-handed agility as a three-quarter. There was no one with whom he could share the sultry guilt of paternal responsibility, since Pegs had been a virgin before Archie seduced her and her carnal knowledge was of this man alone. To Archie, a blunt-headed, squat if nimble lout, hairy and crafty but otherwise not intelligent, it seemed that a partner in paternity would more than halve his fears and indeed would allay them completely, restoring his game and his chance of a Rugger Blue. Surreptitiously he had taken legal advice. And in spite of it all, Pegs remained an immensely desirable mistress.

None of this was disclosed to Meego and his few constant companions who allowed Archie into their outer circle because, I suppose, a potential Blue was an asset to most circles. He knew, as they all did, that Meego drew females in the nude, an activity which to him was synonymous with sexual intercourse or at least implied sexual intercourse as a preliminary introduction. Why else should a girl be undressed? When, therefore, with Peg's agreement he offered Peg as a nude model to Meego, and one who would sit not in the sterile precincts of the Ruskin School of Art, but in Archie's rooms, he assumed that intercourse would occur. So, for that matter, did Meego.

The arrangements could scarcely have been more obvious and crude: nothing left to chance or implication. Meego had been duly excited by false accounts of the girl's sexual expertise which easily annulled the spiritual powers marshalled by Evan who prayed always with a trace of spittle at the corners of his sensual mouth and without knowledge of the enemy forces prowling so closely around. The girl had been similarly, but with no justification, excited. In Archie's bedroom the tryst duly took place and, after the introductions had been solemnised with a bottle of green Chartreuse, Archie withdrew, warning his guests that he would be back in a couple of hours by when he expected—with a leer he hoped—all the paraphernalia of art which Meego had brought with him would have yielded its masterpiece.

The sitting-room across the passage was out of use, so Archie had said, because of a broken window-pane and the gas fire out of action. The bedroom, where the stage was set for art, was grim but at least warm, suffocating hot from the gas fire which, when it was turned down at all, went altogether out, and from the window which did not open but was stuck fast shut. Pegs asked nervously: "You want me in the nood?" When Meego contrived a nod and a grin, attempting the casual sophisticated smile of the professional artist to whom naked flesh was merely his raw material of no more excitement than the usual arrangement of a still life: fruit and an old chianti bottle. Pegs slipped away and returned in her dressing-gown, obviously naked underneath. By this time Meego had set up his drawing-board and pastel chalks. In the room was a plain deal washstand with basin and jug, one wooden chair which Meego shared with a football jersey, a linoleum floor on which slid loosely a square of brownish yellowish patterned carpet, and the overwhelming iron bedstead with brass knobs. On this sat Pegs, swinging her legs and nervously huddled close inside the pink flowered cotton dressing-gown. Awkwardly but gently Meego loosened Pegs' grip and drew the dressing-gown apart. He drew it a little way off her shoulders, down her upper arms. Her head was tilted back, her eyes closed, her lips open. As the moments passed without further action, she opened her eyes and shut her mouth. A resigned expression captured her face, while her body drooped, relaxed, waiting within the open gown. In all Meego's life this was the moment of greatest fear. He was almost overcome with nausea, his mouth dry, his pulse frantic. Until this instant there had always been some adequate reason, plausible excuse, for adjourning the experience which he both desired and feared with so much tumult. In his perfectly healthy body he had no trust: at Rugby he had learnt to despise it; it would surely, when tested, betray him. Previously the occasion had never quite been brought in his ignorance to the point of test. Never before had the dish been fully prepared and put before him. But now it had! Nothing impeded consummation, the pounce, the ending of all doubts and the supreme experience where men and animals met in one consciousness. He had only to throw himself upon her: she was awaiting it. "I'll draw you just like that. Don't move!" he said. And when Archie returned not in two hours as he had forewarned them, but in one, the drawing was quite nicely done, but nothing else. As Meego in all sincerity told Evan at their next private meeting, the power of prayer had again been asserted and made manifest. Blessed be the Lord God of hosts!

CASABLANCA

4

For this modern world we have built up for ourselves must seem to quite a lot of us sometimes so nonsensical and so full of frustration, that even the sorrows of fighting a war can have some compensation in the escape that they offer. Escape to a war is escape to a world hideous enough in itself, but still it is a world in which a man is judged by what he is, and not by what he earns; where deeds are not done for profit, but because they just need doing.

From a broadcast by R.H., 15 June 1944

Admiral Lord Louis Mountbatten sent for Lamego who expected the sack and was ready to get it. He was just about out on his feet, and by now anxious for the merciful knockout punch; for another climactic personal defeat from which, as he knew by experience, there might come revival, a new beginning, another chance. Standing wearily and approximately to attention he heard Mountbatten say: "I consider that you're unfortunate if not disastrous . . ." and he understood at length that General Truscott on behalf of General Patton had chosen him, Meego, to go to America and there to help plan the American assaults on Morocco which were to be a part of the whole North African venture known as Operation "Torch".

The Americans were anxious, or had been persuaded to be anxious, to set up in their country the same kind of inter-service planning teams that were working so well under Mountbatten. Given the pick of C.O.H.Q. for this purpose Truscott had requested Dick Costabadie from the Navy, John Homer from the R.A.F. and from the Army—Meego. "You have ability, I grant you," Mountbatten said, "but you seem completely devoid of tact. Nor do you know when to keep your mouth shut. I should think we shall be at war with America before you've finished." He did not smile; he gazed at the wall facing his desk and scarcely glanced at all at Meego who stood entranced by that excessively handsome profile.

From this aspect the only weak feature of this most genuine of

53

War Lords—the not small, but smallish eyes, too close together by only a fraction—was inevident; and the face represented for Meego all that he would always covet of power, personality and assurance; and ambition justified; a vast ambition that was not reprehensible, because it exactly coincided with public interest; an imperial ambition, superbly equipped for any conquest, armed with a quick, logical mind and an even swifter intuition, with no weakness, except a total inability to judge men correctly, whether they were his cronies or his subordinates, and yet with the power to command an uncritical loyalty from almost everyone; an ambition rather sad to see in an age that offered it too little scope.

"So there it is!" Mountbatten was saying to Meego, who was still standing roughly erect beside the imperial desk. Mountbatten sighed, which, in these circumstances, was as much as to smile. He didn't need to smile nor even look at Meego for his charm to command devotion. Meego felt devoted as Mountbatten continued: "I did my best, I assure you, to persuade Truscott to choose somebody else, *anybody* else. But he was quite obstinate about it. Be that as it may and since he insists on taking you, I want you to know that you can count unreservedly on all possible help and support from my Headquarters and myself. Everything, anything, any time! You have only to make a signal: 'Personal from Lamego to Mountbatten' and I shall personally see to it." He nodded curtly a dismissal, but added as Meego got to the door: "I'm afraid you've got rather short notice. You leave to-morrow forenoon. Time is rather short."

Thus reinforced and reassured Meego set out on his first visit to the United States. There had been yet another last letter, in case of his death, written and left behind in the care of the Bank; another last farewell to his wife. As they embraced she said: "I only ask one thing, darling. You do do such silly things, darling, promise me not to be silly?"

Early in the afternoon following his summons to Mountbatten, an immense black Cadillac with an American driver manoeuvred itself into the forecourt of Albany to transport Meego to Northolt. The driver, something of a thruster, passed en route the two similar cars which were carrying, respectively, John Homer and

54

Dick Costabadie.* Although all three of these relatively junior officers were starting for the same destination from within half-a-mile of each other, each had a car to himself, the biggest kind of car in the world, for America was already their host, and this was American efficiency, and now that America had got going, the war would be over in a matter of months.

The party, headed by (British) Admiral Ramsay and (American) Rear Admiral Bieri, assembled at Northolt Aerodrome. It numbered eight. Apart from the three planners from Combined Operations, there were two British experts in Shipping and Movements, and that curt, saturnine, censorious disciplinarian, Captain Brownrigg, R.N., previously Master of the Fleet to Admiral A. B. Cunningham in the Eastern Mediterranean. Now he was on Ramsay's staff. Ramsay, a merry little man who had come out of retirement to take over Naval command at Dunkirk, was great fun to be with. But it was some days before Brownrigg, as major-domo of the backstairs element, ceased to disapprove of Dick's flippancy and Meego's facetiousness. John was always a quiet one, frequently asleep or else fraternising with his fellow-airmen—Polish, Dutch, French, Belgian, American or British—from whom he collected, for everyone's benefit, such prizes as bottles of whisky, boxes of cigars, candy, chewing-gum and contraceptives. Like Harry Romilly, dear John specialised in providing for his colleagues even more than any of them could want.

A quick hop from Northolt to Prestwick; at Prestwick they said there was "just time for chow"; and everyone was handed a single plate furnished with an assortment of chicken, jam, cheese, salad, chives, jelly, spam and apple, the whole suffused rather than inundated with tomato sauce: Meego's first taste of a fare with which, in the course of much service with the Americans, he was to become nauseatedly familiar. Embarking then in one of the newest kinds of plane—Meego thinks it was the very first of the Stratocruisers, certainly it was pressurised—they took to the air, went comfortably to bed between sheets each in his own curtained bunk with a spring mattress and fled westwards.

They had put back their watches, four hours, or was it five? Many hundreds of thousands of miles has Meego flown since

---

* Group Captain John Homer, later killed flying in India, and Lieutenant-Commander R. de Costabadie, later the youngest Commander in the Royal Navy, died after the war from a tubercular infection.

then, but never in such comfort, never with such exciting prospects of landing in a warless world of no rationing, shops full of everything, no black-out and all aglitter. The flight itself, luxurious in the extreme, was an accurate foretaste of what was to come. Indeed the superb plane had no drawbacks whatsoever, except that it lacked the range to get across the Atlantic. From a dozen hours of deep sleep Meego was woken by Dick standing in florid pyjamas by his bed and solemnly declaring: "The sun rises in the East." The sun was slanting into the cabin from forrard; the plane, having got almost to the point of no return, had, in the middle of the night, turned back and was now heading whence it had come; and all the watches that had been put back had now to be put forward again. John woke only when the plane landed. Told he was back at Prestwick, he said: "It doesn't surprise me in the least."

It was then decided that a Liberator bomber with few amenities and no comforts but a much longer range was a more suitable vehicle; and since, in those days, it entailed the use of individual oxygen, the party was now drilled in putting on the masks and turning on the taps of this apparatus. At nightfall they re-embarked, took to the air and almost immediately returned to the runway. The weather was too bad and the forecast too menacing. It remained the same for about five days, maybe more, nobody can say for sure, since those suspended in mid-travel, just like those in gaol, become oblivious of calendar and clock, aware only of discomfort. This was very real. The party, except for the two Admirals, was reduced to palliasse life, being quartered, four to a very small, bedless room, half a mile from a lavatory or a wash-basin, three Army blankets apiece. The amenities of Prestwick in war-time proved to be even less diverting than expected.

True that on the third or fourth evening there was a break in the storms which enticed the party to pack hurriedly and re-embark in its special plane, ready for flight: all of them, that is, except its boss. Admiral Ramsay had unaccountably vanished. After a few hours the security police discovered that he had gone to visit his laird, his clan, his fiefs, or maybe it was just his family seat, somewhere on the other side of Scotland and not on the telephone. But in a day or two he was back, cheerful as always; and since it was now becoming somewhat urgent that they should get to America, the two Admirals put their heads together and decided it was quicker by sea. A signal was made to the Clyde, and the Queen Elizabeth which had just weighed anchor and sailed, westward bound, was ordered to come back again and wait in mid-stream until the party had reached her. This would have been in an hour or so, but there was no road transport.

By now the staff had lost interest in what had become an improbable project. A sort of oriental apathy had superseded impatience. Night fell dismally; nobody took action, nor even suggested it. Ultimately it was Meego, the junior officer of the party, who collected four antique taxis from waiting at the station to drive all the way to Greenock; or rather they would have done so, if only they had had the fuel. But they had used most of their rations for the month, and Meego, as he afterwards explained, took a calculated risk and relied on finding Black Market stuff. These four taxis were only just sufficient for all of the party with all their bedding rolls and suitcases. It was raining when the first taxi ran out of petrol; and raining very hard indeed, and also very dark, when a second taxi spluttered and fell silent; and it was in a cloudburst that the party re-grouped itself and baggage into the two decrepit vehicles that were still mobile. There passed something like six hours before seven enraged officers, long speechless, reached the Clyde in those two cabs, much of the baggage missing, Bieri sitting on Brownrigg's knee and Ramsay on Meego's. John Homer, as usual knowing a better way, had fallen out. He met his colleagues again on the quay at New York.

Again, in the thick darkness at Greenock, it was Meego who discovered the Naval launch awaiting them and reported it to Admiral Ramsay who theatrically twice asked—"What!" And twice Meego, who should have known better after his many, many months with the Royal Navy, committed the same sin and compelled the Admiral to answer sternly, after giving Meego every chance: "Larnch, boy, not launch; larnch, larnch! As a midshipman I had my bottom tanned for a great deal less than that."

"Aye aye sir," Meego said.

Even in utter darkness one knew, says Meego, that the launch was gleaming and spotless, the drill of its crew faultless, but it could not find the Queen Elizabeth until it had enquired the way of several vessels lying at anchor en route. "Do I look like the Queen Elizabeth?" asked the skipper of one tug-boat, mistaking the question. And still nobody laughed.

At last the great wall, the greatest wall that anyone could ever imagine outside concepts of infinity, stretching upwards with no crest, no joining to the invisible sky, met them with a well-drilled thud. Nothing in the world is so big as the biggest ship in the world unseen from the water-line in the dark. The ship did not seem very affable and no wonder. Costing £100 a minute, or maybe £1,000 a minute, to be kept trembling under power, she had been arrested at the start of her flight, held in mid-stream and kept waiting for seven hours for the seven little men who were now trying to board her. Overhead a rectangular gash even blacker than the rest of darkness was the hatch into which they had to scramble, and be hauled up, home at last, and met by the Captain himself, as their distinction merited. "By God," said Ramsay as he dusted his trousers, "I'm about ready for a drink."

Smugly, or perhaps it was with a sense of poetic justice, the Captain shook his head. The two Queens, he said, being under American charter as troopships, were, by American Naval regulations, teetotal. "You're under the White Ensign," said Ramsay. "You're sailing empty?" The traffic in troops was of course all one-way—Eastwards.

"It makes no difference," the Captain answered with relish. "We have nothing on board but Coca-cola or ginger-pop."

At dinner that night a bad time was had by all. The meal was silently eaten. Only the irrepressible Costabadie dared ask Meego to pass the salt. Yet the next night, well out into the Atlantic, was very different. For forty minutes the party sat at table without food, awaiting its two Admirals. When they came at last, it was arm-in-arm, doing a kind of step-dance, or of course it must have been a jig, down the length of the immense, empty saloon. "By God," said Admiral Ramsay, "that doctor packs a pretty medicine cabinet."

"By God, it's medicinal," Admiral Bieri said. "All you boys need is rank." And, thanks to the ship's doctor, the remaining four days of the journey, even if those without enough rank had not a drop to drink, were relatively hilarious. Brownrigg even smiled as he trumped Meego's ace.

On account of their speed the two Queens were reckoned invulnerable to any but the most fortunate of U-boats striking their trail by accident, wherefore they sailed unescorted but on a zig-zag course. Safe outside harbour at New York, the ship had to wait for daylight before entering. The sunrise by itself was more than spectacular: a poet's sunrise, or at least a novelist's, making inadequate, unfit to live, the plain man swollen with desire to speak, but inarticulate and hurt beneath the ribs by too much inexpressible revelation. The supreme moment was only a moment while the world still slept, but Meego, awake early and on deck, had caught it just as the tops of those pinnacles snatched the sunrise first. The same as everyone else, only more so—Meego thought—he felt everything that he ought to be feeling at the first sight of that ecstatic skyline of New York struck by dawn. Since man had made this scene of crystalline towers and pinnacles then man truly was himself made in the image of God. God could have made the Alps or a Cotswold valley by happy accident; but man had made this skyline with set-square, dividers and the mason's implements. Unwillingly, Meego found himself committed to worship. Then he began to think in practical terms. Either (he thought) he must see no more of it, ever, and keep the vision intact for ever to cherish; or the vision must be broken and the dream explained, understood, by showing himself that this wasn't Prospero's work, nor any magical hallucination, let alone divine, but a plain city in which people lived as squalidly as anywhere else, maybe more so, and man was at his commonest. The more squalid the disclosure, and the more common the people found squatting beneath their own invisible peaks, the greater would be the miracle of what they had created, and the more certain it would be that God had breathed something into them, and the more true was God. In short, Meego wanted to go sightseeing in New York.

The reception committee, which had got up very early in the morning to come alongside in a launch for the Admirals, had in fact planned a tour of the city to be preceded by a semi-official breakfast and concluded with a demi-semi-official lunch. Rooms had been booked at the Waldorf-Astoria where everyone could rest and recover from his voyage—as if the party had been battered across the Atlantic in an ocean-going tramp—before a special plane flew them on to Washington in time for a quite informal dinner that night. John Homer, who had, as so often before, got to the right place at the right time by his own methods and was awaiting his colleagues on the quay, had laid on a special afternoon treat for what he called "the travelling trio," that is

Dick, Meego and himself. "A blond, a brunette and a redhead, chaps!"

No sooner had the party been apprised of these arrangements than duty became obstructive, and Admiral Ramsay suddenly decided that he was duty's embodiment. He vetoed the whole thing. "Time presses," he said. His hosts were desolate; but the more they pointed out that Washington was not expecting anyone till nightfall, the more the Admiral insisted that he must get there by noon. Meego begged Dick to add his nautical pleas to those of the Americans. "Not me," Dick said. "I'm not all that keen on John's cast-off redheads. I've got my promotion to think of." Meego tried even Brownrigg. "Tell your boss there's no possible point in arriving when we're not wanted."

"Try telling him yourself."

Meego did.

"You have been brought here, Lamego, to advise not me, but the Americans," Ramsay said.

Somebody went to telephone to the airport; but by the time he got back with the news that the plane could not anyway be ready before one o'clock, Ramsay and his staff were swept into cars and, preceded by motor-cycle police with sirens wailing, whisked round the edge of the city to La Guardia airport. Inside the aerodrome they settled down to wait. After a long while they moved to a quick lunch counter and had a quick lunch. By mid-afternoon they were air-borne and in ninety minutes or so were at Washington Airport where no one expected them. Here they waited again until, at the time originally planned, they were ceremoniously fetched. Again they were reduced to seven in number, for again John Homer had found a friend and vanished.

Washington in 1942 was not unqualified fun for anyone in British uniform. The ordinary American, informed only by his own Press, regarded Britain not just unsympathetically, but with positive contempt. An extra million of these ordinary Americans, or so it was said, had been imported into Washington to deal with the war, and there was as yet no increase of amenities to deal with the influx. Life for an alien, uncomfortable in this over-crowded city, was not enhanced by the outspoken comments on his country offered by complete strangers who sometimes would approach Meego in the street to explain the timidity of British strategy, the incompetence of British tactics and the timidity of British troops. Why else Dunkirk? And what had Britain been doing ever since Dunkirk? Meego, who had come expecting honour as a representative of the people who had saved the world, was received as a representative of the people who had yet again messed things up, so that yet again America, against all her principles, had to save British imperialism, or was it colonialism, from its overdue extinction. Again and again! "Again" was the savage adverb. Again "our boys" were to be "sacrificed" to save Europe. The Dieppe raid had lately been executed by the Canadian Division and three Commandos, with perhaps a dozen American officers going along to watch, quite enough for certain American newspapers to report the landings in their early editions under banner headlines: "American troops back again in Europe." In later editions, however, when the raid was over with the dusk, the headlines had been changed to: "British again scuttle out of France."

At a Georgetown cocktail party an American Colonel explained it all to Meego: "You Britishers' backsides must be gettin' wore out sittin' around in your offices waiting for our boys to come over and give that guy Hitler a kick in the pants." Even an educated American, even a Colonel, could not understand, he simply could not accept, that his country had not declared war on anyone but had suffered the humiliation of having war declared on her by Germany after being attacked by Japan without provocation. Americans cannot accept such unacceptable facts any more readily than us. And they are less often required to do so.

Unhappy as usual in a strange place, Meego did his best to involve himself in work. American hours made this difficult. The military in Washington knew too well about Whitehall methods, hours and apathy—(hence Dunkirk)—and by contrast with the British, every officer reported for duty not at nine-thirty or ten o'clock, but at eight precisely. Having made his mark he then queued up, in succession to buy his newspaper, enjoy his shave at the barbers, eat his breakfast, get his shoe-shine, and patronise the lavatory. Getting on for ten o'clock he was all set, seated at his desk and all but ready for work. But work was not ready for him. The practice of arriving at the office in ascending order of seniority

61

or importance, as practised in Britain, was plainly undemocratic. In America the most junior clerk was no lowlier than the Commander-in-Chief. Both of them started and stopped work at the same moment, so that the Staff Officer had a few idle hours each morning at his empty desk waiting while the clerks at their leisure opened the mail, filed the various signals, and in general sorted things out. By then it was just about time for lunch. In the afternoon one could work, but only briefly, because everything stopped dead at five o'clock. By that hour all replies to the incoming mail had to be dictated, typed, signed and despatched; at that hour, or slightly before it, the clerks took into custody all the documents from all desks and locked them in their filing cabinets for the night. The clerks ruled the roost: the clerks, the girl stenographers and the female cleaners. If an officer, who might have hidden a few papers on which to work, should try to linger in his office after five o'clock, he would literally be swept out of it.

This procedure allowed quite a number of documents to be drafted, some of them to be typed, all of them to be filed, but none of them to be read. Nor were they readable. An American military "Estimate," the equivalent of a British military "Appreciation," which is the basis of all operational staff-work, was written entirely in jargon as abstruse as a treatise on advanced mathematics, cluttered with abbreviations to keep it short, and then, to make it long, stretched, set out, over-punctuated, superparagraphed, sub-paragraphed and spaced like a typographical experiment on an *avante garde* prose poem of the middle-twenties. Confronted with these papers Meego recalled nostalgically his Staff College teaching on "military writing" and the lecture by his chief instructor "Jorrocks," now Sir Brian Horrocks, which began something like this: "Imagine yourself to be a simpleton with a very limited vocabulary writing for a moronic and reluctant idiot... Unless what you write is not only to the point, but easy and interesting to digest, as well as brief, and even on occasions humorous, the reluctant idiot will not read a word of it."

American staff training and methods were never the equal of the British. An American Headquarters had on its establishment nearly twice as many staff officers as its British equivalent, so that its staff procedure was at least twice as ponderous. On the other hand, the Americans at their best were quite uninhibited by their staff when they really got going. Without staff-work at all they would move a Division a hundred miles, commit it to action and contrive to supply it, while the British "Q" staff of our Movements Control Section would still be proving that the movement was impossible.

Moreover the Americans were always ready to learn, and they learnt very quickly, while we remained obdurately ignorant. Without the least reluctance the Americans would borrow officers from us to teach them a job that we had already learnt, but we never returned the compliment. Our engineers, for instance, were disastrously inefficient by comparison with theirs, but we declined their offer of equipment, instructors and specialists. Yet we were constantly lending them such odd experts as Signals Officers, Intelligence Officers, interpreters of air photographs and, of course, planners like Meego. In fact they were learning to plan from Meego while many British Commanders were still insisting that planning was not something to be learnt at all but something that one just did. They may of course have been right.

After the war the very word "planning" was deprived of its meaning and given a political significance: Socialists planned, others didn't. It was misused to destruction until now, as in 1940, few people have the least idea of what they mean by it. Meego reckons himself to be one of the few, the very few.

After the war was over Meego spent some three years writing a study of planning, illustrated from the secret planning files before they were incinerated in the course of the grand clearance. The book was commissioned by the War Office but was to be put on sale to the public. This could not be. Meego had spent but a few months of research in the archives of the Cabinet Office when it was plain that what he was about to write would have to be censored, and severely so, not on account of security, but for the sake of several reputations, or it would not be fit for publication. Despite censorship Meego thought that he could make it into a popular best-seller which would still have a limited military use; uncensored it would be, he reckoned, a masterpiece. He reckons it is. With the consent of the War Office he produced a treatise too indiscreet for print. A number of copies were stencilled off, numbered, given a security grading, and distributed only to the libraries of certain service and inter-service institutions. Very, very rarely somebody reads a few paragraphs of one of them. This is sad, because Meego knows it is the best work he has ever done, probably the best that he ever will do; and he knows that he knows about planning. The few who have read his "masterpiece" are inclined to believe him—as the Americans did.

To be brutally objective in retrospect, it must be admitted that Meego's contribution to the planning of the Casablanca operation was both unimportant and odd. The operation itself was strategically unsound and tactically crazy, since the very great risks that had to be taken were uncalculated and incalculable, the prize was small, and the journey not really necessary. The British considered it not only unjustified, but pointless. They persuaded General Eisenhower, not exactly to their way of thinking, but at least to be unenthusiastic about the project. It was the American Chiefs-of-Staff who insisted on doing it. They felt it to be an essential insurance to have an Atlantic port in Africa if they were to commit their forces inside the Mediterranean. Otherwise the Germans might come down through Spain and Spanish Morocco, taking Gibraltar en route, and so cut off our armies in Algeria from American and British bases. The American view was that the Germans would do just this; the British view was that they couldn't.

Moreover, so the British maintained, French Morocco and the huge port of Casablanca were not assets, but liabilities. They were equally liabilities to the Germans who were not occupying them at the moment but were represented by a series of missions which issued orders to the French troops and the local French Government. If the Germans should be tempted, by the allied landings in Algeria—and of course the advance of the Eighth Army through Tunisia—to come through Spain, take Gibraltar, take Tangier and Spanish Morocco, and so extend their armies and lines of communication by some six hundred miles, it might in fact be disastrous for themselves and a prize bonus for us. Officially the Spanish liked the Germans, and in reality did not object to them any more than they objected to all foreigners in their country. This was known to be a lot. The Spanish would not have consented to the degree of German occupation necessary to ensure the German lines of communication; and although Gibraltar could undoubtedly be captured by almost anyone, it was not so easy as it seemed to control the Straits of Gibraltar by simply sitting on that famous and relatively useless Rock.

The Americans would not agree: they had a tendency to go rather strictly by the atlas, to which they applied a quite different —and more realistic—set of logistic rules from those in force with the British. In practice the Americans were usually right about logistics. Nevertheless on the question of Casablanca, indeed a major port, but one entailing, if it were to be used to supply the Allied armies in Algeria, a drive by road of 800 miles across the Atlas mountains, which at their lowest pass were ten thousand feet high, their ideas seemed unduly fanciful. As a supply base for Algeria—the British insisted—Casablanca was virtually useless. (In the event the British were proved to be wrong.) Moreover, once Casablanca had been taken, French Morocco would need a garrison of not less than six divisions to secure it against possible attack by Germans through Spain, Gibraltar and Spanish Morocco. (Again, in the event, the British were proved wrong.) Consequently, the British General staff produced a characteristic red herring which the Americans innocently pursued for some weeks: a plan whereby Casablanca should be taken by airborne attack from Oran, a week after Oran had been captured by the main "Torch" assaults, which presupposed a flight of eight hundred miles over the Atlas mountains by aircraft carrying paratroops. Nobody really thought that it would work, but everybody pretended to believe in it. For two long weeks Lamego made idiotic calculations on the plan, working with the American staff as their assistant, each day adding another naval element, a couple of battleships, a cruiser squadron, a few flotillas of destroyers, a medium-sized fleet, which would directly assault the ports of Spanish Morocco simultaneously with the parachute drop. To each suggestion the U.S. Navy gave a flat refusal. Yet by some curiosity of inter-allied concordance it became accepted policy that Casablanca was to be taken either by this impossible airborne assault from Oran, or by direct assault of infantry sailing from American ports, and the whole efforts of a sizable staff including Meego were directed to making an endless succession of comparative studies of the two alternatives.

While the argument was still at its height, the decision was made: Casablanca was to be taken by amphibious assault, an exclusively American operation, on the long, limitless beaches of French Morocco where the only hazard, apart from a few French soldiers, was surf.

On a calculation of meteorological probabilities—with which amphibious planning must always start—the odds were decisively against a landing in early November being possible at all on that exposed coast. On an average, landings might be made on seven days in the month, but not on the other twenty-three. The strong probability was that surf would capsize all the landing craft, if it was attempted to lower them, and that everybody would be drowned.

It was worse even than this. While the odds were roughly thirteen-to-four against the landing being possible on any one day, they were more than ten-to-one against its being possible on two consecutive days, and more than twenty-to-one against three consecutive days of calm sea. This meant that, even if troops could be put ashore on the appointed day, the probability was that they would have to wait for three or four days before they could be supplied and reinforced. It would not be at all unusual if they had to wait a fortnight.

In short the operation was a bad, mad gamble which the American Chiefs-of-Staff decided to take because it was the view of their Intelligence Chiefs that the French would not fight. Our own experience at Dakar led us to suppose they would. The Americans said that the French might oppose a British landing while they might, on the contrary, welcome an American one. The Americans, after all, had not sailed into Oran and sunk almost the whole of the French Fleet. Nor had they even defeated the French at Trafalgar, an incident which each new generation of French Naval officers continues to regard as a personal affront. In other words, the Americans said that the French did not like the British, and while the British knew this to be true—and did not themselves like the French—they resented the Americans saying it.

Actually there were four possibilities. First, if the venture was unopposed and there was no serious surf (which was heavily against the odds), then the operation would be merely an amphibious exercise which would certainly get into an amphibious muddle, as such exercises always did, but would end in success. Secondly, if the venture was unopposed and the surf was bad (which was the odds-on chance), a landing on the beach would be off, but the Americans, masters of improvisation as they were, might be able to improvise something on the spot by sailing straight into Casablanca and other, much smaller ports. Thirdly, if the French decided to fight, and the surf was bad, then the whole thing would have to be called off, despite Patton's protestations that he would personally swim ashore rather than return home without a fight. And the fourth possibility, again against the odds on both counts, was that the French would fight, but that the surf would permit a landing in face of French opposition. This last possibility was the only one for which Patton would plan. He always insisted that the French would fight, and that he hoped they would; and, in the event, even when they declined to do so, he insisted that they had. He had not the least intention of being stopped by either Frenchmen or surf. Anyway, he said, his luck was in and he proposed to count on it.

The plan, which had scarcely been considered when Meego reached Washington—although the plans for the other "Torch" landings in Algeria, both British and American, were then far advanced—was to provide for an opposed landing on a flat coastline. Down in the south, the half of an Armoured Division would be put ashore at Safi. Up in the north, Truscott was to take Port Lyautey with a regiment (the equivalent of a British Infantry Brigade). In the centre the main landings would be made by the Third Infantry Division in the area of Fedala, a small pleasure resort some ten miles north of Casablanca.

Casablanca was defended by a French Division under General Béthouard; in the port there was also the *Jean Bart*, a very powerful battleship which was mechanically incapable of going to sea, but whose heavy guns were still operational and could bear on the American Naval forces and on the whole long expanse of Fedala's beaches. These beaches were also commanded from the north by a French fort, Fort Blondin, which stands on its promontory and cliffs, a notable landmark not only of all that coast, but also of Meego's life. In brief, while the *Jean Bart* and Fort Blondin remained actively enfilading the beaches, landings would be costly, if not impossible.

As has been said, Fort Blondin stood on cliffs which could not be scaled, so that it was not subject to direct assault. A mile or so to the north the cliffs disappeared gently into the sand-dunes characteristic of all that Moroccan coast. To the south, the Fort was equally immune from direct attack, since the cliffs curled northwards or eastwards to form the northern lip of the estuary of the river Mellah which flowed into the Atlantic at that point. The Fort entirely commanded the estuary, and it would be impossible in any circumstances of war to sail craft up it. The river itself was crossed by a bridge, about half a mile inland, carrying the long road which ran the length of Morocco, or most of it, parallel to the coast. On the southern bank of the estuary, there was a fine, long beach leading to a few sand-dunes and scrub before the coastal road was reached. If landings were practicable at all, they could best be made to the south of the estuary, the troops having to force their way inland as speedily as possible in the hopes of reaching the bridge before the French or Germans, or both, had been able to demolish it. Intelligence was conflicting as to whether or not the bridge was already prepared for demolition. If so, then the chances of capturing Fort Blondin against any considerable opposition were more than remote.

All through the planning that fort was dominant in Meego's thoughts. Most of his American colleagues tended to belittle it: its construction was ancient, it was manned only by the French; "Our boys" will "look after it." Meego doubted if they would. It had, he thought, either four or six guns of seventy-five millimetres and one hundred-and-five millimetres calibre, well emplaced in concrete; and the French gunners, if they chose, could be more accurate and stubborn than most. Of course, at the back of American minds there was lingering that optimistic forecast of the Intelligence Section that the French wouldn't fight. But the plan had to be based on the assumption that they would; and if they did, then that fort would be the major obstacle to the whole assault. On this logical conclusion Meego became such a bore that when he went into an office in Washington, its occupant would probably say at once: "We are *not* going to talk about your fort!" But how was it to be taken?

It might have been taken by Commando troops under cover of darkness. But the American assault troops had not had Commando training; they had not had assault training; and few of them had even seen a landing craft; they had not had battle training since, at that stage of the war, the American public would not have tolerated casualties in the course of training with live ammunition. Moreover at that stage of planning, the Navy had not yet agreed to a night assault. Like all navies, like our own Navy at Dieppe, it was insisting that the crews of its landing craft would never find their way to the right beaches in the dark.

If the assault was to be made, as the Navy desired, by daylight, there would be needed a tremendous weight of supporting fire, not only to silence that fort and the battleship *Jean Bart*, but also to engage Béthouard's Division while the landing craft beached in the surf, and the infantry waded ashore, fought their way inland and got gradually reinforced, supplied with artillery and fighting vehicles, and generally established. For such support there could be no aircraft, for none could get there except from carriers; and those being carried by the Navy would be needed for exclusively Naval purposes. A senior Naval officer was said to have promised to "beat hell out of that fort" by Naval gunfire. "What with?" Meego asked. Would the supporting cruisers take "bombardment" charges for this purpose? He suspected not, because he had reason to believe that the American Navy did not possess them. When he expressed these doubts, he was told very properly by the Navy to mind his own business.

On this question Meego went to Patton and explained that "bombardment" or reduced charges gave to a ship's guns the effect of howitzers. At a sacrifice of range and penetration their shells could be lobbed with relative accuracy on to a land target. Without such charges, and using their normal, high-velocity shells, Naval bombardment was not only wildly inaccurate, but extremely dangerous to those whom it was intended to support. If a shot was a fraction high it could whistle inland for miles out of the picture; if it was a fraction short, it would hit everyone on the beach. Patton asked: "Do you think I can't trust the Navy to take along the right sort of ammunition?"

Meego answered: "I think you can't."

"I think so too," Patton said.

Their mistrust was justified. All navies have always reckoned that a warship's job is to engage other warships and not to provide artillery for soldiers who ought to take along their own. No true sailor, if he could help it, would ever waste the limited space in his magazines on reduced or bombardment charges whose lack of range and penetration made them useless in Naval warfare. "They'll never knock hell out of that fort," Meego said. "They'll knock it out of us."

"I think so too," Patton repeated.

The inter-related problems of Naval support and the timing of the assault were solved, as so often in America, by a decision slammed down from the topmost level upon all concerned. All landings, it was decided, in both Algiers and French Morocco, were to take place simultaneously under cover of darkness. With this decision, which over-ruled the Naval objections and was presumably irrevocable, the plans for the individual assaults could now be shaped. Patton agreed that two complete battalions of the Third Infantry Division, his central force, should be detailed to capture the fort: one to be put ashore on a beach to the north of the estuary and promontory, whence it might hope to be approaching the fort as day was breaking; and the other to be landed on the southern lip of the estuary with orders to push quickly inland and get across the bridge under cover of darkness. Patton, with the realism that usually enlightened his tactics, insisted that any attempt to co-ordinate the attacks of these two battalions, advancing in the dark from opposite sides on to the same objective, "wouldn't work out." It would lead only to delays while each waited for the other. Speed, speed—this was always the first demand made by Patton on his troops. "If they're let stop and think, they won't fight," he used to say. "If they don't stop to think, they won't have to fight. The enemy will still be thinking and guessing what's happening by the time it's happened. Let the enemy stop and do the thinking!"

He saw that his two battalions ran the risk of shooting each other up. In which case—"It'll be just too bad," he said. "Let the bastards make a race of it! I'll give a medal to the winner. Medals cost nuthin'."

"That's all right," Meego persisted, "so long as the Navy keeps out of it. If the Navy starts knocking hell out of people at the same time as people are knocking hell out of each other and..."

"I know it," Patton said. But when Meego, importunate as always, tried to extract from him an assurance that he would force this point on the Naval Commander, Patton's face became obstinate—an expression that was soon to become familiar to Meego—and the General changed the subject. In due course

70

Meego learnt that the General was no more prepared to talk to the Naval Commander than the Admiral was prepared to talk to Patton. Between the Military and Naval Commanders there was no direct communication of any sort. Meego, his misgivings still clamorous, went in search of Dick.

On their arrival in Washington Meego and Dick had been put to live in Fort X, a large, hygienic but not very attractive military settlement for officers on the outskirts of the city. Between them they had two adjoining rooms, but decided to put both beds in one room, so as to keep the other as an office in which they would work together at nights. This did not happen, because in fact they very rarely met, since Dick spent most of his time looking for a laundry to compete with his Naval summer-dress. Nothing is so impractical for office-work as the Navy's spotless white; and nothing looks less spotless than the Navy's summer rig after it has been worn once. Soldiers wore khaki drill and anyway worked in shirt-sleeves; but the Navy in those days remained correct. The expansion of laundries in Washington had not kept pace with the rest of that city's war-time effort, and nothing could be got back washed or cleaned in under a fortnight. Dick's plight was desperate. Needing a dozen sets of uniform, he had only three with him; a number more were somewhere between Prestwick and the Clyde in a broken taxi. To solve his problem Dick used to fly the 150 miles to Naval Headquarters in Norfolk, Virginia, where a warship's laundry could restore his rig while he was taking a bath. At Fort X there were no baths, but only showers in common washrooms where, in the morning, officers of all ages and seniority had to queue for a place at a little after six o'clock in the morning. This was the hour when a large piece of artillery was fired with a thunderous detonation to shatter sleep. This had no sinister associations for the local population, whether civil or military; but for Meego and Dick, fresh from London, it was a rude beginning to the day. On their first morning at Fort X, by the time Meego had sat up in bed doing his *sang-froid* act, Dick was prone on the floor asking: "Jesus, have they followed us here?"

Norfolk, Virginia, as sordid a place as most major ports of consequence—witness what the American Navy has done to

Naples in the last decade—soon became Dick's permanent base. Since neither the Navy nor the Army would make the least move of reconciliation, let alone co-operation, the two components of what should have been a joint headquarters engaged in joint planning remained adamantly a good deal more than a hundred miles apart. Meego and Dick, instead of working together in next-door rooms, as at Richmond Terrace, were able to meet only when Dick, his wardrobe temporarily at full strength, could pay Washington a three-day visit. Meego succeeded in getting from Washington down to Norfolk only once. The planes that plied between the two headquarters were almost all Naval and would sooner allow a Japanese General to board them than an officer in their own or the British Army. It is literally true of those days in the United States that the two services hated each other and spoke quite frankly of each other with unbridled recrimination. General Truscott's project of setting up inter-service planning in Washington, on the Combined Operations system of Richmond Terrace, had seemed very obvious in Britain but, in America, was more obviously fantastic.

It is only fair to remember that the same would have been very nearly true in Britain three years earlier, except that we have never dared to make very nasty remarks about our Navy, nor really wanted to, and our Navy, incapable of hating anyone or anything save bad gin and mispronunciation, regarded the soldiers, or pongos, with nothing more venomous than charitable contempt. Nevertheless, even in Britain, it had taken all the tact and perseverance of Keyes, Mountbatten, Burroughs and Haydon to promote the notion of real inter-service staff-work, as opposed to periodic inter-service staff conferences. I remember myself that, as late as that same year, 1942, the new practice of soldiers and sailors actually planning together day by day in teams was described by a British Admiral as—"this boozer's of hermaphrodites." I should add, on impeccable authority, that the Admiral in question was himself described by Churchill as—"that master of negation . . ."

In Washington, while Meego was there, there were no inter-service planning conferences. At Patton's Headquarters in the

Munitions Building, where Meego worked, there was a sad, rather junior Naval Liaison Officer from Norfolk, in touch with nobody at either end. He had no communication with Patton's staff, because he never had anything to communicate. At Meego's instigation the procedure was adopted of giving him copies of military papers; but when he had sent these on to Norfolk, they went straight into a filing cabinet, and were no more likely to be read than those which were disseminated amongst Patton's own staff. Everyone was desperately writing documents to be read by nobody. The result of all this was a very odd incident.

One warm October afternoon Patton sent for Meego. It was then about a fortnight before the Task Force was due to embark —and in the previous month Meego had grown very fond of Patton and of his gracious wife. With both he was on terms of respectful intimacy, so that the summons was normal and not alarming.

When Meego got to the General's spacious office, he found Patton, a very large and always a magnificent, awe-inspiring figure, standing by his desk beneath the American flag and for once quite speechless. Silently he handed Meego a letter just received from Naval Headquarters at Norfolk. It said in the briefest terms that Admiral King, the American Naval Chief-of-Staff, had recently visited Norfolk as a result of which it had been decided—not proposed, but *decided*—that the Army's suggestions for the assault were not feasible and must be abandoned forthwith, and that the assault could not, and would not, be made under cover of darkness, as planned, but would take place in broad daylight. This would enable the crews of the landing craft to find the right beaches.

A layman may not immediately recognise the enormity of this communication at this juncture. It meant, not just changes of plan, but a totally new plan which, even if it had been practicable, and it certainly was not practicable, would have taken weeks to draft in detail and more weeks to put into effect. An "outline plan" for any operation stipulates the objectives which are to be attained, the forces allotted for this purpose, and the timing. The outline plan when made on the highest level is handed to the Force Commander who, in his "detailed plan," sub-divides his forces and gives each formation or unit—call it a sub-force—its individual tasks.

In an amphibious assault involving a long sea voyage, as opposed to a "shore-to-shore" affair across the channel, these sub-forces have to be "married" to ships which take them from a home port into enemy waters and "married" again to landing craft which take them from their ships to the enemy beach. The final product of a detailed plan is a landing table which shows exactly when, where and in what craft, every man, vehicle and wheeled weapon is committed to action. This very intricate time-table has to be matched with a loading table which shows when and where everyone and everything has to be stowed in ships. A loading table is the landing table in reverse. What goes first into a ship is apt to come last out of it. Hence, once a force has started loading —and the process is lengthy—it cannot alter its landing table, which means, of course, that it cannot alter its plan. At the time when Patton got his message from Norfolk, loading had been going on for about a week.

All the old questions about fire support for an opposed landing in daylight were again revived by this message. What, for instance, was to be done about that fort? If there had been time, it might have been possible to improvise something; to put little guns into certain landing craft and use them as support craft; or somehow to put ashore in the first flights an artillery unit and at least a few light tanks. But for anything of that sort it was now far too late. Patton said: "You don't have to tell me, Larry, about that goddam fort."

"This is out of the question," Meego said. "The plan can't now be changed without a postponement."

"Nor do you have to tell me that," Patton said.

Meego said: "You'll simply have to consult the Navy and explain to them . . ."

"Me consult with the Navy?"

"Yes sir."

"Consult with the Navy!"

"Yes sir."

"I'd as soon consult with a rattlesnake."

"If you won't talk to them, sir . . ."

"They won't talk to me. Why should I talk to them?"

"Then you'll have to write them a letter, sir."

There was quite a long silence before Patton said: "No! You write the letter; I'll sign it and send it."

"May I take a copy of their note, sir?"

"Larry, you may wipe your arse with it!"

For once Meego was sensible in accepting his own limitations and those of his position. With Admiral King behind this affair, it became heavy-weight stuff. Therefore he asked Patton: "Do you mind whom I consult?"

Again a pause before Patton asked: "Who have you got in mind?"

"The British Joint Planners across the street."

After a while Patton nodded and said: "So long as I don't know it."

Exactly opposite the Munitions Building, in another administrative palace normally devoted to the organisation of Public Health, there was housed the British Joint Planning Staff. Meego was already well acquainted with this body through whose offices he had, on several occasions, made signals to Combined Operations Headquarters at home.

It was to this body that Meego now took himself with the letter that Patton had received from Norfolk. On his way out of the Munitions Building Meego called at the office of the Naval Liaison Officer who, as usual, was sitting at his desk with the newspaper, bored and out of work. "Have *you* heard anything about a change of plan?" Meego asked him.

"What sort of change, Larry?"

"A change in the timing of the assault."

"Nuthin', nuthin', Larry. I ain't heard nuthin'. Nobody tells me nuthin' in this place. They can't go changing plans as late as this."

"I know it," Meego said. He was learning the language fast.

As Meego came out of the Munitions Building he met Dick coming into it. "I'm looking for you," Dick said. They stood together on the pavement where the shadows of trees were just beginning to stretch from the afternoon heat. Their meeting, the first for over a fortnight, seemed providential. But when Meego told him about the letter, Dick said: "I haven't seen it, but I got a sniff of this down in Norfolk. It stank, I rather thought; so I came up."

They dodged the traffic across the street and paused at the foot of broad, imposing steps that ascended to the marble hall of the Public Health building.

"It can't be bloody true!" Dick said. Meego was feeling the

same; the improbable affair had begun to have the flavour of a joke. He read the letter again, just the two paragraphs, and gave it to Dick. Having read it, Dick said: "It still can't be bloody true. Nobody could be as nuts as that."

They went upstairs feeling rather silly, almost expecting to be told that they were making a lot of fuss about a puff of Naval ill-humour, one more irascible note, nothing more than a trifling move in the game of inter-service bargaining that was always part of any combined operation. But the Brigadier in the offices of the British Joint Planning Staff said: "It's not untrue to form; it doesn't greatly surprise me."

Leaving Dick and Meego for a moment, he went into the next room and returned very shortly with the Naval Captain, his opposite number. "We're agreed," the Brigadier said, "that we'd better meet on this." They moved into the conference room and sat round the table. Although the Air Forces were not directly involved, the Brigadier sent for the third member of their Committee, the Air-Commodore, who had been in Washington longer and had more friends and contacts, and more back-stage knowledge, than the others. In the conference room they were joined by a Major of the Royal Marines, who acted as secretary to their meetings, and also by a Wren officer who was one of the personal assistants. But the Air-Commodore when he came and had read the letter said: "No minutes of this one, I suggest! Whatever we may decide at this meeting, we have definitely *not* held it."

The Naval Captain said: "All right, Major, I know you're up to the neck." The Royal Marine officer left, taking the Wren with him. The Brigadier said: "I'd dearly like to send this back. If this won't make them believe us, we might as well give it up." He was clearly referring to the corner of Whitehall at Storey's Gate, the Cabinet offices.

The Air-Commodore said: "Not on your life! Believe you me, this is dynamite."

The Naval Captain said: "But is it? Isn't that rather the point? This note, though perhaps a trifle brusque, or one might say querulous, may well be realistic. Given the prospects of surf, the state of training of the crews and much else, it may in fact *not* be practicable to beach these craft in the dark."

"Then why don't they say so?" the Brigadier asked.

"They've said so again and again."

"And been over-ruled."

"Against their better judgement," said the Naval Captain.

"Perhaps," said the Brigadier, "Costabadie can enlighten us? He may have seen these crews at practice?"

"I have," Dick said. "They come from the Coastguard Service. They know all about surf, they're the best boat handlers and in-shore navigators I've ever seen in all my life."

"There you have it, Sailor!" the Brigadier said.

"Nevertheless . . ." said the Naval Captain. He interrupted himself. "We must accept what Costabadie tells us." He struggled to placate his judgement. "From the start we've insisted that this operation is unsound. We've been over-ruled here. We're agreed that, if anything, it's less unsound in the dark than by daylight. It's now too late to change our minds." He sat back in his chair and concluded: "Either the thing must be called off or it must proceed as planned. Patton must say so."

"To whom?" the Brigadier asked.

"I should have thought to General Marshall."

Meego said: "The effect of that will be to start the argument all over again up at the top. That must be what King wants."

At this impertinence there was a short silence before the Naval Captain, somewhat surprisingly and reluctantly, said: "I dare say Lamego is right."

"I am quite sure he is," said the Air-Commodore.

"Would it be appropriate," asked the Brigadier, "for Patton to send a memorandum to Marshall, with a copy and a covering letter to Norfolk?"

The Air-Commodore said: "It sounds right to me. Would Patton agree to it?"

"I think so," Lamego said.

"Supposing," the Air-Commodore suggested to Lamego, "You go right along and find him and find out? I've got a date for dinner myself. We could perhaps meet later? We could perhaps meet quite late?"

It was at eleven o'clock that night that they reassembled. In the meanwhile Meego had been to Patton's house. In the hall he met Mrs Patton, a gracious and minute lady of wonderful charm and spirit. She was carrying in both hands a lump of primitive carving in lava rock. Somewhat battered, it seemed to be a carved head with the hair curled up in a peak. "Meet Charlie!" she said

77

to Meego. "He's very, very old, and very, very distinguished. They gave him to the General in Hawaii. He's a warrior. You can tell he's a warrior from his peak."

"Do they have warriors in Hawaii?" Meego asked.

"They used to have, one time," Mrs Patton said. "This is a warrior idol. If you're a warrior yourself, he brings you good luck. But if you're not a warrior, it's quite the reverse. Would you care to have him, Larry?"

"Doesn't the General want him?"

"I don't know what you've done to the General today," Mrs Patton said. "He's in a terrible wax."

Although Mrs Patton must have been twenty or thirty years younger than Meego's grandmother Micholls she seemed to belong to that same generation and to have been brought up on similar traditions which had allowed them to borrow from their brothers at Oxford or in the Army such rather daring slang as "wax," or as "swell" used as a noun but not as an adjective, and as "don't" and "ain't" used in the third person singular. Our grandmother would have said, for instance: "He's no end of a swell these days. He don't have the time ... He ain't asking. . ." All, of course, as a kind of joke borrowed from her kin in the mounted regiments who had got it from the cockney cabby.

"The General," Mrs Patton continued, "came right home and threw Charlie right in the pond. I just fished him out." She thrust the idolised lump into Meego's hands. It was quite a weight. "I warned you about being a warrior," she said. They were walking towards the drawing-room. "One other thing, Larry ... If you take him, you must take him with you."

"Take him where?" Meego asked.

"Take him in the little boats," she said. "I must be promised that. He has to go to Casablanca with the General to bring him luck." Meego was shocked at the indiscretion and must have shown it. "Doesn't *your* wife know where you're going when you go off?" Mrs Patton asked. "The General didn't exactly tell me," Mrs Patton added, "I must have just kind of guessed. I'm kind of psychic like that."

When Meego had finally taken Charlie for keeps, Mrs Patton said: "You must cherish him. That is to say, you must give him plenty to drink. You'll find he's a thirsty individual . . ." And it is true that the porous rock of Charlie's substance absorbs liquor when it is allowed to fall upon the mouth, as fast as a human gullet.

The General seemed quite composed, even genial, when he received Meego and gave him a drink. In his attitude to his staff Patton was more like a British Naval Commander than a soldier, either American or British. The tradition is that of a warship's Captain, who keeps himself aloof, takes his meals alone, and has no social communion with his subordinates aboard, to whom he is the source of orders that are to be obeyed instantly, the local representative of supreme authority, and nothing less. The Captain may not relax or descend either to confide or to frolic.

The cult most popular at that time amongst American Generals was of simplicity, equality and nauseating fraternity, practised to the extremes that a Divisional Commander in the field might even carry his own bedding roll, dig his own slit trench (or fox-hole), line up with everyone else for his meal (chow), clean (shine) his own boots (shoes), press his own trousers (pants) and generally so exhaust himself with the normal chores of keeping himself in good shape that he had neither time nor energy for the contemplations of command. Much less could he build up those reserves of energy, observation, conclusion and even abstract thought with which the born commander saves the day that is otherwise lost. Patton in these respects was unlike any of his contemporaries. He never descended, confided or relaxed with any of his staff—much less did he carry his bedding roll—and none of his subordinates knew the man behind the General. Many of them doubted that there was a man there to know. Patton once said to Meego: "My chief qualifications for Generalcy [sic] are histrionic." (How wrong he was, and not only in his English usage!) It was the product of his histrionics, and nothing else, that was released for his subordinates and staff on ordinary occasions. His intelligence and, yes, his subtlety—that word in this context will raise a laugh but it is veritably apt—his spiritual courage plus his physical fearlessness, and above all his intense study of military history and the art of war made him a great General. But none of his subordinates were allowed to guess it.

Meego was held to be different. Meego, being British, didn't count. In him Patton could confide without threatening the code of discipline which he applied to everyone else, including himself. For such confidences he had a craving that was secret and almost pathological. This splendid person, a great gentleman of exquisite courtesy and manners, when controlled, Master of his own pack of foxhounds in his own shire, Master of his own yacht which he sailed to the Pacific, when his Division was posted there, with his wife and son and only one deck-hand, was built for a public figure which he too often betrayed. Inside the public figure was a lonely man who depended on the privacies of his home to relieve his loneliness. When away from home he sometimes depended on Meego. Much of many nights was spent alone with Meego and a bottle of whisky in long monologues, but sometimes arguments, which continued until the bottle was finished. He would even listen to Meego. Meego could make him laugh when his mood was thunderous. Meego was a kind of court jester with unlimited licence for his opinionated facetiousness. Meego detests whisky, but he had to drink it through many hours after midnight.

This relationship was of course undeveloped at the time, that evening, when Meego went for guidance to Patton's house in Washington and was given Charlie, the idol, by Patton's wife. But it had begun as it was going to continue. And when Larry offered the proposals of the Joint Planners—being careful of course not to mention that body but to present the proposals as his own—Patton answered: "I'll tell you something. Those goddam boats are going into that goddam sea in the goddam dark if I have to stick my goddam pistol into that goddam sailor's stomach. You've got to fix it, Larry, so I don't have to pull the trigger. I don't care how you fix it, so long as it's fixed. You can write what you think best to whomsoever you think best, but don't forget to make it illiterate, else they won't believe it's my own work."

Actually, Patton had a pleasant style of prose, and his half-completed book on the psychological effect of armour, from chain-mail to the tank, was lucid and euphonic. He now said: "They don't reckon on literacy from me, so see they don't get it."

This exacting requirement was the worst of their problems when the Joint Planners reassembled late that night. The lines of the memorandum to be sent by Patton to General Marshall, with a copy to Norfolk, were obvious. The conclusion was brief: the operation, for which loading had already started, must either proceed as planned or be called off. The Army recognised the difficulty of accurate navigation with landing craft in the dark and accepted the risk of being landed in the wrong place on occasions, provided the first flights were ashore before daylight. It was not what had to be said, but how to say it, that was troublesome. How to imitate Patton's style?

"Just season it with expletives," the Air-Commodore suggested.

Finally Meego took the documents away with him, five foolscap pages of the memorandum, and a page of the covering letter, and he re-drafted them completely on his portable typewriter into what he thought was not only American, but Patton's American. A long job, it lasted all night. When he took it to Patton in the morning, the General asked: "Has anyone got a copy of this?" Meego assured him that no copy existed, and that it had been typed on American paper with an American machine. It was completely anonymous. Patton read it slowly. At the end he tore up the covering letter into small pieces but kept the memorandum. He said: "I've been thinking about that letter all night. I've been thinking how I'd enjoy writing it."

There was no further dispute about landing under cover of darkness.

Later that day General Sir John Dill sent for Meego. General Dill, with his gentleness, his air of humility and his radiant integrity, had a strange effect on some people. Meego found it spiritually refreshing to be in his company and to recount the events of the previous day and night. One was talking, he says, to a favourite uncle who got particular pleasure from his younger relatives. Dill listened with calm, relaxed attention, almost like a psychoanalyst. When Meego had finished, Dill gave him a cigarette. (Two months later the same story was to earn Meego an extra cigar from Winston Churchill at Chequers.)

Dill asked: "You've got a clear conscience about it, have you?" The question made Meego acknowledge with a little shame how much he had enjoyed the incident; it had been truly big stuff, he thought; he had made his mark on events; he had worked all night. "You took no copies?" Dill also asked. Even a used sheet of carbon paper could of course be embarrassing in the wrong place. And the typewriter? Dill seemed greatly to enjoy the human trivialities in which he showed a collector's interest. What, he asked, had prompted Meego to bring a machine with him to

Washington? The story of the typewriter was rewarded with a second cigarette.

A stranger in a strange city—and the incapacity to feel at home, to be excited or intrigued, to make friends, to see the sights or even to find his way around in a strange city remains an incongruous weakness—Meego was in his early days in Washington not only miserable and bored, but tired, hungry and in need of a drink. He had no work to do; he couldn't discover the plan with which he was supposed to be helping; he couldn't even discover that the plan, at that time, existed. Nor could he bring himself to work on his own manuscript which was in his suitcase. He was too tired, hungry and unhappy to make himself write.

Considering the amount that he has travelled, Meego is one of the least resourceful of travellers. He cannot even thumb a lift. This was a severe disability in Washington at that time, because there was very little transport. Even to get from Fort X in the morning to Munitions Building depended upon cadging a lift from an officer with an automobile of his own or finding a place in one of the pool of automobiles which the Army sent for this purpose. Meego was pathologically incapable of doing either. Each morning he would bring himself to the point of trying, but either the vehicle would not stop or it was already full up. As soon as an automobile from the pool arrived, a bunch of American officers would plunge and pile themselves into it. "Room for me?" Meego would ask. Silently—because their mouths were otherwise engaged with gum—the occupants of the car would shake their heads. Sometimes, as he had learnt at Rugby, Meego would lower his head for the scrimmage and force himself into a seat, to find, when he was settled, that this particular vehicle was bound for the wrong place. This is the kind of person that Meego was—and might well still be.

Meego therefore had to walk to work. Duly reporting at Headquarters by eight o'clock, as prescribed, he would then hang around until the staff had completed their routine in which he could not join. Shave and shoe-shine, breakfast and even newspapers all cost money which Meego hadn't got. Between nine and ten o'clock he would visit various rooms, whose occupants would look up from their newspapers to greet him warmly: "Hallo there, Larry!"

"How're you keeping, Larry?"

"Fixed up all right, Larry? Swell, swell!"

"Sometime, Larry, when you got yourself fixed up, I'd like to have you come around one evening and meet my wife ..."

"Be seeing you, Larry! Mustn't keep you now. Be seeing you!"

After an hour or so a certain number of documents for which he must sign were often brought to his room. They were meaningless to him, as to everyone else. For a while Meego would study them, fascinated by their style, for the sheer glory of their incomprehensibility. Then, with a dash and a purposeful manner, looking at his watch as he went as if time was short and precious, he would visit the Joint Planners across the street. Here his reception, although different, would be equally unsatisfying. "Morning, Laurence. Hot isn't it? Sorry I must rush ..."

"That you, Laurence? Someone was asking after you the other night. I forget exactly who it was. I'm just off to a conference. It's too damn hot for conferences ..."

"Good morning, Major. I'm afraid the Air-Commodore won't be in today. He'll be awfully sorry to have missed you ... It isn't the heat so much, so they say, as the humidity ..."

"Major Laurence, isn't it? Oh, Lamego ... No, there was nothing for you in the bag. Isn't it *hot?*"

"How's the big plan going, old boy? Mustn't expect too much. They're a comic lot out here. Nothing happens till it happens all at once. Possibly it's the heat."

The heat and the humidity of this over-spaced, blinding city, beautiful in parts but not as a whole, were enervating to all and exhausting to anyone who had to walk about it. Nobody but Meego and the Negroes did in fact walk. Everyone else had either transport or money in his pocket, or both. A couple of miles walk would get Meego to the Paymaster's Office (British); but the staff, being part British and part American, had found a happy compromise between their respective ways of life. Arriving at a White-hall hour approaching ten o'clock, they would follow the American routine which took them through to lunch; and at the Washington hour of five they shut up shop. It made little difference. "I'm desperately sorry, old boy, yours isn't through as yet."

"You owe me three hundred quid."

"His Majesty may, old boy, but I don't know of it, not officially, that is . . ."

"I can't live on nothing," Meego would say.

"I'll tell you what, old boy, I'll take a risk on another ten bucks; but we can't go on like this, it mustn't be a precedent."

Ten dollars could be stretched to two-and-a-half inadequate sessions of mixed nourishment in a sordid eating place. Much later, too late, not until Meego's diary was so full of invitations that he never paid for a meal himself, he discovered that several of his relations and numerous acquaintances had been in Washington all the time, in addition to another score or so of officers, male and female, all as lonely as he was.

By that time, General Truscott had paid a brief visit to Patton's Headquarters, bringing with him, and leaving behind him, Ted Conway.

Of General Lucian Truscott, Meego says, one never could tell what next. In Richmond Terrace he had seemed to be shy, reserved, cautious, unperceptive, indeed I've got to say "dim," withdrawn almost to extinction and almost inarticulate. Like a student, conscientious but not very bright, he attended every conference as an observer and exclusively fulfilled this function, sitting at the table for hours with a perfectly blank face. When invited to comment by Mountbatten or General Charles, he usually shook his head. Outside the conference room he would occasionally, but very occasionally talk a little, but then it was so softly that he was inaudible and so slowly that by the time he got to the end of the sentence one had forgotten how it had started.

When discovered in his office at Richmond Terrace, Truscott was either lying back in his chair looking from his window across the Thames with what seemed to be nostalgic eyes of pale, intense blue, or he would be writing very slowly and laboriously his reports or notes. Some people when disturbed at their work have a subconscious habit of furtively moving as if to hide it. Truscott did the reverse. Pushing his papers away from him and towards his visitor, he would fall back in his chair as if glad of the inter-

84

ruption. "Sit down, Larry..." His rare, warm, slow expanding smile was like the pricked ears of a horse or the wagging tail of a friendly dog. Inexplicably he inspired intense affection.

In Washington he was at once comprehensible. The leisurely, light-moving Texan had somewhere mislaid his horse and came into Meego's room with limitless assurance. That quiet withdrawn manner, which often seems like shyness, reserve and caution in a strange environment, belongs to men who have been brought up with horses, are horsemasters rather than just horsemen, are attractive to dogs and children and often fatal to women. That soft, Texan drawl, inaudible in London, now seemed infinitely friendly, purposeful, easy on the ear and easily comprehensible by contrast with the other dialects to be heard in Washington. That Texan hand-shake and slow, very wide open smile were instantly reassuring to Meego. Gone was his loneliness; he had a friend again; he had a master; he had a great deal of work. And in Ted Conway he had a comrade, a fellow worker.

Ted was another quiet one. In London he had seemed a likeable but most unsoldierly person because, although slim and erect, he had a pale face and a diffident outlook through rimless glasses. Like Truscott, his master, he spoke rarely. Unlike Truscott, his smile was so slight that it was scarcely apparent. So little we all then knew of America, most of us British soldiers, that we could not recognise our professional counterparts. Meego says that, in Whitehall, Ted matched the popular notion of a low-powered business executive from across the Atlantic, too indecisive to carry authority, lacking the drive to get ahead.

After all, we did expect Americans, and surely American soldiers, to look and act tough, to be ruggedly efficient, brash, full of pep, all of a bustle. This might be true of the worst of the amateurs who came our way. The best of the professionals, like Truscott and Ted—but excluding of course Patton who was a singular phenomenon—had what was in fact a "West Point" manner, just as distinct as the "Oxford" manner of the twenties and thirties but exactly the opposite. For their manner was a negation of mannerisms. Unless they had something to say they very pointedly did not talk. Unless there was need for propulsion, they made a point of not driving themselves or anybody else. Until it was appropriate to do so, they did not emanate personality. They were scrupulously realistic, quietly efficient, so highly trained and so confident that, when they were ignorant, they never thought of hiding it. But when you saw these people in command of troops and on the battlefield, as Meego did later and often, they were certainly as good soldiers as anything the allies could produce, and a good deal better than most.

After a minute wasted on greetings, that morning in Washington, Truscott spread his maps and put Meego to work. Meego was happy.

Leaving behind him Ted Conway, who had an apartment in Washington where his wife was awaiting him, Truscott was returning to his regiment to supervise its training. He had briefly outlined his plan, the details of which could be left to Ted and Meego; but the training of his men could be conducted by no one but himself. Not only was he an exceptional trainer of troops for war, but as an American Commander he had had an unique experience in his close study of our Commando Centre at Achnacarry and our subsidiary training establishments for mountain warfare, rock-climbing, demolition, and all the rest of it. In Britain he had already made arrangements for raising and training the First Ranger Battalion, the American counterpart of a Commando, for which Combined Operations Headquarters had lent Achnacarry and its entire staff, guards, drill sergeants and all. And Truscott was already convinced, ahead of many British Commanders, that the "battle school" methods and the toughening process, products of Commando experience and practice, were the best training for ordinary infantry in modern, mobile warfare.

Truscott was very well aware that all American troops, with the exception of the Marines, were too undisciplined and, worse, too soft. Their inept notions of democracy applied to soldiering, and their general training, influenced by uninformed public opinion and the Press, had left them unready to be bloodied in a hazardous amphibious assault. They were not only unfit to fight; they were straightforwardly unfit. Whatever could be done in the few remaining weeks to correct this condition would be done by Truscott. Just for a start, he taught his troops to walk.

Meanwhile Ted and Meego worked on the plan. Truscott, again

influenced by what he had learnt at Richmond Terrace—when nobody thought he was even listening—had suggested sending a ship-load of picked troops straight up the Lyautey River under cover of darkness.

It was a bright idea. The path of planning is beset with bright ideas, diversions, sideshows which cost little and offer a plump bonus. To reject them sternly is to behave like a blimp; to accept them readily is to risk the squandering of forces which are always limited and rarely, if ever, enough for the job. The more inadequate the force, the greater is the peril of the bright idea. Yet, paradoxically, the greater is the need for it. If you can do a Montgomery and amass a superior force before you agree to attack, you can afford the sideshow which you can equally do without. But when your forces are so weak that their chance of success looks slight, you are forced to the bright idea, a desperate remedy perhaps, in the hopes of improving that chance. It often comes off. War, like love, can unjustly favour those who abuse her principles; she rewards the bright idea while punishing the orthodox.

Truscott's bright idea, requiring an extra ship, appealed to his planners from the start. Every hour that they spent examining the operation discovered for them so many new hazards, amounting to so gloomy a prospect, that their hopes were forced back upon the remedy of this one small ship. And every hour that they spent examining this remedy, the more sure they felt that it would work. Dick came up from Norfolk and nautically eyed the project, pronouncing it feasible and writing the Naval paragraphs in what should have been a combined plan for a combined operation. On paper Lyautey was taken. There remained only one snag: a ship meeting their requirements seemed not to exist.

This was the more disappointing in that everyone concerned, from Patton to the Combined Chiefs of Staff, had approved the project with most unusual alacrity. The whole thing was through in a couple of days before the shipping experts had had their chance to denounce it. It was several days before a curt note came from the Allied Shipping Board asking General Patton to inform what it called "General Truscott's light-hearted planners" that every available ship in the allied pool which was capable of sailing the Atlantic had long ago been enlisted for the "Torch" assaults. Ted, a novice at the game, was inclined to accept the verdict; but Meego not. Meego had never yet made a plan which, at some stage, had not been condemned as impossible by one or other of the experts, specialists or vested interests who had virtually acquired the power of veto. Meego was used to fighting the veto and had even come to enjoy it.

Hope lay, Meego thought, in that useful and ambiguous word "available." Often, in his past experience, it concealed a weakness. He went after it. Now that Ted had arrived, Meego had the use of Army transport. He had borrowed money in his wallet. He had paid for his laundry and got it back. He was no longer hungry. On top again, so he felt, he called Dick back from Norfolk and even chased John Homer. The old gang was back on the job. For two days they assaulted by telephone and in person every office of every allied organisation and indeed of everyone who might know anyone who might conceivably know of a ship. Useless! Thousands of ships that had come under allied flags from a score of occupied countries, or had been acquired from friendly neutrals, were scattered about the world: some in the Pacific, or allotted to the Pacific, or others for Atlantic convoys, or convoys to Russia, or in dry dock, or waiting for overhaul or repairs. Only the Shipping Board, whose authority was made absolute by their exclusive possession of the statistics, could say what was "available" and what not.

At last Meego was able to confront the man who was said to be at the top. "I'd certainly like to help you if I could," he said. "I spend my life helping other folk."

Meego said, "This is a project approved by the Combined Chiefs of Staff."

"Sure, sure, feller! I'd certainly like to help the . . . What was it you said?"

"The Combined Chiefs of Staff."

"I'd certainly like to help those guys. They certainly need every bit of help they can possibly get. What was it they wanted?"

"An ocean-going ship capable of carrying * men, at a pinch, with a draught of not more than * eighteen feet."

"Holy smoke—not more than eighteen feet! How's that?"

"It's got to go up a river," Meego said.

"Sorry, feller, you've come to the wrong shop. We don't trade in river traffic."

* Blank in MS.

88

"It's got to go across the Atlantic first," Meego said. "It's got to keep up with a twelve-knot convoy. It's part of 'Torch'."

"Creeping Jesus—whatever's that?"

Meego said: "This request has been in your office for over a week. It's top priority and very urgent."

"Take it easy, feller. Haven't we told you nuthin'? That's too bad, too bad."

"You've said it isn't available."

"Then maybe, feller, it just ain't. Maybe we told you right. I spend my life running ships around the world and my office doesn't . . ."

Meego interrupted him: "I'm damn sure you could find us this ship if you really wanted to."

The big man picked up the telephone: "Say, Bob, there's a compatriot of yours right here in my office asking for the earth and kicking shit out of me because he can't have it . . . Will you, Bob? I'd be mighty glad if you would . . . Thanks, Bob, thanks a lot." He hung up and said to Meego: "He's coming right round." Then he returned to the work on his desk.

The Englishman who came in asked what the trouble was; and when Meego told him, said: "There was a young chap in here this morning, Costabadie I think, I never forget a name, this isn't anything to do with it?" Meego said it was. The Englishman said: "Will you take it from me," and he spoke very angrily but very quietly, "that there is no ship remotely meeting your requirements which can conceivably be sailed to Norfolk, Virginia, within weeks, if not months, of the required date? Will you take it from me that, even if we found a suitable ship, there is no suitable convoy which it could join sailing within that period? Will you take it from me that however unpalatable they may be, those are the facts?"

"No," Meego said. The Englishman went out of the room, and the American continued with his work. Returning not to Munitions Building, but to the Public Health building opposite, where the British Joint Planning Staff had their offices, Meego made his signal: "Personal from Lamego for Mountbatten . . ." describing the ship that was needed and its purpose, he added: "Information essential by Friday latest for final planning conference." This was on the Tuesday. By Monday morning next, when Truscott was expected in Washington to confer with Patton, his detailed plan which, with its appendices, would amount to fifteen or twenty pages of close-typed foolscap, had to be complete and typed in its penultimate draft. So far it consisted of nothing but a mass of notes.

Having made his signal, Meego returned to his room at Patton's headquarters. Ted was looking anxious, tense and ill. He was shivering and sweating with some kind of fever that had struck him down—as years later it was to strike Meego in the same place—in less than an hour. Ted had a message for Meego: General Sir John Dill wanted to see him at once. Dill was as charming as ever. "A complaint, Lamego," he said. He stated with accuracy the charge against Meego and asked: "Is that correct?" When Meego said that it was, he asked: "Can't you take 'no' for an answer?"

"No sir," Meego said. "Not in this case."

"Some people can't," Dill said. "I am one of them myself. I'll convey your apologies to the proper quarter. I wish I knew myself how to find your ship."

Back again in Munitions Building, Meego found that Ted's fever was very much worse. It had increased at a pace that seemed lethal. Sweat was pouring down his white face and soaking his shirt. Soon he could scarcely talk or walk. Meego took him back to Mrs Conway and helped her put him to bed. His temperature read about 105, and she sent for the doctor. Plagued by his knowledge of the time factor, Ted was no sooner in bed than he started to get up again. It was only Meego's promise to press on with the plan and to keep Ted in constant touch with its progress that secured Ted's surrender to his illness. In this job Meego was, of course, Ted's willing subordinate.

By now Ted was incapable of coherence except, with an expletive vehemence unusual for him, to say, repeat and continue repeating: "Will you, for God's sake, Larry, stop worrying, will you, about that goddam boat?"

For several days Ted's fever was to persist and his temperature to maintain its height. He was not back at work for nearly a week. Leaving him in bed, Meego went back to the office. If there was to be no little ship, then some other bright idea would have to be contrived if the operation was to be feasible, even on paper. But Meego, who was never short of bright ideas, was now denied them. His intuition, he says, told him that Mountbatten would find that ship. His intuition assured him that Mountbatten would do the impossible for the sake of helping a subordinate, particularly a subordinate whom he did not much like. Loyalty commands loyalty of course; and the art of commanding loyalty is the first tool of ambition.

Until this faith in Mountbatten had been disproved Meego's mind would not put itself to work on any other assumption but that the ship would arrive at Norfolk, Virginia, in good time to be overhauled and loaded. It was a wild assumption.

Mountbatten's ship must arrive at Norfolk by, say, a week before loading must start, in order to be put in trim for the Atlantic crossing and the subsequent assault. She must be capable of sustaining at least 12 knots. At this speed she could cover 3,000 miles in a fortnight, if she were sailed unescorted and on a straight course. The risks of sending an unescorted ship on the Atlantic routes, and the certainty of the Admiralty refusing to do so, were very well known to Meego but were cast aside by his crazy, obdurate hope. Looking at the chart he persuaded himself, by getting the scale wrong, that the ship could come from anywhere in Britain, or from Gibraltar, or could be diverted from a West-about convoy coming up the west coast of Africa, or ... or ... Wherever she was, Mountbatten would find her and, despite the strictures and demands of time, space and enemy action, would get her to Norfolk by the time she was wanted. Reposing contentedly in this faith, Meego put the plan aside for thirty-six hours and revised a couple of chapters of his manuscript.* By the time this was done the reply had come from Mountbatten. A suitable ship had been discovered, and had been allotted to Truscott by decision of the Combined Chiefs of Staff. For quite a while she had been lying idle in port, with nothing in view for her, at Norfolk, Virginia!

It was now Thursday morning, with three and a half days before the plan had to be in final draft. As yet it was only a folio of calculations and notes. If Meego had been a sensible man and a competent planner, and had not suspended the job in favour of his own work, it would have been ready for a copy-typist. Instead he had to send for a stenographer from the pool. Past experience had warned him, or should have, that these girls, however efficient in their own tongue, were unaccustomed to English which

* Later to be published as *Captain Smith and Company*.

reduced their speed by half. It was not until Friday afternoon, a few minutes before five o'clock, that the draft plan was complete in the stenographer's notebook. The girl said: "This'll take me quite a while to type."

"I know it," Meego said in American. "Will a day do it?"

"I reckon a day'll do it. That'll make it Tuesday night."

"But today is Friday!"

"We don't count on working Saturdays'n Sundays. Monday's a national vacation . . ."

Nothing, no bribe, no contrivance, no appeal to the highest available authority, nothing short of an Act of Congress could get the plan out of that girl's notebook and into typescript by the time it was wanted. Two days of dictation had been wasted; and if Meego was not to betray Ted, Truscott and Patton he must type the thing himself. He had no typewriter. Nor could he borrow one from the pool, because even if the regulations could be waived, the "pool" offices were already shut and locked. In Washington the English week-end operated relentlessly and even more promptly than in its birthplace. Already the whole place was implacably shut up.

The hand of war had touched America but lightly at this time, and there was only one shortage. Nothing that anyone could think of was lacking from American shops, except typewriters. With dollars strange in his pocket Meego tried everywhere in the city, but there was not a machine to be bought. Nor to be borrowed. For once, American and British habits were identical and, mutually reinforced, had caused the simultaneous closure of every office in the city, and the absence for three days of anyone to whom Meego could have turned. By Saturday noon, despairing, he rang up his publisher in New York, Johnnie Farrar, whom he had never yet met. (During all his days of loneliness he had never before thought of this recourse.) Thanks to that astonishing phenomenon of private enterprise, the American telephone system, he was told that Mr Farrar was "away somewheres" yet, in less than five minutes was hearing that effervescent voice, he knew not from where, in a warm cascade of greeting: "My, my, but I'm certainly looking forward to meeting you! Where are you speaking from?" Meego told him the Lee Sheraton Hotel, to which he had lately moved from the hygienic rigours of Fort X. "I'll be right round," Johnnie said and hung up forthwith. He was in the same hotel and on the floor below, a happy coincidence which, in Britain, the Postmaster General himself would not have discovered, nor even tried to do so.

The machine which Johnnie provided served to type out not only Truscott's plan and Patton's memorandum, but also much of Meego's revised novel.

It was due to Johnnie, also, that Meego completed this book in Washington. Brownie, a friend of Johnnie's, spent many unpaid hours of many nights typing while Meego dictated from his illegible manuscript. It was an exhausting task. By this time Meego, feeling heroic, had asked Patton if he might go with him to Casablanca. The General, assenting, gave Meego a hero's handshake. A solemn moment, no doubt! From then onwards the perils, and indeed the absurdities, of the whole escapade, becoming increasingly obvious as the plan developed, convinced Meego that this would be his last book and that, with 60,000 Americans and one other Englishman, he would surely perish off the shores or on the beaches of French Morocco. Inspired by the prospect of imminent death, he put into this book his testament of faith; love for his wife, his inhibited love for his children, his nostalgic sentimentality, his almost hysterical love of soldiers and soldiering that went with his love of home, all indeed that he was truly feeling, all that he would like to have felt. When it was done, he feared, with some reason, that it was not done and would have held it back if Johnnie had not sent the thing, oddly composed of prose in various styles, much of it Johnsonian, and of rhymed and unrhymed verse, to Sephen Vincent Benet. This considerable writer and poet, whom Meego was to meet with Johnnie in New York before embarking for "Torch," was unduly enthusiastic. He agreed to edit the typescript in Meego's absence, to correct the proofs and to write an introduction.

Whether or not this book had any real merits there was no doubt of its religious content. It purveyed the kind of religion which the soldier, despite his chaplain, had found or was finding for himself; and this was perhaps proved by the very large number of copies of the "overseas edition" which soldiers on foreign service bought, read and cherished, while civilian reviewers were condemning the thing—justly on the basis of their own experiences—as "obscure" and "unreadable" and "bogus" and "utterly meaningless."

Happy under Patton and Truscott in America, Meego prepared himself for certain death in the Casablanca assaults. His book had been discussed at a long lunch in New York with Steven Vincent Benet, a short, thick, crippled man with a lovely rugged and eager face. He had a passionate knowledge of war; and he shifted about in his chair with excitement, with a connoisseur's relish, at Meego's stories of Commando operations. "Lay on, lay on!" he cried whenever Meego paused and sometimes, but then in a whisper, while Meego was still talking.

Always, when he is in New York, Meego suffers acute attacks of loneliness. On this occasion, just prior to embarkation, it was worse because he had so little money. During all his days of penury in Washington it had never occurred to him that a relatively large sum was standing to his credit with his literary agents; but when Johnnie Farrar reminded him of this affluence, a telegram was at once sent to the agents saying: "Do not, repeat not, send my royalties to England." Thus, when Meego had installed himself in the Waldorf Astoria, he phoned his agent with confidence and asked for cash. There was none available, they said: in obedience to Meego's telegram they had sent the lot to London. At Meego's enraged protests they looked up his telegram and discovered their mistake. "I guess we're real sorry," the girl said. Meego told her to recover the money instantly; but until his agents had done so—which was not until Meego had embarked— the most they would give him was 200 dollars, representing a part of their own commission on his earnings. Even in those days, with the dollar at five to the pound, New York was expensive.

With no money to burn, and conspicuous in his British uniform which was still an unusual sight, and still unrespected, Meego set out for the Waldorf Astoria looking for fun, looking for company, for adventure, for trouble, for anything. He found, as usual, nothing. At length, in Broadway, he descended a flight of steps beneath a glittering sign of invitation to a long, low, cavernous, garish but dimly lit room where, at one end, a band was playing. At the other end, the bar, there were standing and sitting a variety of people, some soldiers, some civilians, some nearly drunk, some quite. At one end a girl of remarkable beauty seemed to be not only unaccompanied, but almost sober. When she smiled at Meego he offered her a drink. "Why not?" she said. "What?" he asked. "Champagne," she answered.

At the far end of the bar a kindly-faced Major, American of course, had caught Meego's eye and was shaking his head. To hell with him, Meego thought. He ordered champagne and talked to the girl whose attractions, for Meego, were but little diminished by her almost complete incoherence. "More champagne?" he suggested. Again she said "Why not?" Again the Major's warning. Again the champagne was ordered. And again and yet again the whole procedure was repeated until, an hour later, Meego invited her to dine with him. "Why not?" she said, and Meego asked for his bill or check. When the barman held it out, for an astronomical sum, another hand took it, stretched from behind Meego. "Allow me, please," the American Major said. "And allow me to present to you my wife." To his wife he explained: "This is a British Major."

"Isn't that too cute!" she replied. "I was wondering just what he was."

The night that followed may have been memorable but was lost to Meego. With the Major and his wife and several others he left the bar and must thereafter have dined, danced and drunk, because he recalls quite clearly his own patient explanation, to which nobody would listen, that the correct nomenclature for those first signs that the night was ending was "the start of nautical twilight." At that particular moment everyone was extracting from a secret place in his car the automatic pistol without which it was unwise, it seemed, to visit a Harlem night-club. Meego's only other flicker of memory about that dawn is of sitting with another man on a low settee in front of a mirror which covered the wall behind them. Somebody flung a bottle which, missing its target, missed also the heads of Meego and his companion and smashed itself in the looking-glass. The man beside Meego kept on repeating—"High jinks, high jinks . . ." or was it— "Hi, Jinks," since people are sometimes called "Jinks" in America? Before Meego could enquire, the shooting had started. He woke up in bed, his own bed, at noon, unhurt, feeling fine and with no headache. In the pocket of his uniform he found the broken head of a small gilt charm.

The next day his son and daughter, aged 12 and 9 respectively, arrived from the school in Connecticut to which they had been sent by their guardian in America, a friend of his family, Admiral Lewis Strauss. They were to stay with Meego in New York for the next five nights, but he did not know how to afford it. On the recommendation of the poet Benet he moved from the Waldorf Astoria to the Berkeley, just round the corner, which was much cheaper and nicer. He put his problem to the manager who listened with the dead-pan face that, by now, was familiar to Meego and infinitely dispiriting. In a cold voice the manager said that the only solution was a suite. Meego might have one at a reduced price. "How much?"

"No more than you can afford," the manager said. He would neither smile nor elaborate his answer. There was always the chance, Meego thought, that his royalties would get back from London before he left.

The suite was full of flowers which were being reinforced, as was a large box of candy and a huge basket of fruit, when Meego and the children got to it. Most of their meals were had in the hotel, in the sitting-room of their suite. On the fifth day Meego asked for his bill. "Shall we say fifty dollars?" the manager suggested. It was not a fifth of the normal charges.

"Why are you so good to us?" Meego asked.

"I guess," the manager said, "you British have been fighting this war alone for long enough." He smiled at last. If, in all America, there was anyone else who took that view of recent events, Meego had not met him. Even Johnnie, dear Johnnie Farrar, who loved everyone nice, kept discreetly away from the subject of the British at war as if, between friends, it needn't be mentioned. With a Limey then, and later with a Wop, one could be pals despite their cowardice.

The impact on Meego of this generosity at the hotel, and of the parting with his children, which he then believed to be final, left Meego's emotions in an elated state, close to the heroic, which was not abated by the return to Washington that night, the long drive in convoy to Norfolk, Virginia, at dawn the next morning, embarkation in the *Joseph P. Dickman*, to which Meego had been consigned with others of the Staff, since there was very limited space in the cruiser *Augusta* where Patton had his headquarters, and the long, languid voyage across the Southern Atlantic, during which the formidable fleet rolled and pitched, but never with

96

much violence, for it seemed endless days unseen by the enemy, to within three miles of the enemy-occupied coasts of French Morocco.

Patton had given Meego strict orders that, first, he should wear American uniform, so as not to provoke the supposedly anti-British French into more anti-American action than would otherwise be met; and secondly, that when they got to the other end, Meego was to remain aboard ship and not to go ashore without the General's personal and express permission. At no time had Meego intended—or had Patton thought that Meego intended—to obey this second instruction very literally. But as regards the first, Meego disported himself aboard the *Dickman*, sunbathed in rubber rafts, carried Charlie around to see the sights, argued with those war correspondents who happened to be in the same ship, persuaded the official photographers to take his photograph, and with his own Leica took many snapshots himself, always dressed correctly, or very nearly, as an American officer. He was guilty of one mutinous anomaly. Patton had decreed that insignia of rank should be borne not only on shoulder straps, but also welded to the front of an officer's helmet; and in both of these places Meego sported, instead of a silver leaf, his own legitimate gold crowns of a British Major.

No other passenger could have shared with Meego his foretaste of disaster—only a few of the others had his complete knowledge of the plan and its circumstances—nor, if they had, could have assessed the probabilities on the basis of Meego's experience in planning and operations. He was possibly, probably, alone in his preoccupation with a soul that was so soon and so certainly to be parted from its body. He had written, and consigned to safe custody, yet another "last letter" to his wife ("to be opened only in the event of my death") a practice which resulted, at the end of the war, in the return from various custodians of seven such letters, inspired by a similar number of last farewells. These last farewells were to Meego the soldier's symbol which, more than anything else, distinguished him from the civilian. The British civilian might quite likely dwell in greater peril than the soldier; he might be bombed nightly; his physical discomforts might be similar; but he was never for long out of range of his wife's voice. On the subject of last farewells Meego had written in *Captain Smith and Company*:

It was better not to glance back from the head of the stairs to the closed door of the bedroom, from the side of an army truck to the curtained first-floor window, from the road-tipped crest which overlooked the house for a last refreshment of regrets. One could not have borne a last retrospection: the end was too final to permit the luxury of added pain; the sense of repetition too keen for a part to be played in this ancient drama. One knew the blind sequence and inevitable laws which had always ordered these occasions; the inescapable future, beyond knowledge, which had so often struck down the past. So many men with their changing implements of war had seen the spring bud but not the summer foliage, had looked on the blossom that would never fall and the bloom that never wilted. The play was an old revival, but one would not wave the hand and go with a gay smile and a gallant jest; honour was not enough beloved for such glamorous deception, or for this intimate withdrawal to be anything but dully tragic. The rift must be final and complete, without expectation of return or hope of renewal; for the worst must be over and done with in this ultimate hour, so that it could not again intrude on adventure and threaten resolve. . .

A man could not easily forget the approach and the ultimate: the bright and lovely security that had to be so soon relinquished; the black foresight, the desolate wastes of future, the soft, warm, comfort that scarcely remained. He could never forget the last cup of lovely assuagement, the soft cheek with the salt tear, the lips half opened in unutterable plea. He could not forget the going, nor the penultimate knowledge that the going must come.

During the night of 7 November the Western Task Force approached the Moroccan coast. Soldiers should have been sleeping (Meego's best repose was always before battle, or even during it) and he was dismayed that none even tried to rest but, on the contrary, made sleep impossible for anyone by their excited tramping up and down the companion-ways and along the decks. Long before it was time, everyone was fully accoutred for the assault and, since everyone was carrying primed grenades, not to mention weapons of all sorts with their magazines charged, Meego kept to the relative safety of his own bunk. (In fact, Americans in general, being far more accustomed to firearms in the home, are much safer than the British in handling them.) Meanwhile Meego had made a satisfactory arrangement for himself. It partly, but only partly, contravened Patton's orders. Although he was proposing disobediently to leave the ship, he was not going ashore, but would observe the proceedings with Buck in his special support craft.

As the senior officer of the Coastguard Service on board the *Joseph P. Dickman*, Buck was in command of all the landing-craft and responsible for the planning and execution of all their operations. To give support where needed, his boat was specially armed with automatic weapons and a small searchlight, so that Buck, accompanied by Meego, could first lead his flight of landing-craft almost to its beach and then, turning away, could cruise up and down the coast, close inshore, engaging any opposition that was particularly troublesome and also exercising some measure of control over subsequent flights by imparting to his subordinates encouragement, exhortation or appropriate abuse. During the voyage, Meego and Buck had developed a friendship which was responsible for this happy arrangement.

Before embarkation began there was a religious service for each denomination. This healthy usage, common to American forces, was rarely practised by the British. The former reinforced the pre-battle perorations of their commanders, when God was invariably invoked; whereas the latter, having slipped the Almighty into an "Order of the Day" were content to leave it at that. Since there was no Rabbi aboard the Dickman, the Jewish element in the forces would have had to assault without bothering the Deity, if it had not been for the Roman Catholic Chaplain, Father Flinn. He approached Meego, who happened to be the only Jewish officer in the ship, and offered to stage, although he could not conduct, a brief Jewish Service

U.S.S. *Joseph P. Dickman*
7 November 1942
Jewish Service Before Action
Announcement by Chaplain Flinn
Prayer for the Government: Lieut. Cmdr. Strongin
Captain Cohen reads: (page 69)
        a) "Oh My God The Soul"
        b) "Bless Ye the Lord."
Page 7: Lieut. Cmdr. Strongin: "Shma Yis-ro-ayl."
Capt. Cohen: (page 71–72)
        a) "I will lift up mine eyes unto"
"Holy, Holy, Holy, is the Lord of Hosts."

Lieut. Cmdr. Strongin: 23rd Psalm. (Congregation to join in.)
    (Page 332, Holy Bible.)
Major Henriques, British Staff Officer: "Adon Olam."
Chaplain: The Lord's Prayer. Blessing.

Accordingly, when the rest had finished their prayers, the twenty-
two Jewish soldiers and sailors of the *Dickman* assembled on a
mess deck. The Priest told them that if they truly believed in God
according to their own teaching, He would hear their prayers;
and if they truly repented their sins before God, they would be
forgiven as surely as if, being of his own faith, he could give them
absolution. He bowed his head while his little flock of Jews prayed
standing, as they must, and while Meego and several others
recited such prayers or declarations that they happened to know
by heart. It was a moving ceremony that lasted no more than ten
minutes. To end it, the Priest raised his hands and gave them his
blessing. For Meego it was a quick, tense and very real experience
which some people might explain as hysterical but which he
insists was religious. He was accorded a vision. What he saw was
a certainty, it was certainty itself, an efflux of doubts like a swift
ebb, an influx of faith like an irresistible tide, that there was
some meaning in life and some direction in death. In a state of
exaltation he took his seat in the boat which by now was hanging
fire on its davits.

Once again, and once only, and it was years later, Meego
experienced this same sense of certitude. It was—he has to confess—after a superb lunch of *bécasse flambé* with his close friends,
Hilary and Joan St. George Saunders, at the Restaurant Palmer in
Bayonne. That day in January, the year before Hilary's death, was
cold, bitter, bleak. The afternoon was black with rain; the day
was slipping away into dusk without ever ripening. While Joan
went shopping, Hilary (a scholar and writer as well as Librarian
to the House of Commons) took Meego to the Cathedral which is
lofty, spare, frigid and was then, at that hour, deathly dark. The
setting, the light and the sparse colour were of Goya; and towards
the altar, lit by scores of tall candles, the priests and choir were
singing vespers, all in green robes and raiment, with heavy chant.
This island of light, in that surround of darkness, was of such
beauty that it struck the two men unconscious. Ten minutes later
they came awake, holding hands like children and with childish
tears on their cheeks. During the previous minutes they had

100

known—they knew not what. They had not believed, thought or felt; they had just been given certainty. "Certainty of what?" I have often asked Meego. He cannot answer.

Armed with this certainty, on that previous occasion at sea off the coast of Morocco, wearing American uniform with a miniature American flag on his upper arm but a gilt crown on his American helmet, Meego clambered into the boat, settled himself in the stern and fell fast asleep. His somnolence was due neither to his state of exaltation, nor to his sleepless night, but to barbiturate. An hour earlier a sergeant had handed round a plate of small, white pills, of phenol barbitone, prescribed by the U.S. Army Medical Corps not only to allay sea-sickness in the swell, but also to soothe the nerves and prevent the assaulting troops from taking fright. Each man was supposed to take one pill; but since Meego, even in those days, was accustomed to sedatives and was rarely able to sleep without them, he took his customary dose of two. For once, they worked instantly. By habit a very light sleeper, he was on this occasion so deeply unconscious that he saw nothing of the three-mile passage shorewards and heard nothing until he was awoken by Buck's boot prodding his ribs and Buck's voice saying: "Hey there, Larry! The shootin's started. Don't you wanna wake up?" This story of British *sang froid* travelled far and wide and fast throughout the U.S. Force, and there are some Americans who still remember and repeat it. Meego has never before confessed to the barbiturate. But when he awoke there was indeed quite a racket and a certain amount of shell-fire. The craft was caught in the dazzle of a searchlight. A couple of machine-guns were firing, but the bullets were passing high, very high above the boat. In the first, scarcely perceptible traces of morning dusk, the coast was visible ahead. There was very little surf.

The battalion (of the 3rd Infantry Division) which had taken passage in the *Joseph P. Dickman* had a task which might have been tough. It was to land on the southern lip of the estuary, to advance inland to the road, to cross the river by the bridge and attack the fort from the east. At the same time, following the agreed plan of operation, another battalion was being landed north of the promontory to attack the fort from that direction.

The landing-place on the southern lip of the estuary was easy to find, and Buck took his landing flotilla into shallow water before turning away, watching them beach and then cruising northwards

101

until, coming opposite the fort, he opened up with his machine-guns against the searchlight. Meego said "That's not a bit of bloody good. Nobody ever shot out a searchlight with a machine-gun."

"Maybe not," Buck answered, "but there's guys manning it." And in fact the searchlight was doused. This incident caused Meego to suspect that the garrison of the fort was not really anxious to fight.

Returning southwards across the mouth of the estuary Buck now came upon a flotilla of craft—three or four of them—which was heading to seawards and still loaded with troops. He hailed them and asked—"What's up?" The coxswain of the nearest landing craft answered that he couldn't find the right beach and was looking for it.

"The way you're looking," Buck said, "is Norfolk, Virginia."

"I know it."

"Godammit," Buck shouted, "nobody could miss that goddam beach."

"We did," the coxswain answered.

"He's a yellow-bellied bastard," Buck said to Meego. "He's plain yeller. You c'n find that goddam beach?" Meego thought that he could. "How would it be, Larry, if you was to get aboard that craft? Push your pistol in that bastard's guts and get him to take you to the beach?" Meego agreed and, when Buck brought his boat alongside, transferred himself to the landing-craft. He did not draw his pistol as instructed, but stood beside the coxswain in the stern on the raised platform or poop from which the craft was steered. In that exposed position any tendency to courage was speedily diminished.

In a few minutes the keel grated in shingle, and the craft stopped. Nobody got out. They shouted back from the bows that the water was too deep. "Nonsense!" Meego said and, pushing his way forrard, leapt into the sea which, in fact, came almost to his neck. Aware of this possibility he had held his Leica camera safely above his head.

Since Meego is over six foot tall, and many of the men were much less, they would in fact have been out of their depth. Meego having neglected to tell the coxswain, before beaching, to put on full speed, which would have run the craft into shallower water now had to persuade the tallest men to get out first and to form a human gangway for the support of their shorter comrades. Wha

102

happened to the rest of the flotilla Meego never noticed. When all the complement of his own craft were ashore, he followed them, stiff, very cold and stumbling. The need to keep his camera dry, as also the lop-sided weight in his haversack of Charlie, that lump of larva rock, made wading difficult.

Ashore the cry was—"Foxholes!" Everyone was shouting it and digging like mad, in proper accordance with the training which, at that time—but not of course later—was American Army policy. A few shells of field-gun calibre were bursting—some of them uncomfortably close to the water's edge—and had probably come from the 75 mm armament of the fort. But the distant tapping of machine-guns from both flanks was quite innocuous. As so often, they were sited far too high to be harmful. Duty bound, as he thought, Meego did his best to urge his neighbours onwards. They took no notice and went on digging, except that one sergeant straightened his back and said calmly "Shucks!" before continuing with his work.

Meego walked inland, as twilight grew towards dawn, until he came to a profusion of shrubs and spindly trees, and then the road and, on his left, that girder bridge. On the seaward side of the road there was a ditch, filled to overflowing with troops who were not so much frightened as simply acting as they had been trained, taking cover underground as soon as they were shot at. Most of them were digging, unalarmed, unexcited. Meego, cold and wet, lay down beside them. His cigarettes were soaked. The sun was now rising. He observed that the shells falling in this area were much more numerous than on the beach and of a far heavier calibre. The ditch was as good a place as any to be in at that moment.

But at that moment there appeared on the road an extra-ordinary sight: a trio that had just come across the bridge: a small, dapper man, smartly dressed and wearing a "Maurice Chevalier" straw hat; an enormous woman in her Sunday black, glittering with brooches, pendants and necklaces of jet; and between them, holding their hands, a small boy in a sailor-suit, aged perhaps eight. It was too much for Meego. He got out of the ditch, greeted them in French and started to ask them about the garrison of the fort. The woman looked at this soaked, dripping and bedraggled figure. She showed no surprise. "*Mon Dieu, Monsieur, que vous êtes mouillé!*" was all she said.

"You're too damn right!" Meego answered in English. "Wet is just what we are; dripping bloody wet!" A very large shell fell quite close. There in the ditch he spotted an American senior officer digging democratically like everyone else. It was very urgent indeed that someone should take that fort, and at once, since otherwise it would continue to shoot in broad daylight enfilade fire down the whole length of the beach where, all day, successive flights of craft were due to reinforce, supply and build up the first assault. "Major," Meego said, "hadn't we better get across that bridge?"

"My Command Post has to be right here," the Major said. It was true, it was theoretically correct, that the Battalion Headquarters should be just here to collect the troops as they disembarked, re-form and re-deploy them. "There's a platoon gone on across that bridge," the Major added. In accordance with his training he continued to dig his fox-hole.

"We ought to go across that bridge," Meego said unhappily. "We ought to take that fort."

A big sergeant clambered out of the ditch. "I guess I'm coming across that bridge. I don't like it here," he said to Meego. Turning to his comrades, he called: "Any of you guys comin' with us across the bridge?" Several men joined Meego and the sergeant.

By now the crossing of that bridge had become quite hazardous. Shells were falling close and fast; several men had been hit, some killed, some wounded; splinters were clanging against the iron girders; Meego and the sergeant were spattered with earth, and they moved quickly.

It then occurred to Meego that the emplaced artillery of the fort, which was invisible at the top of the hill on their left front, could scarcely be brought to bear on the bridge: it was most unlikely that it could traverse 180 degrees to shoot inland; and it was almost certain that, at this close range, it could not be sufficiently depressed to bear on the road and bridge beneath it. He was in fact wondering if some of Béthouard's divisional artillery, medium stuff by the feel of it, had not been deployed and brought into action, when he recognised the truth. These were six-inch shells coming from the twelve guns of the cruiser *Brooklyn*. The ship, engaging the fort from far out to sea, had not brought bombardment charges. Moreover the area of sea from which she was shooting—(warships always keep moving and usually cruise in an elliptical course while engaging shore targets)—was in direct prolongation of the line of advance which this battalion had to take. It was happening exactly as Meego had foreseen. All the *Brooklyn's* shells that were missing the fort—as indeed were most —were falling amongst the American troops. The *Brooklyn* was employing what was then called "ripple fire" which meant that every one of her twelve guns was fired automatically the moment it was loaded and laid. It was the most rapid type of fire of which any ship is capable—or any military unit of artillery, for that matter—and it was highly effective.

As Meego saw it, these circumstances increased the urgency of getting across that bridge, getting up to that fort and inducing its commander to haul down his French flag and replace it with a tablecloth. This, by depriving the *Brooklyn* of her target, would persuade her to stop helping. These facts of life Meego explained to the sergeant as, with three or four other soldiers, they ran across the bridge. "Sonsabitches!" the sergeant said. "They's aimin' at us. I got a brother in that goddam ship."

Across the bridge they left the road and turned again to seawards. Following now the northern lip of the estuary they started to climb the moderate slope which led to the fort at the top. Steeply below them now, the river's mouth and the sea sparkled with the approach of dawn. And scattered about the slope were a few soldiers, the best part of a platoon, waiting for orders and, in default of orders, very sensibly digging. Meego could find no officers except one olive-skinned boy with huge, dark eyes, obviously of Italian blood, who pleaded: "Please, I gotta a mortar. Sir, I got orders not to shoot my mortar without orders. Sir, please may I shoot it?"

"Certainly," Meego said. "Shoot at that fort." The top of the fort was now visible and quite close, only a few hundred yards over the brow of the hill. "Aim at the flag," he said. At that moment he had cause to throw himself flat as another cluster of six-inch shells fell all around them. A couple of men were hit.

When Meego thought fit to regain his feet, he found the Italian boy in American uniform still beside him, still upright. "Say, what insignia is that?" he asked, pointing to Meego's crowns. When Meego said he was a Major, the boy asked suspiciously: "What kind of a Major would that be?"

"British."

"C'n I start shootin' on a Britisher's orders?"

"We're allies," Meego said.

"I guess that's right." The boy went off, apparently satisfied. Whether or not he fired his mortars Meego never discovered. The shells of the *Brooklyn*, whose bombardment was now reinforced by the crippled French battleship, the *Jean Bart*, from her berth in Casablanca, were making such a noise that one or two mortars the more could not have been noticed. Meego does not know where the twelve-inch shells of the *Jean Bart* were then falling, but it was somewhere audible, and even loud.

This was the fog of war at its thickest in the Moroccan dawn sunshine which was already nicely warm and drying Meego's clothes. He found a couple of signallers, but their wireless set was useless from its submersion in the sea. They had also a Very-light pistol, and when a small aeroplane with American markings, probably from a carrier flew low overhead, he tried to use their pistol as an identification. But the cartridges also were soaked and would not go off.

To the sergeant, who was still beside him, Meego said: "All anybody need do is walk a couple of hundred yards up to that fort and ask them to haul down their flag. They've just forgotten it."

"I guess that's right," the sergeant said.

But the ground ahead was still being subjected to a liberal bombardment from the *Brooklyn*. To walk across it would be neither very dangerous nor very safe. Seen in retrospect, Meego thought, if there was to be any retrospect, it would be a job for the V.C. or its American equivalent, the Congressional Medal of Honour. How nice to have it! But how nice to live! While Meego was debating whether or not to be heroic, he remembered very clearly his wife's voice and her parting injunction. "You do do such silly things, darling. Promise me not to be silly? That's all I ask." Would this be silly or not? Pondering the question, Meego suggested to the sergeant that he try to find an officer somewhere on the slope, failing which he might take charge himself, to dispel not alarm (there was no alarm) but natural lethargy, to restore some kind of order and to find a dozen or so men who would walk with him and Meego up to the fort. On this project the sergeant went off.

Thus left to himself, Meego began to observe more acutely and

106

to think. Close by there was a cottage, a coastguard's place, sited to overlook the river mouth. He could see that it was on the telephone, the wires still intact; and from there he might speak by phone to the Commander of the fort. Approaching the cottage for this purpose he was met at the door by a minute man with a huge, bristling moustache. He had pinned to his breast a row of glittering medals; on his head he wore his helmet from the earlier war. He kissed Meego on the cheeks and took him inside where his wife, repeating the embrace, at once fell on her knees, lifted a corner of the carpet, prised up a floorboard and, from beneath it, took out a small packet of real coffee which they had not tasted for the past two years and which they had conserved for this moment of liberation.

Had Meego pursued immediately his idea of telephoning to the fort, it might have been an interesting experiment. Instead he sat in the sun, by the window over the sea, smoking the coastguard's cigarette, drying himself and chatting with his host while his hostess ground the coffee and made it in a saucepan. Naturally, the coastguard said, the Commander of the Fort, who was a most amiable man, was not wanting to fight against American troops; certainly he would welcome them. Certainly the coastguard would telephone to the Fort whose *Adjutant* (sergeant-major) was a close friend, devoted like the coastguard, to both fishing and "*la chasse.*" But first the coffee. Madame said that it was ready; the cups were on the table which had been spread with a checkered cloth, and the chairs drawn up. The two men took their seats. Madame fetched the saucepan from the stove.

At that moment Meego felt the blast. He saw the entire window-frame, from which he had just withdrawn, sailing sedately across the room. He plunged under the table and, feeling a violent blow, knew that he had been hit. This was the death that he had so surely anticipated: death under a table in a litter of shattered glass. The *Brooklyn* had done her worst.

It was not death. The blow on Meego's head was from the helmet of the coastguard who, *ancient combattant* that he was, had taken the same action as Meego at precisely the same moment. On all fours under the table the two men looked at each other. Madame, out of inexperience of war, was still outside the shelter, still on her feet and still holding the saucepan. "*Vous pouvez sortir, Messieurs*," she said. "Come and drink the coffee while it is still hot." The coffee was excellent, but there was no longer the chance of telephoning. The *Brooklyn* had removed the telephone post, and the wires were cut.

When Meego had finished his coffee he returned to the field of battle. The French flag still flew above the fort; the *Brooklyn* was still firing, but with rather less vigour; there were no signs at all of any French opposition; and the American troops were still where he had left them, only a little deeper downwards. Meego, advancing warily, skirted the top of the cliff until he came to a ruined cowshed which, it was clear, had recently been hit by a shell. From inside it there came an appalling odour and a terrible sound: a sound at the very top of, and almost beyond, the tonic scale; a sound that was a prolonged shrieking but with no voice to it. Forcing himself to look inside, Meego saw the debris of a milking-stool, a milk pail, a cow and a deep black Senegalese soldier in French uniform. Meego was instantly sick. Then, forcing himself to advance through the slime of blood and milk with which the floor was awash, he had to observe that neither the cow nor the man were dead but only horribly broken. Both their bellies had been blasted open, and their inwards were intermingled. This was the cause of the stench. The sound that Meego had heard was issuing from the man's tattered mouth, but the man was quite unconscious.

With his pistol Meego shot the cow at once. What could he do about the man? Nothing in his "field dressing" was of any use for a wound such as this. There was no other person in sight from the vicinity of the cowshed. He already knew that there was no American doctor—though there were several medical orderlies—on his side of the bridge or even as yet ashore. He had not realised how near the fort he had got—that the cowshed was almost an annex to the fort—for the ground rose so steeply at this point in a convex slope that the closer he got to the fort, the less he could see of it. From the cowshed it was invisible. Again and again he stumbled out of the cowshed, pursued by that thin, voiceless scream, and again and again he returned to the scream's source. The man by now was nothing in Meego's mind but the scream's source; and Meego was engulfed in a frenzy of rage, horror and helplessness, an utter panic such as he had never before experienced. He shot the man through the head.

That night, eager to unburden himself of guilt, he told the

horrid story to a senior Army doctor, a southerner, from the very deep South. "The man couldn't have lived?" Meego asked.

"He probably could," the doctor said, "with these sulphur drugs. These days we'd have stuffed his guts back with sulphanamide and stitched 'em up, and he'd have been all right..." Observing Meego's distress, he patted Meego's shoulder, adding, "Don't you worry, son! What's one nigger the less?"

As soon as he had fired his shot Meego went towards the fort. In fifty yards or less he reached its surround of barbed wire and saw that the flag was down. He noticed that the *Brooklyn* was at last silent. A few Americans were standing about but none of them spoke any French. Meego took a photograph of a gun which the *Brooklyn* had hit. The French officers, with whom he talked, agreed that the battery was a reasonable target. But they had been hit four times in all—four times in less than two hours—and it was too much. Why, they asked Meego, had he or his guns set fire to the Officers' Mess? This all ended at about nine o'clock on the morning of "D-day," 8 November.

Nobody has ever discovered who it was that eventually took the fort, or first entered it, for I doubt if it needed any actual "taking." Certain American war correspondents, none of whom were eye-witnesses, have described how Patton boarded a light tank and personally led the assault against Fort Blondin's gates. This is improbable since, at the time when Meego photographed the interior of the fort, Patton was still aboard the cruiser *Augusta* and, in fact, being carried seawards, out of sight of shore, a reluctant and indeed apoplectic passenger in the middle of a naval engagement with five or six French destroyers and the stationary *Jean Bart*. Both the battalions allotted to the task of taking the fort claimed to have done so.

There was, in addition, a *dossier* compiled of eight separate and independent reports rendered by American officers and non-commissioned officers, all of whom had seen with their own eyes the British major running up the hill, through a hail of fire, and capturing the fort single-handed. Some days later in the Shell Building of Casablanca, where Patton by then had his headquarters, the General showed Meego these reports and asked if they were true. Meego had only to play his part as a modest Britisher and answer: "Actually, yes, I do seem to remember something of the sort..." and probably he would have been the only foreigner ever to have won the Congressional Medal of Honour. But he thought of it too late, and what he actually told Patton was: "When the fort surrendered, I personally was elsewhere drinking coffee." In spite of this reply, Patton recommended Meego for a D.C.M. (the equivalent of our D.S.O.), and Meego was actually awarded the Silver Star (the equivalent of our M.C.) for his part on that day.

Meego's day continued as it had begun: always extravagant, occasionally gruesome, but much more often funny. Returning from the fort to the road he found there, relieving himself behind his car, a short, very thick Frenchman, excessively swarthy and hirsute, in expression a little like Laval. This man, when questioned, declared himself to be a merchant. "Merchant of what?" Of everything, he declared. From the assortment of produce in the back of the car, he was clearly a black-marketeer, which was not necessarily a dishonourable profession at that time in Morocco. Obviously also, from his inimical manner to Meego, from his well-nourished figure, from his confidence, indeed arrogance, and from the mere fact that he had a car with petrol in its tank, he was, if not an outright *collaborateur* with the German and Italian Commissions, most certainly not a member of any of the very numerous pro-allied factions which, however much they warred against each other, were united against authority and in favour of being liberated. The man in the road, on the contrary, declared that he had no desire for liberation and no intention of giving Meego a lift in his car. Meego therefore took it away from him. At the same time he took the cumbersome revolver with which the Frenchman attempted to defend his property. This was Meego's only act of violence throughout the war. During the next two days this car was of great use to Meego, after which it was stolen by somebody, perhaps its owner, from the streets of Casablanca.

Leaving the Frenchman to walk, Meego drove southwards towards Fedala. As always, the Arab inhabitants seemed not only unperturbed but uninterested in their liberation by America; they squatted by their shacks, or continued their cultivations, or drove their beasts of burden through the middle of military operations.

Although dangerous, these operations were one-sided. American soldiers were shooting fast and no doubt accurately, for they are always good shots, but at nothing. There was nothing to shoot at. At the same time, some of the junior officers were restoring control and were bringing their platoons down the road, where the possibility of resistance, or even ambush, could not be entirely ignored, in good, tactical order.

In the pleasant little town or suburb of Fedala, Meego found the cafés, restaurants and shops all open. No Americans were as yet there—or if they had come, they had already gone again—and he had the place to himself. There was one excellent and very modern hotel where Meego chose himself a room and duly registered. The manager, a rigid, unsmiling gentleman, very correctly dressed in a starched white collar, black coat and striped trousers, had been many years in London, learning his trade, and spoke good English. With a caution that was very proper—since events might easily have been reversed, and rapidly at that—he required Meego to complete all the documents decreed by the wartime regulations for a visitor: Coming from where, Monsieur? *Washington.* Going to where, Monsieur? *Casablanca.* Purpose of visit? *Tourism.* Occupation or profession, Monsieur? *Homme de Lettres,* said Meego pretentiously. And now, Monsieur, *vos Pièces d'identité?* Meego produced the identity card that had been issued to everyone. It bore the American flag, together with instructions in English, French and Arabic.

The manager shook his head. It was not at all regular. Meego took out his pistol. The manager, wagging his finger, said: "Exceptionellement, mais tout exceptionellement, Monsieur..." and Meego was in. Having secured his bed for that night he chose a bistro where he had a cognac with some very nasty coffee of the ersatz kind; and then at the largest of the restaurants, where the patron was ecstatically pro-allied, he reserved a table for lunch. In exchange for the black-market cargo in the car, which provided the restaurant with more *viandes* than it had seen for months, the patron took Meego across to his friend the pharmacist. The pharmacist, M. Klein, was a cultured young man, quite delightful, and quite delighted at the sight of an American uniform. Meego wanted some Leica film to replace the cartons which had been ruined by the sea during his wade ashore. The possession of film was of course illegal, but the pharmacist had hidden some away and now, refusing payment, got it from its hiding place and gave it to Meego in an ecstasy of welcome. Promising to return that evening, and leaving his car outside the pharmacy, Meego took his camera back to the beaches.

The scene there was chaotic. There should have been what we called "Beach Groups," and the Americans called "Shore Regiments," established by now and operating "Report Centres," recovery gangs, engineers and signals. They were in fact there but they were not operating. They were all deepening their foxholes. Meanwhile the sea had increased with the dawn and there was now considerable surf. Handling their boats with extreme skill, but with no guidance or help from ashore, each coxswain beached his craft in what seemed a suitable place. While the troops disembarked, the craft were swept broadside-on by the surf and had to be abandoned. And the troops, lacking direction, wandered inland in search of their units.

There was no excuse for this lack of organisation and this obsession with excavation. There was very little danger; nor did anyone seem frightened. They were prompted not by fear, but by doctrine. So precious was human life, that the first charge on a soldier or a sailor ashore was self-preservation. This was what, in obedience to public opinion, "our boys" had been taught in training.

Even so, there was really no reason for it on those beaches. The Naval battle was continuing far out to sea. There were no aircraft over the beaches, not one. A few, but only a very few, shells were falling very occasionally on the soft sand or in the surf, where they were all but harmless. But on their account the order was—foxholes!

Troops disembarking in the surf behaved with vigour and resolve. But those who should have been receiving them, helping them ashore, directing them inland, reporting their arrival, recovering their bogged-down vehicles and salvaging their craft, were all digging. With one or two officers, both naval and military, Meego did attempt a reasoned persuasion. Usually he got no reply. Once he was told very properly to mind his own business. This he did by taking a great many photographs. Being inexpert with a camera, he produced nothing very impressive, except evidence.

After an hour or so of photographs, during which Meego—as

cautious as any man when bullets are about or shells falling—never once had to take cover, he went to lunch at the restaurant. Afterwards he returned to the beaches, just in time to meet Patton as he landed from an assault craft. This little scene was later described by an American journalist who wrote a book* about Patton:

> In the midst of the naval and land battles, General Patton came ashore in an assault landing craft ... he resembled a hunter harking to the distant baying of hounds, except that the music on this November morning was the percussion of battle. As the rifle fire inland grew sharper, Patton exclaimed: "Christ, I wish I were a second lieutenant again."
> It was a beatific moment for this warlike man, as he leaped on to the beach ... In the air sang the noises of war, the crack of rifles, the whirr of machine-guns and the grunt of cannon. There were planes in the sky, screaming with the torture of combat. Everything was violent, so that to stay alive, a man had to look all around, at the earth and the sea and the sky. Across the ground men ran or fell or crouched. They swore and grunted. The sweat shone on their faces. Their backs were bowed. It was loud and dust-ridden and confused. It was war.

To be fair to the author of this fantasy, a reputable war correspondent who saw much active service, I must explain that he was not personally present, nor ever pretended to have been present, with Patton on that occasion. This early part of his book was presumably compiled from hearsay. If so, he must have listened to the wrong people.

Meego is not a man to belittle the dangers or gore of an engagement. Nor would he want, by doing so, to detract from the value of the American decoration which he got for his activities that day. But he is bound to say that there was no battle on, or anywhere near, those beaches. As Patton stepped ashore, Meego met him with Charlie in his hands. Patton said: "Goddamit, Larry, didn't I tell you to stay in your goddam ship?"

Meego said: "Mrs Patton made me promise to bring Charlie ashore with the assault."

Patton said: "So she did!" Then he asked what had happened and was happening. Meego told him and explained also that the

---

* *The Man in a Helmet* by James Wellard. (Eyre & Spottiswoode, 1947) pp. 50–51.

chaos, which Patton was reviewing at the time, was due mainly to the dereliction of the "Shore parties."

Patton stood there, with his two pearl-headed pistols, surveying the long beach. The scene was silent, sunlit and tranquil. An Arab was leading a donkey laden with sacks along the stranded craft. He was filling the sacks with such oddments and trifles of American equipment as he thought were of worth. Nobody else was doing any work. They had even stopped digging, for they had no longer any pretext of danger to dig against. This picture of total idleness and untroubled chaos provoked Patton to say—and he said it then, and he said it to Meego and to nobody else—he said:

"Jesus, I wish I were a corporal!"

At this moment Meego took the General's photograph. Shortly afterwards he took another photograph to record the historic occasion when Patton actually consulted with the Navy. In Mr James Wellard's account Patton "immediately assumed the role he liked best, that of the General on the field of battle. He walked up and down Red Beach calmly and quietly . . ." at which reassuring spectacle men became active and began to do their jobs. "Under his cold eye, they shut out the noise and chaos of the fighting, and moved back and forth from the water's edge to the dumps inshore."

There is an element of truth in this. In fact two things happened. First, while Patton was talking to the naval officer, he saw the itinerant Arab with his donkey come upon a rifle which some American soldier had let fall rather than carry. As the Arab was stowing it away in his sack, Patton sent a shot across his bows from one of his pearl-handled pistols. The result was satisfactory. Not only was the rifle let go, and the donkey sent scurrying in panic, with the Arab after him; but also, and more important, helmeted heads popped up from scores of foxholes to see what it was that had disturbed so rudely that sunny and silent afternoon.

Secondly, Patton decided—and Meego claims a vital part in this decision—to discontinue landing on the beaches and to use instead Fedala's small harbour. Meego was astonished to see how quickly and competently, once that decision was taken, it was put into effect. At the time he thought that Patton's intervention was indeed a touch of magic, as Mr Wellard seems to suggest. But later, when Meego had had more experience of Americans, he learnt that Americans are like that. Like everyone else they can make a mess of things; but they are unlike anyone else in the speed with which they can put things right—if and when they are ordered, persuaded or led to do so.

All that day and the following night unloading continued in the little harbour. Before going to bed Patton walked down to watch it for a while, taking Meego with him. This was after an extremely poor meal in the hotel; a meal to which the unfriendly manager had declined to contribute so much as a bottle of wine until Joe Stiller, one of Patton's *aides*, had threatened to blow the lock off the cellar with his pistol, unless it was opened forthwith.

This was one of the rare occasions on which Joe was heard speaking. An astonishingly silent man, he was expert with his pistols. It was commonly said that if you sent a tin plate spinning in the air, Joe could put twenty-four shots through it before it returned to earth. It was said that, while Patton was the American Army Champion with a pistol, Joe was the best in the world. It was said that he packed five pistols, two being visible on his thighs, two more being under his armpits, and the fifth being in a place that even his best friend didn't know of. Later, in Algeria, it was said that Patton and Joe Stiller had stopped their car on a long journey; and that they were relieving themselves against a large rock when, from the other side of it, an Arab popped up and took a shot at them with an ancient flintlock; and that as this Arab was running away up the open hillside, Patton emptied two pistols at him, and Joe emptied all five of his, but the Arab was unhurt. Nevertheless both Patton and Joe were extremely good shots.

Late on that first night outside Casablanca, Patton with Joe and Meego walked back from the harbour to the hotel. The cafés of Fedala were all packed with American soldiers. These were not clerks or orderlies or headquarters units, because none had as yet come ashore. Nobody had come, this first day, but the "fighting men" of the advance battalions. On their shoulders they all wore the blue and white flash, later to become renowned all over the world (later to be worn by Meego as a mark of exceptional reward), the symbol of the 3rd U.S. Infantry Division, a Regular Division of crack troops who, at that moment, were supposed to be in close contact with Béthouard's hostile French, locked in bloody affrays, edging in the dark towards Casablanca, being ambushed, suffering casualties, sending out fighting patrols, standing sentry or snatching a few hours' rest: in short, they were supposed to be in the middle of a battle, not drinking ersatz coffee in the French bars.

On a corner there was one large café which, like so many, was completely walled with glass. It must have held a hundred or more American soldiers. Patton's little group of officers stood on the pavement, jostled by other troops who were thronging past, while Patton glared through the glass at his men, and they gazed innocently back. It ought to be said that of the officers and men of this famous, and justly famous, Division, not more than forty per cent were regulars. The rest were National Service men, totally inexperienced, drafted to the Division just before embarkation.

Moreover there was no harm in it, because there was no enemy. What was needed to enter Casablanca instantly, that night, to the cheers of the populace, was not an undisciplined division, but the band of the Grenadier Guards in American uniform. Only the French Navy at Casablanca wanted to fight. On land there was no fighting outside the imagination of a few reporters, all of whom were still at sea on that first day and night. The battle that they concocted passed smoothly into history. Meego's medal was only one of many awarded for that day's work.

All the same—since we are offering our modest contribution to military history—it is worth remarking that, if Béthouard had been less of a patriot, less pro-Allied, and had decided to make even a token resistance, all these men who were now in the bars of Fedala would have been either dead or made prisoner. It was not really their fault. Most of them were untrained soldiers who had never even found their units. Spewed on to a beach in isolated sub-units from individual craft which capsized in the surf, seeing or hearing an odd shell falling somewhere in the middle distance, receiving no orders from the Shore parties and only the order "Foxholes!" from any officer or non-commissioned officer of their own, they ceased to be soldiers and became isolated human

116

beings looking for somewhere to go and, as darkness fell, naturally gravitating to the nearest lights. The lesson was plain. No unit will ever collect itself on the beach as a unit in an amphibious assault. The only unit (or sub-unit) which will survive a landing intact is the complement of a single landing-craft. On this assumption every plan must be based—and most were subsequently based—so as to provide a competent and active authority on the beach to collect and re-direct the strays—and almost all will be strays—and generally to sort things out. Meego had always known this and had said as much on countless occasions in Washington. To allay Patton's fury, his white, almost speechless rage and humiliation, he said it again outside that café in Fedala.

By now Meego had been promoted. Perhaps the anarchical state of his command induced Patton to take notice of the one irregularity which he still had power to correct: Meego's dress. "Goddammit, Larry," he said, "didn't I tell you to wear American uniform?" Meego replied that he was doing so. "Those goddam crowns!" Patton shouted, pointing to Meego's shoulder and helmet. "There hasn't been any goddam crowns in the American Army since the Declaration of Independence."

Meego said nothing. He wore that dumb, obstinate expression so often used at Rugby. Patton said: "Are you holding out on me? Are you reckoning, maybe, that an American Major isn't the equal of a British Major? Is it that?" Very quietly he then said: "Judging by today, you're too goddam right!" He was joking in his way, but grimly, with no touch of a smile. "Hey there, Bobby!" he called to his Chief of Intelligence, a full Colonel and a particular friend of Meego's. "Have you gotten a spare set of insignia?"

"In my kit I have," Bobby said.

"Then gimme those there!" He took the Silver Eagles of a full Colonel from Bobby and, with his own hand, put them on Meego's shoulder in place of the gilt crowns. "Git that helmet fixed likewise!" he ordered. "I'll have it entered in Orders . . ."

It was as a full Colonel in the American Army that Meego masqueraded for the next week. It seemed a satisfactory arrangement since, so far as Meego knew, there was no other British Army Officer within 500 miles of him, while his own immediate superiors, Brigadier Antony Head and General Charles Haydon, were safely in London. Secure in this illusion, some three days later, he was standing on the steps of Patton's Headquarters in

Casablanca when he felt a tap on the shoulder. Turning in response to this summons, he found himself face to face with Charles Haydon. "Well, well, Laurence! And who salutes whom today?" General Haydon asked.

The General, on a sight-seeing tour, had thumbed a lift to Gibraltar and another lift in a special destroyer which General Eisenhower had sent from Gibraltar to Casablanca in order to find out what, if anything, was happening in Morocco. Owing to a complete breakdown of wireless communications—or more possibly to Patton's reluctance to report to higher authority, in case higher authority told him to do something that he didn't approve of—no news of the Western Task Force had been received by the Supreme Commander since the operations began.

But again this narrative has leap-frogged events. By the time General Charles Haydon met U.S. Colonel Larry Lamego in Casablanca, the latter had been into and out of serious trouble. It began on the morning of D plus 1, November 9th, when an American civilian called Leo arrived in Fedala. He was a charming man of the international variety, in which Americans excel, and he held theoretically the appointment of U.S. Vice-Consul in Casablanca. The appointment in itself was not particularly distinguished or distinctive; it meant almost nothing, since at that time there were a great many American agents and intelligence officers in Morocco, most of whom had adopted a consular title for convenience. Leo was exceptional in that, when the consular offices in Casablanca had shut down during the night of 7 November, according to plan, and the staff evacuated the city for prearranged hide-outs in the country, Leo had been left behind for various duties. During the previous day, the day of the assault, he had quite openly watched the *Jean Bart* firing on the American convoys, the French destroyers putting to sea for their naval engagement with the American escorting fleet, and a small detachment of French marines ashore showing pro-Vichy and anti-Allied sentiments. He had now motored to Fedala in order to tell Patton that, apart from these hostile activities, there was no other opposition between him and Casablanca and nothing to prevent his marching immediately and ceremoniously into the city.

118

Patton never got this information, because by the time Leo arrived, the General was out and about, driving around in search of his army. Nor was there anyone else with much authority left in Fedala, since the great majority of Patton's staff were still afloat on board the cruiser and flagship *Augusta*, or dispersed like Meego's cabin mate, Red, in various transports, and were not due to be put ashore until later that morning. In fact Meego, who had gravely overslept, was alone in the sun, breakfasting on ersatz coffee with disgusting, grey wartime bread and ersatz butter, when Leo joined him. Leo said: "We can provide you with a better breakfast than this in Casablanca. We've got good contacts with the black market."

The results of the conversation that followed were two-fold. In the first place, Leo and Meego agreed that since General Patton was touring the country himself, he would inevitably reach the very conclusions that Leo had come to convey to him. This persuaded Leo that his undischarged mission was unnecessary and that he would return at once to Casablanca where his presence was important. Secondly, Leo had of course detected that Meego was British, and there was an urgent job which, in Leo's opinion, could best be done by a British officer. This was to prevent the uprising and uncontrolled escape of some 600 British members of the Navy, Army, R.A.F. and Merchant Marine who were interned in a prison camp some 70 miles east of Casablanca. Through his various contacts with the French, Leo had learnt that the British internees, having got news of the American landing, were already out of hand, and that the French Commandant of the prison camp had been frantically calling for reinforcements. There was a real and imminent danger, Leo said, certainly of widespread pillage, and possibly of bloodshed, if the British broke out of prison and dispersed uncontrolled all over Morocco.

They had good reason to be very angry. The survivors of crashed aircraft or of warships, troopships and merchantmen which had been sunk by U-boats, they had reached French territory where they had certain legal rights to be treated as internees. These had been denied them. Instead they had been treated as convicts; they had been housed in semi-derelict barracks which had once been designed for Senegalese troops, but had long been condemned as insanitary; they had been deprived of medical attention and even of disinfectants or the means to clean them-

119

selves and their premises; they had been underfed and given no clothing. If and when they cut loose, somebody would obviously pay for the deprivations and maltreatment that they had suffered.

Leaving behind him a note for Patton explaining what he was up to, Meego took passage in Leo's car which drove straight down the main road to Casablanca. There was not so much as a road-block or control post, either French or American; a few American soldiers who were lying on the roadside observed them without interest; half a mile on, a few French soldiers who were seated in a café scarcely glanced at the travellers.

In Casablanca they drove to an hotel where Meego selected a room with a balcony that overlooked the sea and a corner of the port. The manager here was most friendly. From an intimate knowledge of England he saw at once through Meego's disguise and was delighted to welcome an Englishman. He assured Meego that, whatever happened, his room would be inviolate; so that without further concern for his own comfort, Meego could now drive with all speed to the internment camp at X.

Of Casablanca, where Meego spent the best part of a week, he remembers nothing except that, for an African city, it seemed unusually undistinguished, with less than the usual proportion of native squalor, picturesque or merely dirty to contrast with its occidental concrete. Of his drive inland that day, he has equally no memories except of flatness, a dull landscape, a long, unbending road for many kilometres, and a growing apprehension about what he was doing. Surely somebody would take a shot at them? Surely he was playing truant for too long? But truant from what? For he had no specific duties.

Of the camp, he recalls the high double fences of wire, the watch-towers commanding them, an office block on the right, an argument with the guard at the gate . . . but all this is very vague and fragmentary, as were all those hours, and his clearest sensory picture is of dung-coloured smell.

Of the camp he recalls very little; visual perception was submerged in the insanitary smell. There were, he thinks, the usual high wire fences commanded by watch-towers, the rows of dilapidated huts, an administrative block of white buildings, with the Commandant's office and the French flag, on the right as he entered. He remembers a brief argument at the gates when the guard admitted them with surprisingly little protest, almost with welcome. No wonder! At these disgraceful conditions of this camp imposed on them by a former ally the men had cause to be savage. They were in so savage a mood that Meego had a job to make them listen. In the absence of their officers, who had been segregated at another and much better camp, some 20 miles further inland, they were about to become, but had not yet become, an uncontrolled mob inspired by mob lusts and resorting to mob violence. At any moment the sentries might have been assaulted, and the guard overwhelmed. From the guards' point of view, Leo and Meego must have come as saviours.

For half-an-hour Meego talked, argued and pleaded with the men. It was not easy. He assembled a number of naval petty officers and army and R.A.F. non-commissioned officers and asked them would they take charge while he made arrangements for evacuation. His difficulty now was to persuade his compatriots that, despite his uniform, he was in fact a British officer. Reluctantly they agreed to his proposals, but only on condition that evacuation began that very day and that nobody would be held responsible for the behaviour of the Merchant seamen. These, being subject to no discipline, were beyond the control of anyone and were also beyond reason.

Throughout these negotiations Leo had engaged the French Commandant in a parallel argument. Meego now joined them. He found the Commandant talking on the telephone to the French Deuxième Bureau, or Intelligence Department, in Casablanca. On no account, said the Deuxième Bureau, were the British to be released. On the contrary, those demanding their release—whoever they might be—must be at once arrested.

The French Commandant was old, tired and grey, with a drooping grey moustache. Sitting at his desk beneath a portrait of Pétain, and looking almost as old as the Marshal himself, he reported his conversation with Casablanca. His air was of helpless dismay. What could he do, he asked Leo, he asked Meego. Obviously his was an appointment which neither required an officer of much promise nor was rewarded with many amenities. He would be only too glad to be rid of it, he almost said, spreading his hands in despair. But he had his orders. "Everything depended on orders. Orders, gentlemen..." Evidently—he quickly added—Meego and Leo were not men who would allow themselves to be readily arrested. One could see that. He would

121

be glad to report that they had escaped, if only they would please do so at once. But as for releasing his charges, he did not dare, he did not dare . . .

Feeling very foolish at so melodramatic a gesture, Meego took out his pistol. The Commandant looked reassured. Was it, he asked hopefully, a question of *force majeure*? Meego agreed that it was. With a sigh of relief the Commandant produced a pistol of his own and handed it courteously to Meego. "It is not loaded," he assured his conquerors. Neither, for that matter, was Meego's.

The next step was to persuade the Commandant to telephone to his colleague at the officers' camp asking him to send over a group of officers from each of the three services. The trouble here was that nobody had any transport; the best that the two Commandants could jointly promise was that the ration lorry belonging to the officers' camp, which was due back at any moment, would be loaded with officers and dispatched forthwith. Officers would arrive perhaps within an hour, perhaps within two hours, it depended on the lorry-driver, on the staff at the ration dump, on this, on that. One must hope . . .

This arrangement, not entirely satisfactory, was all that Meego could contrive. Leo had to get back to Casablanca in a hurry; Meego felt that, equally, he should hasten to Patton's headquarters where he might make arrangement, if it was not already too late, for the orderly evacuation of these British subjects. Meanwhile he selected a Naval Petty Officer, of evident standing with his colleagues and of typical characteristics, whom he appointed to take charge of the camp, the Commandant and the Commandant's telephone. A grizzled, burly man, he accepted his charge phlegmatically. "Aye, aye, sir," was all he said.

Before finally quitting the camp, Meego supervised the peaceful disarming of the French sentries and their replacement by British. Already, before Meego could intervene, the French flag had been cut from its mast. But the Petty Officer was taking charge, was already passing instructions to a small group of other Petty Officers and N.C.O.s; and Meego, like the two French Commandants, could but hope . . .

As it happened, his hopes were realised, and all went as planned except that—as had been foreseen—the merchant seamen refused to obey anybody, or to listen to reason. Breaking camp they looted their way at leisure towards Casablanca. So leisurely were some of them that they failed to reach the port until long after the ship which was sent to evacuate them had sailed. So far as Meego knows, they may still be in Morocco.

On their way back to Casablanca, Leo and Meego came upon a gay young man who, they suddenly realised, was in R.A.F. uniform. This is not quite accurate. They had in fact driven some way past this lonely and brisk pedestrian when Leo, putting on his brakes, said: "Hey, wasn't that an officer or something? He looked too smart to be French. Maybe he's British?" The man was wearing khaki shirt, shorts and stockings, all very neat, with the badges of a Squadron Leader on the shoulder straps of his shirt. Having made his own individual break, he was immediately preoccupied with freeing the occupants of the camp which Leo and Meego had recently left. He got into the car which, after dropping Leo in Casablanca, Meego drove on to Fedala.

It was by then late afternoon, and Meego entered headquarters with, no doubt, an air of purposeful haste, a certain panache. He was very quickly deflated. He found himself under arrest. He was told so very curtly indeed by a senior member of the staff who had come ashore that day, after Meego had left. "What for?" Meego asked. He got no answer. He put the same enquiry to several of his former friends, but none of them would even speak to him. Had he been sent to Coventry? Did they have a Coventry in the United States? Even Bunny Carter, even Charlie Codman, even Red, would scarcely meet his eye. But hadn't Bunny drooped an eyelid? A hint of sympathy, perhaps, but not an honest wink.

It was all very awkward being under arrest in a foreign army. What did one do? Oughtn't one to have an escort? One should surely at least surrender one's pistol to somebody? But to whom?

Meego was not without feelings of guilt. He had overslept; he had played truant; without authority, he had meddled with men who were in an explosive state; he had taken the kind of un-authorised action which, if it goes right, is praiseworthy but, if it goes wrong—and this well might—would earn him disgrace and punishment. What was to happen next? Since nobody seemed concerned with confining him, and since arrest seemed to be a spiritual exclusion rather than a physical restraint, he walked down the hotel corridor to the rooms at the end where Patton had his office. In the narrow ante-room he was stopped by Joe, the silent aide, the pistol expert. Joe touched Meego on the arm and

123

pointed to the settee against the wall. When Meego sat down, Joe sat down beside him. Meego asked Joe what it was all about. Silently, but not inimically, Joe shook his head. Meego felt that now he had at least an escort, a prisoner's status. It was almost a relief.

Staff officers, all of whom Meego knew, were coming and going. And still none of them would look at him. Time passed, amounting to an hour or more. Time was pressing, if something was to be done about that British camp. At length, and suddenly without pre-consideration, almost on an impulse, Meego got up and walked quickly into Patton's office. Joe followed him.

By now Meego knew most of Patton's moods, his elations and sudden depressions, his various angers, his noisy fury, his speechless rage. He had not before met the cold, quiet cruelty with which Patton said: "Get out!"

Standing properly, very properly, to attention, Meego said: "I am told, sir, that I am under arrest. What for?"

"Get out!"

"I have a most urgent matter to report to you, sir. It needs your immediate decision."

"Get out!" Patton's voice had never changed: it was soft, very high-pitched, but without a squeak. He often had this high-pitched voice; and when he used it, and when his face also became blank like a baby's and equally uncreased, he inspired hate. This was one of his moods, of which he had several, when he could pass beyond the control of himself and everyone else. He stood up. He might easily have struck Meego. But it just happened that Meego, who by now was angry himself, hit upon the right thing to say and the right way of saying it. He became very pompous.

"I am a British officer, sir," he said, "detached on a personal mission for Admiral Lord Louis Mountbatten to yourself. I have the right of access to you at all times and I am now exercising that right. I insist on making my report."

It was not only pompous, pretentious and presumptuous, it was rather silly. But it happened to do the trick. Patton sat down again and said: "The French authorities, with whom I am negotiating an armistice, report to me that you have been up and down the country releasing dangerous and convicted communists. Twice today I have sent officers under a flag of truce right through the

124

lines to Casablanca itself ..." He was becoming calmer. In the process his voice grew louder and dropped lower. His sentences were shorter, more natural. "The French have sent emissaries to myself. General Béthouard is contacting me tonight. General Noguès is making a bid. All this you have prejudiced by letting loose a bunch of dangerous convicts ..."

"Of *what*, sir?"

"Communists. Did you or did you not?"

Meego told him the truth. While he was speaking it seemed to him strange, as indeed it was, that neither the British nor American Intelligence files had contained any reference to the British internees of the two camps. When Meego had finished, and had explained the dangers of letting loose upon the countryside some 600 very angry compatriots of his, and how he thought, he hoped, these dangers had been prevented, Patton said: "I asked you—are they, or are they not, communists?"

Meego said: "They are sailors, soldiers, airmen and merchant seamen of the British Forces."

"Are they, or are they not, communists?"

Meego lost his temper. He became still more pompous. "I don't know and I don't care," he said. "If His Majesty doesn't care what political opinions are held by members of his forces, what business is it of mine? And what business is it of any American General?"

Patton gazed at Meego for long moments before he blinked, smiled and said: "I guess that's right." Rising again and coming round his desk he put his arm round Meego's shoulders and led him from the room. In the ante-room several members of the staff were waiting, together with a couple of French officers come to negotiate. Patton said to them: "I've just got to give this goddam sonofabitch a big drink, and I'll be right back."

While drinking champagne with the General, Meego got him to promise that he would arrange with the French emissaries for the immediate provision, that same night, of ample rations, clothing, medical supplies and disinfectants to the internment camp. With Patton he made out a list of what was to be delivered. He also wrote a brief note to the Senior Officer now in the camp, telling him what was happening and begging him to keep his command where it was until transport was sent. This note Patton took personally and gave to the French. Meego, although very much tempted to return in Leo's car that night and to establish himself in less disturbed quarters in Casablanca, thought he had better not. He went to his hotel bedroom for a wash and found there a horrid sight.

By now the whole of Patton's staff, his specialists, administrators, political advisers, and most of the war correspondents and official photographers had been able to get ashore. Fedala was overcrowded. In the hotel, officers were three or four to a room; and Meego found that several sets of bedding-rolls and officers' kits—including, surprisingly, his own—had been dumped in his bedroom. There was also a disgusting smell, the source of which was inescapably obvious. Some member of the fatigue party which had delivered the officers' baggage had mistaken the *bidet* for a water-closet. Meego decided first to be very sick and then to get quickly out. Humping his bedding-roll and baggage, he went along to his friend Monsieur Klein, the pharmacist, who most gladly took him in. They made a splendid night of it, and the pharmacist's wife provided a superb dinner. Afterwards they went into the library: a beautiful, semi-circular room filled with books. And about books they talked.

At their previous meeting M. Klein had not noticed or interpreted the crowns that Meego was wearing. He had assumed, and continued to assume, that Meego was an American. Since they were talking only in French, he had no reason to think otherwise, and it was Meego's duty to avoid disillusioning him. In this duty Meego failed. The temptation was too great when, in the course of an argument about modern novelists, M. Klein had suggested that there were many promising young writers, particularly amongst the English. Meego disputed it. "You Americans," M. Klein said, "are never willing to admit that the English surpass you in anything. There are many excellent new novels, more by Englishmen than by Americans, which have recently been translated into French. True, the events of 1940 put a stop to that. But there is one which I received only last week and have only just read . . ."

He went to find the book. Meego took it but was so fervently committed to the argument that he did not at first look at what he had in his hand. It was quite a time before he realised that he was holding the French translation of his own first novel.* Until then he had not known that the book had even been translated into French, much less published in Paris during the German occupation—and in fact on German orders. Meego, a man who can never resist the chance of a dramatic gesture, especially of self-advertisement, took out his pen and autographed the book.

The Germans had not unwisely decided that the book should be published in France as anti-British propaganda. Being a narrative of the regular British Army between the wars, this novel naturally contains a number of remarks, made by various characters, which are unflattering to the British High Command, the War Office and, in particular, the type of General who was then fairly common, the General who looked first at a young officer's riding boots, next at the cut of his breeches, and only then at his face. In the course of translation, before the fall of France, many of the remarks to this and similar effect had been cut by the Allied Censors and replaced by asterisks. This gave the Germans the chance to insist on an "Introduction" in which the publishers, explaining the asterisks, were required to add: "Since events make it no longer necessary to spoil a work of art in this fashion, the extracts that were previously censored can now be published and will be found in an appendix at the end of the book . . ."

The next copy of this French edition that Meego saw was back in London. Its translator, Denise Van Moppé, had escaped from France through Spain without baggage of any kind, with nothing except a copy of this latest work which, since she knew no one personally in Britain, might serve as an introduction to Meego and as some kind of credential. Choosing the escape route through Barcelona she was, like so many others, arrested in that city and temporarily imprisoned. In prison she met another compatriot, Tony Schumann, with whom she ultimately got into conversation. Did he know any English people in Britain, she asked. He answered that he had no English friends except one family that he had known for twenty years, since childhood: the family of Lamego. The first person to read that copy of Meego's book, and to cut its pages, was Tony in prison in Barcelona.

* *Sans Armes, ni armour,* Albin Michel, 1941.

The next day was a bore. There was nothing left in Fedala to eat or drink except American emergency rations ("K rations") which, good as they were, were not susceptible to the *cuisine*, even the *cuisine* of Madame Klein.

The "war" of course had been promoted on the previous day to a great bustling to and fro of American jeeps and French motor cars, all wearing their large white flags. Bunny Carter and Charlie Codman, the only members of Patton's staff who spoke good French, were worn out with interpreting. To relieve them Meego had earlier been given a try-out; but his French was inadequate for those subtleties of the negotiations which, as it happened, the negotiations would have been far better without.

There need have been no subtlety at all: the facts were plain. Béthouard, being a loyal ally, was unwilling to fight; and even if he had been, his men were not. Like the majority of the population, they also were pro-Ally. And even if they had fought they hadn't by now a hope. Some sort of order had now been restored to the 3rd Infantry Division which had sent a Regiment (Brigade) inland, so that it now sealed the city from both North and East. Far to the South, at Safi, the 2nd Armoured Division which had landed in the port without opposition had sent northwards a "Combat Command" (Armoured Brigade Group) which was already within 40 miles of Casablanca on that side. The General should have driven into the city to the cheers of the populace. He should have advanced instead of talking. Since he had been ordered to talk, he could and should have laid down his own terms. But he had also been ordered to play politics. For this he was totally unqualified. He made a dreadful mess of it.

Patton was in a good mood when Meego saw him and surprisingly, unwisely, signed the following document which Meego had had typewritten in French and English: "*Colonel (British Major) Laurence Lamego is hereby authorised to travel in French Morocco without let or hindrance. If anybody is requested and able to assist him in any way, will they please do so?*"

"I would have worded it differently," Patton said as he signed. "That doesn't read like American . . . Don't get me into any more trouble."

This document was necessary since the American and French Divisions, being about to sign an armistice, had now established road-blocks on the main road. But with the aid of his *laissez-*

passer and a white tablecloth borrowed from the hotel, Meego was able to return that afternoon in Leo's car to Casablanca. The city was still calm, and even dull, although the Armistice was not declared until just before Patton was really going to attack, early on the following morning, 11 November. The previous night, General Noguès, who was technically French Foreign Minister to the Sultan, but was in effect Governor of Morocco, had visited Patton at Fedala. Meego missed the occasion, since he was dining in the Hotel Miramar, in Casablanca, where he spent a disturbed night. Secret agents of the British, having heard that he was there, kept on scratching at his bedroom door and trying to report to him. One or two of them were female, but none was beautiful.

In the morning he took breakfast on his balcony. Next door, divided only by a low railing, the French Commandant of the Port was also breakfasting; but when Meego tried to start a conversation, the Frenchman only turned his back—and continued to do so on each successive morning. Later that morning, Meego went out to watch the American entry into the city: a pathetic spectacle.

The whole tragic story is now history and has been "explained away" by General Eisenhower who accepts full responsibility. His explanations or excuses are not valid, as anyone who was there will testify. The French authorities, under the subtle and ruthless Darlan, built up a bogey about anarchism, communism and the Arabs. Anarchism and communism existed to the extent that there were literally a dozen or more anti-Vichy groups, all warring with each other as much as with the official Pétainists, and representing between them every shade of political opinion. A lot were nominally communists, because communism and resistance to Vichy had almost become synonymous in the minds of many Frenchmen. And as for the Arabs, they were neither anti-Ally, nor organised, nor armed with anything more than a very few rifles and a larger number of flintlock muskets.

To the problems of administration there were half-a-dozen different solutions which would have worked. The Americans chose the only one which wouldn't and didn't. They endorsed the authority of Darlan and Noguès, who were regarded by 80 per cent of the French population as the traitors that they obviously were. The results were fantastically ludicrous and, of course, sometimes tragic. Casablanca had to be entered not ceremoni-

129

ously, but by the unobtrusive approach of troops through back streets. This was perhaps just as well, since the American Army had not yet learnt to smarten itself up on active service. Indeed it was contrary to its tradition, the frontier tradition, that it should do so. With chins unshaven and shoes unshined, uniforms creased and soiled, plodding out of step, the Americans caused disillusion and dismay as soon as they showed themselves. Was this the product of American power and invention, of glittering New York, of the world's saviours? The French, rarely very smart themselves, could put up a show which was tenfold more impressive than this. The not unobservant Arabs took note of it: it was at least a bargaining factor with Darlan and Noguès who used Arab opinion as a bargaining factor with the Americans upon whom they imposed almost every kind of condition that Pétain or even Laval himself could have wished.

The results were instantaneous. Many of the leaders of pro-Allied resistance groups, known to the police (who were often pro-Ally themselves) but left at large for lack of proof, were now arrested on the orders of the military Deuxième Bureau controlled by Noguès. One pro-Allied French newspaper which had gallantly fought for its principles, and had survived the whole period of administration under the German and Italian "Armistice Commission," could at last be suppressed. And it was. The remainder of the local Press were instructed that exactly equal space and type must be used for the German and Allied communiqués, the former being received by wireless. When a Casablanca newspaper infringed this rule by giving a banner headline to the Allied news, its publication was instantly suspended.

General Béthouard, who had refused to fight General Patton, was arrested by Noguès, tried by court-martial and condemned to death. The death warrant was sent to Patton for signature. He almost signed it. Noguès explained to Patton, as soldier to soldier, that Béthouard had disobeyed orders in not resisting the American landing, that this amounted to treason, and that unless it were punished accordingly, the whole discipline of the French Army would be threatened. It was the kind of argument to which Patton was susceptible, and he almost fell for it.

Someday somebody should tackle in detail the pitiable apologia which General Eisenhower published in 1948 explaining his political decisions of 1942 and '43. Always the Allied policy was guided by immediate expediency; never once did anybody do what was obviously right if what was obviously wrong seemed to offer a temporary advantage. Particularly disastrous, it seemed at the time, and still seems today, was the acceptance of the traitors Darlan, Noguès and others, on the grounds that there was no easy or obvious alternative. History can already foresee plenty of alternatives: for instance, an Allied military Government, with full and increasing French representation from the Resistance Groups, under the shelter of which the French could have organised and established without haste their own, properly constituted democratic substitute. What was needed, above all, was time for the right Frenchmen in North Africa, or amongst the refugees in Britain, to emerge from their lives of clandestine resistance, to make themselves known to their fellow-Frenchmen, to win their respect and confidence, to get themselves elected and, ultimately, to sort themselves out into an administration which, pending the liberation of France, would have constituted temporarily a French Government. Everybody said this at the time— except those who were in control; and they made such arrangements that the right Frenchmen, instead of emerging as leaders, were thrown into gaol.

General Eisenhower's excuse that he lacked the available force to impose a temporary military Government is not valid. First, it ignores the plain fact that the *majority* of Frenchmen in North Africa were pro-Allied and at heart anti-Vichy and would have backed him. Secondly, the Allied forces needed for the job would have been minute. Plenty were hanging around Algiers and Oran with nothing to do. General Patton needed practically none at all in Morocco, although he was constantly asking for more. But then what General isn't? It was simply that he was not qualified to judge the political situation—and calamitously he misjudged it.

Things were, it must be admitted, made no easier by the presence and attitude in Britain of de Gaulle, whom the French of North Africa wrongly regarded as a charlatan and refused to accept as their leader. For all his qualities, he was an impossible man. Meego met him only once when, on being summoned to Mountbatten's office, he found de Gaulle standing there, refusing to be seated, refusing a cigarette, refusing even to speak. De Gaulle spoke not a word of English and always refused to learn any. He was a champion refuser. Mountbatten speaks fair French, and the conversation, which amounted to a duologue between him and Meego, was mostly conducted in that language. De Gaulle had come to insist—as Mountbatten now explained to Meego—that since one or two "Free Frenchmen" were normally sent as guides and interpreters on Commando raids to France, he, de Gaulle, should be given full details of all such raids before they were actually launched. What did Meego think?

Meego answered that there was a carefully kept list of all people who had such advance information; it was headed by Churchill and the Chiefs of Staff; Meego, and the other planners concerned in the actual affair, brought up the rear. The list was slightly different for every operation, since each would require the help of individual specialists or staff officers. On an average it would number eighteen. If there were a leakage, therefore, there were only the discretions or indiscretions of these eighteen people to be investigated. There would be no harm in making it nineteen. Certainly they could inform General de Gaulle, provided he would guarantee to keep the information to himself alone and not to disclose it to his staff.

For once, it seemed, Meego had expressed a wise opinion which Mountbatten instantly endorsed. "You hear that, *mon General*," he said in French. "You will not mind giving me that guarantee?"

De Gaulle, with his face and voice expressionless, answered: "*Je connais la guerre.*"

"Naturally, *mon General*," Mountbatten said politely, "but that is not an answer to my question."

"*Je connais la guerre.*"

Mountbatten, exquisitely courteous, persisted. After all, it had been the indiscretion of the French Staff, who toasted the venture by name in front of the cosmopolitan waiters of a fashionable hotel, which had led the Vichy French to expect us at Dakar and to refuse our overtures. But de Gaulle would say nothing else, and indeed had said nothing else throughout the whole interview. After repeating three times that he knew, that he understood war, he stalked out.

The attitude of Prince Bernhard, who was in a similar position regarding the use on Commando raids of Dutch troops, and indeed the function of Dutch "Troops," or sub-units, within the International No. 10 Commando, was very different. "It would be quite wrong," he told Meego, "for me to know anything about the operations until afterwards. It would be nice to know then whether they have done well or . . . not so well." They always, of course, did admirably.

No, it is not surprising that de Gaulle could never have commanded the affections and loyalties of the French in North Africa and Morocco. But we found no substitute who could.

There were two interesting incidents in Casablanca in which Meego personally participated. The first occurred when the German Commander of the Armistice Commission was arrested by an American intelligence detachment accompanied by officers of the French Deuxième Bureau.

The German Commander was a man of fastidious habits with a great variety of clothes and a multitude of bottles, powders and lotions. He was also, as a military commander, a very careless man, or had been otherwise preoccupied, for he had not destroyed the most secret of his papers which were contained in a large brief-case. It was a valuable, and maybe an invaluable, prize of war.

The Commander was allowed to pack, a prolonged and elaborate procedure in the course of which Meego, who had come to Morocco imperfectly equipped for hotel life, borrowed—and possesses to this day—one of the German's many dressing-gowns: a robe of deep crimson silk. Nobody, not even the German, objected to this little bit of ignoble and illegal looting. But when Meego took charge also, and legitimately, of the German's precious brief-case, there was an instant and furious clamour from the outraged French.

By virtue of the eagles which he wore, and which commanded American support, Meego was able, once more by the exercise of *force majeure*, to keep hold of the brief-case and to deliver it personally to a Senior Intelligence Officer at Patton's headquarters. By the time Meego got there by car, it was too late. He had been forestalled by protests on so high a level that the brief-case was returned to the German unsearched and even unopened.

It was subsequently discovered that this brief-case had

contained most secret cipher telegrams as well as the codes and ciphers to translate them. It was also learnt that the Germans, assuming very naturally that the brief-case had been opened, searched and re-locked, acted accordingly—on the assumption that the Allies knew its important contents.

The second incident, which was similar, occurred when Patton was setting up his headquarters in the Shell Building. This had previously been occupied by the German and Italian authorities who had of course requisitioned for their use not only the building but also all the office furniture and equipment of the Shell Company. To this they had added in every room the necessary portraits of Hitler, Mussolini and Pétain. Now that the advance party of Patton's headquarters was arriving (Meego present) the French military authorities, under the Deuxième Bureau, were removing everything, stripping the place bare, except the portraits, leaving the Americans to hire what they needed, by private arrangement with the French shops.

Watching this curious scene, Meego saw a couple of American soldiers, commanded by an American corporal and directed in sign language by a French *sous-officier*, staggering down the steps into the street with a large black tin box, locked, sealed, bearing a German inscription and obviously full of official German documents. Meego intervened and told the American corporal to take the box back. The Americans started to do so. The French responded furiously. A French Captain arrived, followed shortly by a Major. The American corporal had been told to do what the French said. Between loyalty to these orders and allegiance to the eagle on Meego's helmet—which was now somewhat suspect, since everyone had learnt that he was British —and not uninfluenced by the French detachments which were now being reinforced at a fast and furious pace, American tendencies were towards the line of lesser resistance. "Anyways, Colonel, sir," the Corporal said, "why's all the fuss about a goddam tin box?"

To Meego's aid there came, at this critical moment, an American top sergeant, an enormous man, a regular soldier, jaws chewing sturdily, red-faced, blank-faced, tough and cross. To him Meego explained with patience the possible importance of the tin box. Like an English country policeman he scratched his head while he thought it out. At length he pointed to the lettering on the box.

134

"That's Heine writing, isn't it?"

Meego assured him that it was.

"I thought as much, Colonel. I got no use for the Heines myself. Anyways," he added, "I knows an eagle by sight, a good, honest-to-God American eagle. You fellows, take that box back!" He advanced alone upon the French. "And as for you . . ." he started to say. They fled.

Meego got busy on the box. Sending an orderly with a message to some of his trusted friends in the Intelligence Section which was still at the Hotel Miramar, he asked for urgent help. Meanwhile, with the aid of the American top sergeant, he extracted the documents, replaced them with files of Moroccan newspapers which had not yet been removed, and corded the box up again. When Ben from the Intelligence Section arrived, which he did quickly in response to Meego's message, the documents were smuggled off the premises wrapped in ground sheets and whisked away in Ben's jeep.

In a couple of hours, when the inevitable French protest had arrived and Patton had given orders for the release of the box, it was ceremoniously surrendered to a French detachment. It took them a further hour to discover and report Meego's trick. What the box had originally contained, they quite openly said, was a complete dossier, made by the Germans, of all the resistance groups in the whole country. It was urgent that the French authorities should get possession of these papers, and so arrest and punish communists who, while they remained at large, seriously endangered internal security. The word "communist" invariably worked with Patton at that time. He spoke sternly to Meego who prevaricated for a while until he had been assured that "inadvertently" Ben had burnt the entire contents of the box. When at last Meego made a full confession, Patton unaccountably laughed.

It was on that same day that General Haydon made his surprise appearance. And three days later Meego took passage in the U.S. cruiser *Augusta* when she sailed for America. Meego was to return via Washington so that his first reports could be made to General Sir John Dill and to the British Ambassador, Lord Halifax.

On board the *Augusta* Meego found a truly remarkable dislike of the British among the junior naval officers. It all came to a head one evening in the ward room where, since all American ships were "dry," coffee was kept constantly on top of an electric heater. Over endless cups of coffee, Meego had to keep his temper, and did so, while half-a-dozen very young officers told him about the incompetence of the British Navy, the dirty state of her men and ships, and what a filthy smell, what an invasion of vermin, when a decent American vessel had to tie up alongside a British warship. At first Meego thought it was a joke. After a while, however, when the only two senior officers who had been present made ostentatious departures, Meego realised that it was all venomously earnest. Their malignance, as the attack developed, was astonishing and inexplicable. For once Meego was speechless. When he ultimately walked out, he found one of the two commanders who had preceded him waiting outside the ward room. "We thought you'd come out with us," he said, taking Meego by the elbow and leading him to the surgeon's cabin. Here there was medicinal whisky, legal provided it was drunk from a regulation medicine glass.

"I simply don't understand it," Meego said.

"Neither do we, Larry," the commanders answered.

"You know it isn't true?"

"Of course it isn't true, Larry, the reverse is true."

"Then why didn't you say so?" Meego asked.

"It wouldn't have done to say so."

"Why ever not?"

"We'll be saying so later." Their reprisal must have been prompt, since the young officers who had made those astonishing assertions were not again seen in the ward room throughout the voyage.

In the course of this voyage the *Augusta* was hit by a torpedo which apparently did not work very well, for Meego would never even have known of the event if it had not caused the ship to reduce speed by a few knots. When they got to Bermuda, and stayed there for a few hours, the British Naval Commander sent his launch for Meego. The way this gleaming craft was brought alongside the *Augusta,* and the perfect drill of its crew, so infinitely smarter than any that could then be seen in the American Navy, was the final assuagement of Meego's pride. It is strange

136

how the poor pongos, so often derided, frustrated and infuriated —although equally often rescued—by the Royal Navy, cannot bear to hear criticism of the Senior Service.

To the Commander-in-Chief in Bermuda Meego made a report which was enciphered and sent home. In Washington he made the same report to Lord Halifax and Sir John Dill, both of whom enjoined absolute silence on Meego, so far as the Casablanca operations were concerned, while he was in America. Any critical remarks by him at that time might, when repeated and repeated, have done untold harm to the very delicate fabric of Anglo-American relations.

By now Meego's American royalties from his first novel had been returned to America and he found himself wealthy. He went shopping, first in Washington, for all such luxuries as scent, silk stockings and extravagant feminine underwear, which had long been lacking at home. At Elizabeth Arden's in Washington, he was choosing for his wife a garment called, I think, a *négligée*, and had described to a very charming and helpful assistant his wife's figure and colouring, at which the assistant had produced a garment which she thought appropriate, when the manageress of the shop, a woman of infinite command and light blue hair, majestically approached. "For whom is this being chosen?" she asked. "For Mrs Lamego! For Mrs *Laurence* Lamego! My poor child," she said to the assistant, "you must be out of your mind. You really ought to know better. *That* wouldn't suit Mrs Lamego; she wouldn't *dream* of wearing it. Get me the shell-pink, the oyster and perhaps the pale rose..." She was of course from Bond Street, where Meego's wife was a regular customer, or I think they call it "client." It was a wonderful sales act, and Meego spent a fortune in that shop.

In New York, where Meego spent a brief day before embarking for home, he learnt more of American salesmanship. At Bergdorf Goodman's famous store the management paraded several girls from whom he selected the one most closely resembling his wife. From one department to another, throughout a couple of hours of unbridled extravagance, she accompanied Meego, not only trying on for his inspection whatever he was thinking of buying, but

137

also and quite ruthlessly rejecting anything that she thought unsuitable. So efficacious were these methods that Meego had to buy three large new suitcases in which to carry home all this feminine appeal. To this he added all the silk stockings which he had been asked to buy by his colleagues on C.O.H.Q.: 112 pairs.

He returned in the *Queen Mary* which, with a strong following wind, behaved abominably. Several of the 12,000 American troops aboard were quite seriously damaged; and—the ship being strictly teetotal under the U.S. law of its charterers, it was only the illicit liquor smuggled into their cabins by the few British officers that made the journey tolerable in those overcrowded conditions of military *mal de mer*. Two adjoining cabins housed, respectively, eight British Lieutenant Commanders and eight British Majors, including Meego. The Navy, a jolly lot, chalked on the door of the Majors' cabin—"The Crown Colony." But the sailors included amongst them one brooding, elderly disciplinarian, a misanthropic teetotaller, who happened unfortunately to be the senior of them all. Having imposed prohibition on his mates of his own service he now attempted to extend it to his army neighbours. When they laughed at him, he reported their alcoholic delinquency to the American military commander and compelled him to carry out a search. Nothing could dispel the smell of liquor prevailing over spilled disinfectant and hair lotion, and even Chanel No. 5 and Arden's Blue Grass liberally sprayed, in the Crown Colony; but not a drop was found. "Perhaps," somebody suggested, "the smell was coming from next-door?" The Provost Major, being a regular soldier and thus well accustomed to inter-service warfare, pursued his search with enthusiasm into naval quarters. One, but only one, bottle was found there. It contained only a little whisky, and that had been ungenerously diluted. It was of course in the kit of the misanthropic teetotaller, the informer.

When the *Queen Mary* dropped anchor in the Clyde, and the Americans were preparing to disembark, they were subjected to the dissertation which was then common practice, on every kind of occasion, in their Army. Two generals were involved in this ceremony, the first having travelled with the troops, the second having been in England for some time and coming up from London for this occasion. The first general said:

"This country is called England which is a part of Europe. In Europe there isn't the hygiene you've been accustomed to. You gotta fix your own hygiene wherever you go. You gotta expect bed-bugs, if you go to a hotel. I don't advise it . . . You'll be going on from here by rail. I understand the trains are dirty and verminous. Nobody don't ever clean 'em. England is like that. You gotta expect it . . . If you go to London, oh boy, the taxis there! You'll split yourselves laffin! They look like just nothing you've ever seen before . . . They're as tall as they're long, and they ain't no longer than they're wide. They come out of the ark . . ."

The second general had listened impassively. He was the senior of the two and, apparently, had not intended to speak. It was not until the first general had given the order to dismiss that the second rose and said quietly: "Just a minute, boys! I've been in this country for just about a year. I want to tell you that it's a great country, the greatest in the world, and you're mighty privileged to come to it. Somebody mentioned hygiene. I've been seeing the hygiene of the hospitals here. Let me tell you it's way above our own. We've got doctors right now in British hospitals learning hygiene from them . . . Somebody mentioned trains. Let me tell you that the folk in Britain have got something better to do than wash trains that are kept running day and night, no matter the bombs falling . . . Let me tell you that in Britain every man and woman, and some children, are getting on with the war. There's girls doing men's work; and there's men, old men, doing the work of two or three young fellars . . . Somebody mentioned the London taxis. Maybe they do look funny when you first see them. London is a great old city, very great and very old. It was old when New York was still swamp and Chicago was all Indian. Some of its streets aren't all that broad, and the London taxi is a little masterpiece of engineering made to turn round in them . . . If you should happen to find yourself in a London taxi when a bomb falls at the end of the street in front of you, you'll be mighty glad that cab is made the way it is to turn quickly . . ."

Meanwhile a couple of Customs Officers had come aboard to deal with the British passengers. "Anything to declare?"

Meego said: "I've got these three new suitcases full of new clothes for girls including 112 pairs of silk stockings, nine bottles of scent and . . ."

The officer bellowed with laughter and called to his mate. "Listen to this, Joe! The Major here says he's got nine bottles of scent, 112 pairs of silk stockings and three suitcases full of clothes for his lady!" To Meego he said: "Now, sir, what have you *really* got?"

"Nine bottles of scent, 112 pairs of silk stockings and three suit-cases full of . . ."

"Come on, sir, a joke's a joke and you've had it. Now then, sir, what is it?"

"Nine bottles of scent, 112 pairs of silk stockings and . . ."

"You will have your joke, sir," the officer said as he made his chalk mark on all Meego's baggage including the three new suit-cases. The other officers were bitterly complaining at the duty levied upon the odd night-dress, the box of half-a-dozen silk stockings, the little bottle of Chanel. Thus Meego made his triumphant return just in time for Christmas.

A pause for contemplation and disbelief. Re-reading my account of the last four months of 1942, I have perhaps inevitably felt that it contains a good deal of happy exaggeration and that not infrequently the narrative, in search of a smile or some other effect, has strayed rather deep into invention. At least, recollection must surely have been bent during the past twenty years, and one's memories are usually bent in only one direction, that is to say in one's own favour.

There had been no evidence, much less proof, of anything so far written, no access to secret documents or archives, no personal diaries kept by Meego in contravention of the regulations. He must rely on generous credulity, and in view of what is to follow, some of it much less easy to believe than that which has already been told, surely that credulity would turn to active disbelief. Surely, somewhere in the mass of rubbish which had accumulated in his country house, Meego would be able to find some scrap of paper which supported some part of his improbable stories. And this is exactly what he did find: a brief-case which he had brought home with him just before Christmas 1942 which had been dumped with a lot of other miscellaneous baggage in his country home at Winson, locked and unopened and forgotten ever since. He opened it and there found an assortment of dockets and papers all stamped, in the most forbidding letters, "MOST SECRET," some of them bearing an even more secret title which it is probably unwise to specify even at this distance, and many of them suggesting that Meego, in his recollection of those events at the end of 1942, so far from exaggerating, had wandered towards understatement.

It is particularly interesting to compare two of the documents. The first, four pages of foolscap typescript, is the copy of a memorandum prepared early in September 1942 at the request of General Patton, for the benefit of all the units under his command who were training, issuing orders and preparing plans for the Casablanca assaults. It is tactfully headed "Typical extracts from 'Operation Instructions' issued in amplification of 'Operation Orders' for a British combined operation." It contains all the lessons that Meego and his colleagues had learnt from two years of amphibious warfare, and it was Meego's attempt, prompted by General Truscott and endorsed by General Patton, to prevent the Americans in their first hostile sallies from making the same mistakes as the British all over again. The second document is a copy of a respectful note written by Meego on 18 November 1942 from on board the U.S.S. *Augusta* lying in the port of Casablanca just before sailing for the U.S.A., to General Patton. In it Meego thanks General Patton: "May I once more be permitted to express my very great gratitude for the wonderful hospitality, courtesy, helpfulness and forbearance shown me by you, by the Assistant Chief-of-Staff G2 [intelligence] and by all members of Force Headquarters, and for the tremendous privilege of accompanying you on this operation and observing with admiration United States troops in action in an amphibious operation." And to this letter there was attached, as Meego put it, ". . . a brief extract of the notes I have taken on which to base the report I am submitting to C.C.O. [Chief of Combined Operations, Lord Louis Mountbatten] in London." These notes, although phrased with a tact uncharacteristic of Meego, contain the gist of damning criticism of the American forces at war. They began: "This operation never was (and never could have been) a militarily sound operation of war. . . Nevertheless, it is felt that the operation could have been rendered much less hazardous and less subject to fortune and political action if the following conditions could have been achieved. . ." There are some nineteen of these conditions, each of which implies, but sternly declines to state explicitly, that there had been a grave fault in the conduct of the

141

Casablanca operations. And the note itself is of significance to this biography in two respects. First, it contains the whole substance of Meego's famous or notorious Report which led, during the early part of 1943, to a somewhat unusual sequence of events constituting between them the pinnacle of Meego's life. And secondly, comparing the criticisms contained in this Report with the Memorandum prepared early in September for Patton (in which Meego attempted to warn the American forces against the operational mistakes which he had previously witnessed) it is interesting, it is strange, it is almost fantastic, to see how closely the first document predicted the second: how precisely Meego, who was in fact only retailing to the Americans what had become accepted Combined Operation doctrine at C.O.H.Q., predicted the faults which inexperienced troops might make and, since they largely ignored the Memorandum, did in fact make during the operation.

For the sake of those who are interested in military affairs (to be ignored please by those who are not) it is worth making this comparison in a little more detail. For instance, in the September Memorandum Meego had written that assault troops should land "in light assault order" with each rifleman carrying not more than 100 rounds of ammunition and two grenades, and specifically *not* carrying "respirators, packs, greatcoats, blankets, waterproof sheets." The beach at Fedala, it may be remembered, was littered with, not respirators, but packs, greatcoats, blankets, waterproof sheets which the infantry had lugged ashore only to abandon them at the first opportunity under cover of darkness. "All weapons will be wiped clean of all oil and treated with graphite before landing, in order to prevent sand from clogging the mechanism and causing jams... Each man will personally clean and polish his ammunition before charging magazines." Almost every American weapon landed at Fedala had jammed before daybreak on the morning of the assault. There was no graphite issued, and American soldiers are or were notoriously averse to polishing anything, even boots, much less rounds of ammunition.

There was a warning about electric torches: "Unless special sea-water-proof torches are provided, all torches will be carried round the neck, as far as possible clear of water. We have had many cases on operation of torches which got wet in sea-water and consequently 'shorted,' lit up and could not be switched off."

142

Meego had forgotten, but now remembers, that after wading ashore before dawn on the Fedala beaches, the hinterland was lit as if by glow-worms by the scores of electric torches which, illuminated by sea-water, could not be extinguished and had to be discarded. There is a warning about success signals and pyrotechnics, that they were undependable, that very few should be prescribed in the operation order, that they should be used only on the highest authority, that success signals must be made by rocket and not by Very light, and that both sides in a battle were likely to be using identical pyrotechnics to indicate different emergencies. No small part of the confusion at Casablanca was due to the multitude of signals used within a single battalion and listed (in a document dated 4 November on board the vessel U.S.S. *Joseph P. Dickman*) to a total of twelve different pyrotechnical adventures, with diverse combinations of amber, green, white, red and yellow pleasantries, with a warning that distinction must be made between the "star cluster" and the "star parachute," the Very light fired from a pistol and the rocket fired by any distracted soldier who had a dry box of matches somewhere about his person. The confusion was kept within bounds, as it happened, by the unexpected depth of water or the potholes in the beach which fortunately turned most of the military pyrotechnics into damp squibs. American warships, French forts and American aeroplanes continued to exchange unwitting signals with each other until the bright sunlight of an African morning at last put a stop to it.

There was a particularly interesting warning about the beaching of landing-craft: "All naval and military officers in charge of craft will be reminded that however intense the enemy opposition may appear to be, it is useless to attempt to change the landing place within a few hundred yards of the beach. Any such attempt will lead to loss of formation and confusion, will show the wake of the craft and will provide a broadside target for the beach defenders. The safest course lies in the speed of beaching and landing." It was, of course, neglect or ignorance of this amphibious rule which led to all Meego's exploits ashore, releasing him from General Patton's orders to remain afloat.

The comparison could be continued further but has become a bore. Meego must be content with this evidence of how wise he was before the event in support of the evidence of his truthfulness about the event in retrospect.

Some of the other documents discovered in the forgotten brief-case disclose the patchiness of recollection. There are strange gaps in it. For instance, there is a Minute of a meeting held on 1 December 1942 at 10.30 a.m. in the Combined Chiefs-of-Staff Building, Washington, with Lieutenant-General G. N. Macready in the chair, supported by Air-Marshal Evill and Rear-Admiral Patterson, and attended by an eminent company including two other generals, another rear-admiral, an air-vice-marshal, an air-commodore, three brigadiers, two group captains and a various assortment of full colonels, naval captains and commanders. The Minute is brief: "Operations at Casablanca—Major Henriques and Major Thompson outlined the operations of the Western Task Force at which they were present." Who was or is Major Thompson? There are no initials. There were lots of Thompsons. But Meego can remember no other British officer present at the operations of the Western Task force. If Major Thompson subsequently appears, how much of Meego's story will be discredited?

However, there is some comfort to be won from a long envelope which was found in the brief-case *unopened*. It is addressed simply to Meego, Royal Artillery, and it is printed with "War Department, Washington D.C., Official Business" on one side, and on the other "Penalty for private use to avoid payment of postage, $300." He opened it with interest but not much expectation of enlightenment. It turned out to be a letter from General Patton which Meego had presumably not received until he got to England and which he had somehow failed to open. Addressed from the Headquarters, Western Task Force, Office of the Commanding General, Casablanca, Morocco, and dated 17 November 1942, the day on which U.S.S. *Augusta* sailed from Casablanca carrying Meego back to the United States, it read:

Before you leave Morocco I want to send you my best wishes for a safe passage and my most sincere thanks for the very effective help which you have given these headquarters during these past weeks. Your long experience in the field of combined operations, and the intelligence and patience with which you passed your knowledge on to us have all proved quite invaluable.

Hoping that we shall be meeting again before very long.

Sincerely yours,
G. S. PATTON, JR,
Major General U.S. Army, Commanding.

And there is one last snippet of evidence which modesty should preclude but which, since Meego seems to be telling such a tall story and asking such a lot of those who are inclined to disbelieve it, he is persuaded to quote. It is the Citation supporting the Silver Star awarded to Meego by the President: "For gallantry in action on 8 November 1942 near Fedala... As liaison officer with a task force during landing operations against French Morocco [Meego] accompanied the assault wave. While still at sea he voluntarily transferred to another landing craft to guide it to its proper beach. After landing, instead of seeking a covered vantage point from which to observe, he chose to advance with the men despite heavy fire from artillery, machine-guns and naval batteries. He constantly remained with forward elements, secured useful information by questioning local inhabitants, and always encouraged and assisted our troops. His actions, performed without thought of his own safety, were a profound inspiration to our troops and reflect great credit on himself and the military service." This somewhat exaggerated summary of Meego's exploits that morning is signed by General G. C. Marshall, Chief-of-Staff. But he does not doubt that this is still very far from the truth.

Returning from Winson (his Gloucestershire home) to London after Christmas, Meego found his stars set fair, rewards awaiting him, and his sins of the previous spring, of arrogance, impertinence, ill manners, brashness, tactlessness—as catalogued by Mountbatten three months earlier—now seemingly purged by his success. Thanks to Antony Head and the General, Meego was about to be restored to the rank of Lieutenant-Colonel at the head of an enlarged planning department occupied with all kinds of strange new projects, which stretched his geography to Formosa on the one hand, and to the north of Norway on the other. In between, there were plans concerning almost every part of the world with which Meego's new staff were dabbling. Favourites for the coming amphibious season were the capture of either Sardinia or Sicily, both of which had been planned by Meego the previous year but now had to be replanned to take account of American forces, and Meego's unique experience with American

145

forces put him for the time at a great advantage over his colleagues and superiors. Too often for their liking they had to wait upon his words. And he had to wait all through January to put an extra pip on his shoulder-tabs, and to hear that blessed word "Colonel" preceding his own name. But first he had to compile his Report of the Casablanca operations, based on the nineteen points of criticism which he had sent to General Patton before leaving Morocco.

It was a difficult task, which commanded a greater literary effort than anything Meego had ever written or was ever to write. He had to escape from his own literary style—a feat which is no less difficult for a professional writer than to change his calligraphy. But it was essential. For the Prime Minister a memorandum could with advantage show some literary merit; but for senior officers in any of the services—with the notable exception of Air-Marshal Tedder, who would pick with delight on a neat turn of words—the least literary flavour in a report would make the whole thing suspect. The Report must declare itself in every sentence, every phrase, to be the work of a man who was exclusively a soldier by profession.

Moreover the document was bound to be explosive. It is scarcely an exaggeration to insist that, at that stage of the war, the U.S. army and the U.S. navy hated each other more bitterly than either of them hated the Japanese. (Neither of them had as yet, of course, learnt to hate the Germans in the least: in the United States the Germans were still considered rather nice.) And if Meego were to put in writing the serious criticism of the U.S. army at Casablanca which the operation had in fact earned, his words would be widely quoted by the U.S. navy in their passionate warfare against their sister service. On this score, Meego warned everybody and perpetually warned himself. Yet a report which avoided criticism would be not only untruthful, but also very much worse than useless. In all the plans that were then being made for forthcoming operations, an assessment of the value of American troops in battle was a vital factor. In the United States the operations at Casablanca were still proclaimed as fierce and bloody, as unadulterated victory and as evidence of the valour and effectiveness of Americans at war. The faith of America in her military power and competence was immeasurably enhanced rather than diminished by the news from Morocco. It was not easy for the British Chiefs-of-Staff to belittle American achievement and capacity when planning jointly with the Americans for the campaigns ahead.

The first to listen to Meego and to believe him were his own immediate superiors, Antony Head, Major-General Haydon and Mountbatten. They looked at the great bundle of photographs which Meego had taken of the Moroccan beaches and could read there the chaos which he described and attributed to American inexperience and ignorance of amphibious warfare. And shortly after Christmas Mountbatten took Meego to a meeting of the British Chiefs-of-Staff in the War Cabinet Office. He can remember little of that occasion, except that he was allowed to talk for thirty minutes without interruption. The two generals—the CIGS and General Ismay—the Air Chief Marshal and Mountbatten, looked steadily at the blank sheets of paper in front of them throughout the whole time that Meego was talking. He had no view of a face expressing reactions to his tale. The First Sea Lord, Admiral Sir Dudley Pound, lived up to his own legends: he slept deeply and noisily. His head drooped forward, chin on chest, while a kind of aquatic bubbling snore was rhythmically indrawn on a high note and emitted on a low one. It was entirely the Mad Hatter's Tea Party until the moment when Meego recounted the message sent from the navy at Norfolk, Virginia, to Patton in Washington, requiring a last-minute change of plan from an assault under cover of darkness to an assault at day-break, when Patton had sent for Meego to show him the signal and ask his advice, and when Meego had answered that the only course was to consult the naval staff immediately at a round-table conference. When Meego recalled Patton's answer—"Consult the navy? I'd as soon consult a rattlesnake!"—there was a quick, muffled explosion from somewhere in the depths of Sir Dudley Pound, a rasping escape of breath followed by the exclamation:—"Ha! Rattlesnake eh?"—as if the Admiral had been listening to every word of Meego's narrative. After the exclamation he returned to his apparent slumbers, each indrawn breath rising up the scale and then sharply ejected in the bass continuing thus until Meego came in his story to the fatal bombardment of the cruiser *Brooklyn*, its lack of bombardment charges, and the casualties inflicted on American troops, when there was no comment except a long period of stillness and silence while it seemed the Admiral held his breath and all heads were for the first time lifted and turned towards him. Meego waited but was shortly told to continue.

This occasion is dimmed in Meego's recollection by what followed immediately afterwards. It happened that the Chiefs-of-Staff were, at that particular time, in direct conflict with the Prime Minister on the subject of the warlike reliability of American troops. Winston Churchill insisted on accepting their own estimate of their proficiency and effectiveness. The Chiefs-of-Staff, unanimously ranged against him, their collective opinion supported by all the reports sent home by British observers in the United States, were equally adamant in discounting the value of American troops who had never been tried in battle nor even subjected to the battle training with live ammunition as practised in Britain. It was thought that Meego's evidence, supported by his great bundle of photographs, might lessen the Prime Minister's obstinacy in this respect; and the Chiefs-of-Staff decided that, if it could be satisfactorily managed, Meego should tell his story personally to Churchill. It was a tricky contrivance. If the Chiefs-of-Staff recommended to the Prime Minister that he should listen to Meego, his evidence would immediately be suspect, and Meego himself would be suspect as a tool of the Chiefs-of-Staff. Therefore it was arranged by devious means that the Prime Minister should learn, behind the backs of the Chiefs-of-Staff, of this young officer, an eye-witness of the Americans in action, who had just come back. If he were true to form, the Prime Minister would then indulge his favourite pastime of collecting evidence not through the proper channels, but direct from some junior officer relating his own experience, evidence which the Prime Minister would use subsequently in his bitter arguments against the Chiefs-of-Staff. The operation of getting Meego into the presence of the Prime Minister was no less complex and difficult than that of insinuating agents into enemy territory.

Warned of the plot and of the chance that he might be meeting the Prime Minister, Meego waited incredulously. It was too improbable to be given much thought; and he was anyway too deeply engaged with Sicily, Sardinia, Formosa, the north of Norway, the Greek islands, the Channel Islands—all the old favourites—to spare more than an occasional thought to all the bright ideas, long nurtured, the proposals for winning the war, even the grievances that, given the chance, he might insert into

148

the topmost level of government. When the summons came on a Tuesday, he was inclined to believe it to be a practical joke. The Prime Minister's staff was incredibly punctilious in its courtesies. A secretary rang up Meego's P.A. and, observing that the Prime Minister knew well how busily Colonel Lamego was engaged at this particular moment, nevertheless wondered if he could spare an hour to go to 10 Downing Street at six o'clock on the Thursday evening. Moreover, the secretary would not accept Mrs Ball's assurance that Meego would be there, but insisted on her finding him, passing on the invitation and telephoning back again. It was astonishing to Mrs Ball, with Meego standing beside her, to find that she had only to pick up the scrambler telephone and ask for the Prime Minister's principal secretary in order to find herself speaking to him in a few seconds. There followed several postponements. On one occasion the Prime Minister had to meet a visiting Head of State and deeply regretted the inconvenience caused to Meego by the unavoidable postponement of the interview. The next day it was an unexpected Cabinet meeting, or a prolongation of a Cabinet meeting, which prevented Meego from taking lunch in Downing Street; and finally, but only with profuse apologies, the Prime Minister's secretary asked if it would not be upsetting the Colonel's plans too much if he were to drive down to Chequers for lunch on the Saturday. One of the Prime Minister's cars would be sent to fetch the Colonel if the Colonel could possibly make this new arrangement convenient.

It was a bitterly cold day very early in January 1943 when the Prime Minister's car, a very ordinary Humber Snipe driven by an army driver, came sprinting out of Downing Street across Whitehall to the entrance of Richmond Terrace almost directly opposite. Meego with his bundle of photographs got into the back, and the army driver remarked that he had forgotten the rug and would go back for it. As the car drew up to number 10 Downing Street, the front door opened automatically and a butler shouted from the doorway to the driver, asking him what he had forgotten this time. "Give us a rug, Joe!" the driver shouted back. The man-servant returned with a rug and wrapped it tenderly around Meego. The adventure was already dreamlike and totally improbable.

The drive took some fifty minutes. Since the driver proved to be no conversationalist, Meego spent the time rehearsing again

149

and again the story that he had to tell and pondering the best way of telling it. At the approaches to Chequers there were surprisingly no military defences, pickets or police in evidence, and only a single sentry, who sloped arms reluctantly in order to present them at Meego, some little distance from the house itself. At the front door there was nobody in sight. Meego got out of the car and, with a feeling that the whole occasion was passing inadequately, rang the front-door bell, as if this house was no different from any other. The car drove instantly away, the driver being evidently anxious for his lunch with old friends among the staff, and Meego stood outside the front door and waited. After a few minutes he rang again, and then again. It was after 1.30 p.m., the time at which he had been bidden to arrive, and the afternoon was growing very dark. After three or four minutes Meego tried the front door and, finding it unlocked, entered. He can only remember the hall as large, gloomy, unlighted and cold, and there was nobody about. He stamped his feet and rapped on the inside of the door, trying to draw attention to himself, with a slight feeling of apprehension that a detective might suddenly appear and shoot him before he had time to declare himself. Eventually a manservant did appear. "Are you wanting anything?" he asked. When Meego answered that he had come to lunch, the man said gloomily that it would be a long time yet. Meego asked to be shown the lavatory, but the butler was content to point down the corridor and tell him to take the second or third door on the left. And when Meego returned from the lavatory the man had vanished.

Concerning the next hour or so Meego's recollections are insecure. He seems to remember a large and exceedingly dark central chamber with a fire burning. There was certainly a tray with sherry and glasses to which Meego, after half an hour or so, helped himself. He seems to remember large gothic windows looking on to the gardens. There was certainly a gallery running along one or two sides of the first floor whence came sounds of great activity, typewriters at work, doors opening and shutting, the subdued voices of men and, suddenly bursting out enraged the voice of Churchill himself. A wide staircase led up to this gallery, and eventually, some time towards three o'clock, a lady came running down the stairs. It was too dark to distinguish her, but she moved brightly like a young girl. When she saw Meego she gave an exclamation of surprise and asked—"Oh dear, have you come to lunch?" but before Meego could answer, Mrs Churchill added—"Of course, of course, how stupid of me, you must be Colonel Lamego. Would you please give me a glass of sherry; I am so glad that you have helped yourself." While Meego poured the sherry, the illusion of Mrs Churchill's extreme youth persisted. "Oh dear, that dreadful man," she cried. "I've tried everything to make him punctual, I even put the clocks forward an hour until the Archbishop of Canterbury made me put them back again."

Meego was wholly confused. He even asked: "What dreadful man?"

"Winston of course."

"Why the Archbishop of Canterbury?"

"He's one of the Trustees," Mrs Churchill said. And with an unequalled and unforgettable charm she continued to converse with Meego in such a way that he was even convinced that truly she was interested in what he had to say for himself. She asked him about America, but when he started to tell her his experiences, she stopped him. "You will have to go through it all, every word of it, every detail, for Winston when he comes at last; it isn't fair that you should have to do it twice."

At last, some time between three and four o'clock of the afternoon, Meego was seated at lunch between Mr and Mrs Churchill with one secretary sitting silent at the far end of the table. The manservant was now dressed as a regulation butler, but the footman who helped to serve the meal wore battledress as a member of the Home Guard. Meego talked and talked, and at first the Prime Minister asked only occasional questions. Soon he enquired about the photographs: "I heard tell of photographs," he said in an almost greedy voice. Meego said that he had left them by the sherry, and the Home Guard footman was sent to fetch them, about forty enlargements of all the snapshots that Meego had taken on the Fedala beaches. The Prime Minister seized them with delight, questioning Meego intently, even angrily sometimes, about every detail of the scenes that they represented. What sort of vehicle was this stuck in the sand? This craft beached broadside and abandoned seemed different from the assault craft delivered to the British from the Pittsburgh factories. How was it different, where, why?

151

Once Mrs Churchill tried to intervene, telling her husband that his guest had not been given the chance to eat a mouthful of lunch. "He doesn't *want* to eat," Churchill answered quite correctly. Meego was far too enchanted with the occasion to be bothered with food. But he did drink his wine, as did the Prime Minister, the latter finishing three or four glasses. Once, when his glass was not immediately refilled, Churchill called: "More wine!" Nothing happened immediately and he repeated his cry twice, his voice rising: "More wine... More wine!" The butler hurried to the decanter, but it was empty. The footman in battledress hurried from the room while the Prime Minister in anguish cried for the fourth time "More wine!" and Mrs Churchill leant across Meego to assure her husband that the wine was coming. But when the footman returned with a new decanter of wine, he went first to fill Meego's glass. "It is I who want the wine!" Churchill cried in an agonised voice.

"Other people want it also," said Mrs Churchill.

Among the photographs there was one of two dead French soldiers, and for some reason this particularly appealed to the Prime Minister. Two or three times he asked: "Where are those dead Frenchmen?" While Meego extracted the photograph for his benefit: "France—that country upon which has been heaped every indignity known to man...." Churchill said as he looked at the photograph. The remark seemed to call for no answer. "I said —that country upon whom has been heaped every indignity known to man," Churchill repeated, for some reason substituting whom for which. "It's all right dear, we all heard you the first time," Mrs Churchill said. At the end of the meal cigars were brought in a large silver box, and Meego took one, a real Havana cigar, extra large, but still not so large as that which the Prime Minister extracted from his pocket. By this time the pace had slackened a little, the questions had grown gradually less swift and less pressing.

Spread across the table were all the photographs of havoc on the Fedala beaches, landing craft broached, vehicles and guns abandoned, the French battleship *Jean Bart* afire and smoking in the far distance, an occasional shell-burst, scenes of chaotic inactivity with soldiers and sailors sheltering in foxholes while more craft came undirected to beach in the rising surf, all the evidence of naval and military incompetence... There were a few moments of silence while the Prime Minister looked finally at the photographs and then hard at Meego. At length he said: "If you could see the seamy side of many victorious battles, Colonel, I have no doubt that it would present a picture very similar to these photographs and to what you have told me."

Then they rose from the table and went back into the central hall, when it was made clear to Meego that it was time for him to leave. The Prime Minister shook hands with him and then asked: "Is there anything else that you would like to tell me or ask me, Colonel?"

What a chance! The bright ideas, the proposals, the complaints, perhaps a funny story about all the British officers in Washington being left penniless for a long week-end while the Pay Corps was on holiday in Hollywood. "Nothing sir," Meego said.

"Now is your chance, Colonel," Churchill insisted; "you'd better take it, for it may not come again. Nothing more to tell me, nothing to ask of me?"

"Nothing, sir," Meego said.

"And have I listened, Colonel, to all that you have to tell me?" Churchill asked.

"Yes sir, of course."

"Have I listened with attention, with interest indeed, but with attention and with patience?" Meego stood bemused. "With deep attention and patience?" the Prime Minister insisted.

"Yes indeed, sir."

"Then go back to the Chiefs-of-Staff and tell them so," Churchill answered. It was a nasty blow for Meego, a sort of a slap, to feel that he had been part of a plot which all the time Churchill had detected. As he now recalls the moment, he felt that he was almost slinking away, whipped, as he turned to go. But the Prime Minister called him back. "One moment, Colonel." And when Meego returned, Churchill said: "Have another cigar, a proper cigar this time!" and he took his cigar case out of his pocket and gave one of his own special brand to Meego to take away with him.

Meego smoked the cigar at once, in the car on his journey back to London. He carefully kept the butt, which lived for many years in the head of one of those ornamental silver fishes with jointed tails. It was only quite recently that an over-zealous Spanish servant found this trophy during her spring cleaning at Winson and threw it away.

Much impressed by the occasion at Chequers, and by Churchill's personality, Meego found that the drafting of his report had been made not easier, but more difficult, by Churchill's comments. Meego did not want to spread among all those who would naturally read a report of this nature—at least several hundred officers on various staffs and in training establishments—his description of the seamy side of American operations. Therefore he tried to modify his report, to examine his memories with more sympathy for his American hosts, and at least to produce a document which could not be used against the U.S. army by their inimical sister Service.

It has to be said for Meego that he is almost physically incapable of writing untruths, although quite prone to uttering them verbally, so that the most he could allow himself to do in modifying his report was to change words and phrases, savage adjectives and adverbs for those less harsh, positive verbs of incompetence and cowardice for negative expressions which implied such easily remediable defects as lack of training and experience, and such normal human defects as lack of zeal and steadiness under fire. And by the time he had come to apply this kind of modification to successive drafts of the report, each one less definite in its criticism than its predecessor, making such charitable verbal exchanges as "lack of speed" under fire instead of "lack of zeal" the teeth of the document had all been drawn and Meego found himself the author of a courteous and flattering account about the Americans at war as already seen by the American press and public. In this form the report would be worse than useless, would be in fact dangerous.

Briefly, public opinion in those circles where strategy was determined and plans made was divided into two conflicting streams: the one emanated from the Prime Minister's belief that "the Americans are wonderful"; the other, spreading like an infection from the reports of various British officers in the United States, that "you can't trust the Yanks." Meego's dilemma was that he did not believe the Yanks were untrustworthy, yet knew from the evidence of his military eyes that they would be of little use in direct contact with the enemy until their individual officers and men had learnt at least something about war from battle training with live ammunition. Yet he knew it was useless to state this as a recommendation, since it was still being stated categorically throughout the United States, as a first principle of war, that "not a single one of our boys must risk his life in training" or "the roof will blow off Congress."

Meego in fact found that he had to choose between issuing a toothless blurb which presented the Americans as the Americans chose to be seen, and which certainly would encourage a false sense of dependability on American prowess, or else a lethal document which would warn its readers that, in a real battle against Germans, the Americans would be almost useless until they had been well and truly blooded. The more Meego sweated over his dilemma, the more certain he became that he must write the truth and describe the seamy side, as he had seen it. But a corollary of this conclusion was that the numbers of people who should read his poisonous or explosive document must be restricted to as few as possible.

Taking his dilemma to the Chief of Combined Operations, Meego was enormously impressed, as so often before, by the extraordinary speed with which Mountbatten grasped precisely what Meego was trying to express. When Mountbatten's thoughts were let loose on a precise subject such as this, it was as if a famous pack of hounds from the cream of the Midlands were hunting for a lost scent. The Vice-Admiral, the Lieutenant-General, the Air-Vice-Marshal cast his thoughts far and wide, expressing them as they hunted along every probable line, foreseeing cause and effect, reaching Meego's own hard-won conclusions before Meego could deliver them and pronouncing his decision in a brief, terse interview of less than fifteen minutes. Meego was to write the absolute truth as he had seen it, but no more than three copies of his report should be made, one for the Prime Minister, one for the Chiefs-of-Staff who could make their own copies within the security of their own office, and a third for Mountbatten himself. Meego was to keep no copy, and there should be none in the files of Combined Operations Headquarters. These were the circumstances, and this was the decision, which guided Meego in the final writing of his report. And within

155

twenty-four hours of discussing it with Mountbatten, the three copies of the report had been typed and delivered, and all previous drafts had been carefully burnt. Even the carbon paper was destroyed under the supervision of Meego's P.A., Mrs Ball, who was herself supervised by the Security Officer.

Meego's document was based on, and restricted to, the nineteen points in the memorandum which he had sent to General Patton before leaving Morocco. There was nothing else added; nothing was included which had not been covered by that paper. But it was all turned the other way round. For instance, whereas Meego's nineteen points sent to General Patton had all been positive conditions which, had they existed, could have rendered the operation "much less hazardous and less subject to fortune and political action," in the Report which he now produced, each of those points was expressed negatively, so to speak, as a dereliction, a lack of efficiency or of some other virtue, even courage, on the part of the U.S. forces. For example, one of the points which would have rendered the operation less hazardous had been expressed to General Patton as "a much closer degree of co-operation and co-ordination between military and naval staffs during all the planning stages, during the assault and follow-up and on the actual beaches." In Meego's report this became a forthright denunciation of the complete lack of any sort of co-operation or co-ordination between the navy and the army at any stage in the affair, concrete proof of this deficiency, examples— such as Patton's "I'd as soon consult a rattlesnake"—and a detailed demonstration of the near-calamitous effects of the U.S. navy fighting one war and the U.S. army fighting another, and the two meeting never. Worse still, when another of Meego's points that would have rendered the operation less hazardous was that "assault troops be given previous battle training with live ammunition and high explosives," this got turned round into a plain statement that green American troops coming under fire for the first time behaved with some cowardice.

It was all fair and truthful, and the report was probably a very useful document in so far as it was read by those for whom it was written. Unfortunately it might be said to have won a very large readership, indeed to have become a best-seller. Exactly how this happened was never made clear. But it was at least established beyond doubt that the only copy which could have been seen by an officer in the U.S. navy, which was what in fact occurred, was the one sent to the Chief of Combined Operations. And it was also obvious that this copy had not only been glimpsed briefly, nor its substance told indirectly from one person to another and thence passed out into the wide open spaces of recrimination, but that some U.S. naval officer had had the report in his possession long enough to copy out two or three foolscap pages of extracts repeated verbatim in Meego's own words. Within a couple of days these extracts, chosen specifically for their savagely critical remarks about the U.S. army, its proficiency and valour, had been spread throughout all the upper ranges of the U.S. naval hierarchy where they had been venomously quoted to the discomfiture of the U.S. army in every inter-service dispute throughout three or four continents. And the news of what had happened came with equal swiftness back to C.O.H.Q. and to Meego's office.

Antony Head was abroad in Africa; the General was in Scotland; and so Meego was entitled to go directly to Mountbatten and to confront him with the ghastly situation that Meego's highly confidential report had become public ammunition for denigrating the U.S. army generally and Patton's forces in particular. Meego must appear disloyal and treacherous to all those American friends with whom he had gone so happily to war. He had certainly betrayed—or so it must seem to them—the real friendships he had enjoyed with General Patton, General Truscott and many of their staff.

It was characteristic of Mountbatten that, once again, he understood instantly the situation and all its implications; that he never attempted to suggest that the leakage was anywhere but in his own personal office, and that he turned to Meego with his invincible charm and asked what he should do to help repair the situation. Meego asked that the full report should be sent forthwith to General Patton together with an explanation of the circumstances in which it had been written, its restriction to three copies only, and the unfortunate accident which had caused it to become all but public knowledge. To all of this Mountbatten agreed at once. He dictated the explanatory letter to General Patton in Meego's presence, and he arranged forthwith for a courier to take the report and letter by air to North Africa, where Antony Head would himself take it to General Patton. No doubt Antony Head, when he went to see Patton, added his own balm

157

and supported Meego no less loyally than before, as if this had been the first occasion rather than the tenth on which he had had to do so. In any event, the result was electric. Patton read through the report, the damning criticism of his troops amounting to verdicts even of cowardice, and he did so while Antony Head waited. He had an excellent and well-trained poker-face, which showed no disapproval. And the outcome of the interview was an immediate signal to Mountbatten in London: "If Lamego can be spared, please send him to my headquarters top priority to help plan Sicilian assaults."

The next morning Meego took plane for North Africa. When he returned to Patton's headquarters now in Mostaganem, Algeria, he was summoned at once to the General's office. He got the warmest possible greeting. "About that report," General Patton said to Meego, "I just want to say that I agree with every word of it, except that you were far too complimentary to me personally and my generalship." He then discussed how Meego could best help to prepare more effective plans for the Sicilian operations, as a result of which Meego entered upon the two or three most productive months of his whole life.

A STATEMENT, 1944

5

I have had this pamphlet in mind for over a month. Yesterday I decided that it should not be written: I could not believe in myself; in the sincerity of passion; in the truth of those simple beliefs, assumptions, conclusions that seem so obvious to me but are disputed by others. I could not believe in myself: I was a crank and an impostor. I was not a writer at all. Quite a good staff officer, perhaps; a soldier with an average degree of moral resistance when terribly frightened by loud bangs and sudden death nearby—but no artist. So I could not believe in myself.

But this morning the B.B.C. has just said that it is six o'clock Greenwich Mean Time, eight o'clock Double British Summer Time. And our fourth child is about to be born in the room next door. There is no disbelieving myself at this moment. My eyes see quite clearly, in focus, and I can recall with determinate vision those little scenes of violent death—and the reactions of my own soul—that were becoming indistinct and incredible. If the rest of the world disbelieves the few paltry little propositions that I propound, if no one in the world believes in my sanity and reason, then the world is wrong and I am the only sane and reasonable man who treads it. For it is a wonderful morning in September, and a child is being born. The spirit of truth is allied to the myth of life to be deliberately reassuring.

Against a pale celandine sky a flock of tame white pigeons executes an aerial evolution. This small group of birds catches the sun which has not yet flowed into the valley but is caught by the uplands on either side. From my window I can look up and down the valley, and the sun has now blessed the tops of the trees, the stone roofs of the great barn, and no doubt of our own home, and reduces the long, shadow distortions that lie on the white-frosted grass. The chickens are on the lawn—their wartime privilege—and their shadows are as big and stupid as goats. A man goes out to feed them. They assault as he sweeps his arm in great curves to scatter the food. They converge on him with the

161

resolution of soldiers who have got to go in now that the barrage has lifted. The sun touches the man's head and reveals that most of his hair is now grey. In the twenty years that I have known him, he grew older but his hair was scarcely seared. This morning everything is revealed. The flood, breaking into the valley lays gold or silver tints upon the trees according to the claims of their species. It melts the frost; dispels the river mists that mingle with blue, heart-ache smoke as it rises, slowly, for there is no wind. But there is a moon in its last quarter high, high, high in the western regions of pure blue. It is now ten o'clock.

Walls and roofs cast incisive shadows: there is shadow and light as two distinct and opposite properties; wrong and right. The trees are now green and blue and yellow, without claims to the nebulous gold and silver, the tinsel claims, of dawn. A passing aeroplane flicks my face with shadow, for I have moved to the terrace beneath our bedroom. The doctor has come in battledress, from a Home Guard parade. Labour is as indisputable as this infinite, aching void of absolute blue that opposes the sun, as the things that one knows, not by the intellect, but in the heart. It is those things that require a writer to write.

This valley is so beautiful, the curves of each hillside so sensuous, that one is assured of man's pure, sensuous, will—and intuitive impulse—in which the intellect has no part. It is a heritage from the valley and the hillside. In response to this impulse he goes— at some times and for some things—to the deep, possessive tranquillity of woman. For other things he goes to the society of men who are drawn purposefully together, dependent one upon another, bound together in love. Man is not born in sin, but in love. And love binds men together into one inflexible will until . . . until there enters the devil of greed. This is the real theme of all that I have, so far, tried to write: the sanctuary of men in manly company. I have not yet written of the sanctuary for man that lies in the depths of woman; because that subject has exceeded my powers of truthful and lucid interpretation.

My last three books have had as their hidden, ultimate theme the sanctuary of men. Each was written from the sanctuary of woman. I have written either from the security of woman, or lost in nostalgic remembrance of what woman had to give. Man's conception of woman as his shelter, his anchorage, and woman's conception of man as ... what? ... there were other beginnings. It was man and man that had, in the past, seemed to demand expression: not the individual relationship of one man to another; but the power and the honour of men who were bonded together in mutual love, to fight a battle, to survive the womanless desolation of a soldier's life, a corollary, the opposite properties, spiritual impotence and hate, that belonged to men who were gathered together (e.g. convicts) without purpose or, far worse, for the purpose of temporary oblivion. A carousal of friends was a beautiful thing. It was staunch. The revelry of casual acquaintances was often bestial.

But one cannot be moved only by the collective qualities of men; and there has always been beauty apparent in intimate friendship between man and man. This was another harbour. If one man could find another in sympathy with his purpose, eager to receive and to give the spontaneous disclosure, a friendship, this was again security, never to be sought, ever to be desired. This is an adolescent yearning. And it is desirable to add that its physical consummation in the form of homosexual intercourse such as buggery has always seemed to me both unnecessary and disgusting. Intellectually I can comprehend its part in emotional fulfilment. Emotionally and sensually I find it revolting because it pollutes the conception and remembrance of that last tranquillity which is near-death, near-oblivion, and which pertains to heterosexual intercourse.

My first book, a travel book, was an accurate, quite vivid, but otherwise negligible piece of objective description. My next book (*No Arms, No Armour*) was more important than its artificial success and adolescent philosophy could lead me to suppose. It was written in the last year of peace and has been described in more perceptive and flattering terms than I could myself contrive. Then came war.

The acknowledgement of myself as "a writer" that followed the publication of *No Arms, No Armour* made me ambitious for more of that self-esteem and assurance that comes with success. That assurance was to be secured: I must always write. I dared not stop. If I ceased to write, my self-esteem was gone.

There was more to it than that. Out of the agony of the pen

there sometimes comes a great peace. Writing was a drug for which, once it was discovered, there was no cure. As one took the drug, the truth emerged; strange and unthought words appeared; passion, long forgotten, was recalled. This drug defied the antidote of war. The craving continued, increased, was irresistibly insistent through the desperate years.

And last of all was English Prose, complete in capitals, for me a newly-risen sun. At Rugby nobody told me about English Prose: I read to escape, to open a door and lock it behind me for a few moments: lock it on those loathsome little boys who recognised me, justly, for a boy more loathsome than themselves. I read books as I drew pictures and was beaten, justly again, several times a week. The beatings were less burdensome than the gibes, the casual buffets and dislike of all those other little boys whose friendship I desired in vain. I learnt to step into a book, any book that came from the library shelf. My reading was determined by the whim of the man who chose the books.

The liberty of Oxford was so entrancing that I did no work and little reading. I edited a periodical—that published Auden's poems, by the way—but the utter tastelessness of what I wrote is now beyond belief. I never discovered English Prose. I never discovered anything very much. I was too busy being aggressive. I was very properly still disliked. I decided—God knows why, and literally no one else—to be a soldier.

The liberty of the Army was like a sea breeze. "Try me and prove me," each man said to the rest. I was found to be all right. I married young and was secure. I read a lot with little understanding. I just hadn't the intellect or the purpose. And I was happy. In the evenings, I read contemporary prose for the most trifling diversion: V. Woolf, D. H. Lawrence, Graham Greene, E. M. Forster, Jack Priestley, Willie Maugham, H. M. Tomlinson, etc. I got a different sort of pleasure out of each but was quite unaware of what each was trying to do or, indeed, that each was trying to do anything at all except write a book in the same way that I rode a horse. There was never a more "Common Reader." Some years later I wrote my first three books, of which the first and third were published.

After the publication of *No Arms, No Armour*, a stranger wrote me a very flattering letter. "You are just worth while my taking

164

this trouble," he said; "but have you ever heard of English Prose?" A little more flattery, a curt "yours truly," a signature and a postscript: "P.S. Read Rasselas."

"What's Rasselas?" I asked a bookseller, and was sold a copy.

"High and —— in —— lands glimmered an Islet . . ."

I realised then that some ten years of solid reading lay ahead of me before I could hope to write a book. Yet I had to write. (As didn't Rousseau have to paint?)

So far, I have had a reasonable war . . .

The child is born, though it is not yet noon. A dark daughter. Brightness falls from the air and is replaced by a hazy radiance of satisfaction. Nothing is any longer incontrovertible, utterly distinct. There is a beautiful sentimental aurora around the world; a falsity of happiness and pride. But one must continue, remembering always that the heart and the sensuous instincts speak more truthfully, potently, importantly than the intellect: no new lesson, this creed of the artist, but one which reason, figures in a ledger, power, the obsequiousness of waiters, the obedience of military subordinates, the response of man to the proffer of money, all so insistently deny.

In retrospect it is easy to see the motives which drove my pen through the pages of my first novel. First, there was the adolescent voyage that a man must make to reach agreement with himself, to answer the first of all questions: which or what, of all these things within me, is ME. Second, was the naïve belief—that may not be so far from the more complicated truth—that ME is ultimately God. Third, was the claim that man is good, born in God's image, born *not* in sin. At the back of it all was the joy that is found in the company of men, *when* those men are islanded from ordinary life, excluded by distressful storms—sorrow, separation, poverty, danger, boredom, and the rest—from the western mainland, the way of living that has grown from the power of gold. The worst of war, that is the sorrow of separation, the annoyance of poverty, the boredom, these things were suffered by a soldier in peace. And in spite of it, or because of it, the soldier in the company of soldiers was a fine and selfless man. This was said in my first novel.

FRAGMENTS

6

A Return Journey

In 1960 Henriques wrote the following, calling himself John Winter instead of Laurence Lamego, but again he writes directly, through a third person, of himself. This fragment follows the reception of a letter from a man called Goodman asking him to take part in a B.B.C. programme called Mood of the Moment; *only the place names and names of people are altered. The facts behind are true.*

It was a blue Aegean day with a December sparkle but John Winter was seriously contemplating suicide. If he could have died negatively, by a sin of omission, by failing to do something positive, he would certainly let himself slide into death. Certainly he wanted to die. But probably he would not have actually shot out his brains or overdosed himself from the large assortment of analgesics and sedatives which the doctor gave him for his nagging arthritic pains and insomnia . . .

From his fine assortment of sedatives and analgesics John Winter had often considered what combination would provide him with the easiest way out. He had white pills of pethidin to staunch the perpetual aches in his back and legs, and ampoules of omnopon and a syringe to turn pain into a dream. From this beginning he could fill himself up with so many chemicals to invite sleep that he could count on no awakening: pale yellow nembutal capsules, the white zeppelins with a blue waistband of carbitral, bright blue sodium amytal, or the cupric blue of tuinal, the twin capsules containing respectively distilled water and a white powder for injections of phenol barbitone *alias* luminal. Death would be soft. His only regret about dying—so he told himself facetiously—was that so much knowledge and experience of analgesics and sedatives would moulder away with his body. His only real fear of dying was of the mouldering away.

After reading and re-reading all the most promising parts of the Bible, both Testaments, and after reciting—but only super-

169

stitiously—such prayers and fragments of prayers as he could remember to compose in sleepless watches of the night, he still had to disbelieve in any continuing after death. There was nothing to come but the mouldering of all the fine sensitivities of the brain into fertile soil from which, at best, grew new life, vegetable life, coarse grasses, thistles, dandelions, docks. Weeds! It was this mouldering into weeds which was an abhorrent thought: this no-continuing; this notion of nothing; this nothingness but earth.

Nearly a year ago John Winter had rejected the lure of the microphone and television cameras, a public name and face, all of which had seemed incompatible with the sincere and personally lit writing which he believed was still within his power. Yet he had been proved sadly wrong... Nowadays he could not get through the barrier of logical thought into the soundless, timeless chamber of the imagination, of invention. It was now an impenetrable wall: to write as he once used to write, and as he longed to write again, meant passing through the barrier in an agony of initial effort and then, in the timeless regions beyond, finding memories and transmuting them into new experience. When one could no longer pierce that barrier, and must for ever remain in the kingdom of the conscious mind and the clock, the experience of writing, real writing, inventive writing, creative writing, was no longer to be suffered and enjoyed. During the five previous years he had watched the light go out of his writing. To the Aegean he had come hoping to restore the light. He had failed. Here was the old familiar B.B.C. envelope, and inside the flattering invitation ... Accept and he would be back in the life from which he had fled, believing it to be a lethal pollution of artistic powers.

He accepts by telegram and as he leaves his island the couple who had cared for him weep profusely. The narrative now continues at the airport in Cyprus where John Winter should have only an hour to spend.

An hour which was constantly renewed by another hour so that it became a legend—this hour Winter had to spend on the verandah of the shack, which, in those days, was Cyprus airport. Here the R.A.F. Regiment provided as sloppy a bunch of men as you could find anywhere in the world, not excluding the American and Egyptian armies. A sentry in R.A.F. blue, cumbered with what seemed to be an unfamiliar implement—a rifle with a fixed bayonet—smoked, not overtly as a French soldier would have done, but surreptitiously with a cigarette held in his cupped hand. This man had many of his buttons undone, including his fly buttons, and indeed more were undone than done up. One of his officers came past and was accorded a theatrical wink.

This man's mates—they deserved no term more military in its implications—comprised a gang who were loading Christmas mail into the belly of Winter's aircraft. They did their task noisily, with raucous jokes and ostentatious laughter, as if they were ashamed of being caught publicly at work. From hand to hand they heaved the sacks which were ultimately slung aboard the plane. Often a mailbag would hit the tarmac with a delicious crunch, a whiff of scent intended for somebody's wife or girl, and a ribald cry of triumph. "Here she comes, Jimmy." Crash and Crunch! "Hoo, hoo, hoo . . ." they were swept into glorious abandon by their own mirth. A mailbag disintegrated leaving a china doll seated sadly by Jimmy. "A fucking doll! It hasn't got it, Joe. . . A fucking doll but it won't."

If Winter had been asked at that moment to define his mood it would have been one of savage contempt for the young men, less qualified for their job by upbringing and temperament than the Wogs, Wops, Dagoes or Yanks who were defiling British uniform.

Just then the loudspeaker declared: "Commonwealth Airways regret to announce a further delay in the departure of their flight CA 47 for Rome and London."

The jeers from the various groups on the verandah and in the lounge behind it suggested that this was one of those flights that had long since abandoned its schedule; one, moreover, in which a long sequence of mishaps had created a state of war between passengers and crew. . . More important perhaps was the coagulation of individual passengers into a company, a company into which Winter and the three other passengers who joined the plane at Cyprus had yet to earn admission.

Those three other newcomers were not a credit to humanity. Orthodox Jews, so orthodox that they opposed the State of Israel on the grounds that prophetically it was not due until the coming of the Messiah, and the Messiah had plainly not yet come, they were young men with an unhealthy translucent glaze to the skin of their unshaven, bearded faces, with greasy ringlets and strange

171

clothes, both appearance and dress pertaining to a tradition no more ancient than the eighteenth- or nineteenth-century customs of the Polish ghettoes. Their wives had shaven heads and wore wigs to avert the dangers of providing men with sexual pleasures in either wedlock or adultery.

Like three malevolent black creatures, more bird of prey than beast, nodding their fur-trimmed hats at the pivot of their assemblage, smug in their triumphant bigotry, these young men seemed to flaunt their power like a private joke. Well they might! Their power was grotesquely disproportionate to their numbers and came from votes and money. Owing to the ridiculous system of suffrage which persists in Israel, the ultra-orthodox religious party holds the balance between centre and left wing and uses it to impose oppressive legislation demanding ritual observances from a vast majority which despises the orthodox doctrine, believing it to be either delusion or humbug. As for money, it came from the orthodox communities of the United States, where these young men were now bound with yet another crop of appealing stories about their persecution at the hands of the rest of Israel— to tap the cheque-books of those American Jews who were both very rich and fairly orthodox. In this situation John Winter could claim a legitimate interest on account of a maternal grandmother who was Jewish, thus making him, under Jewish law, a Jew himself, and therefore with his claim to call himself a Jew he felt that he had a right to be anti-semitic about these creatures.

Looking at these three ghouls, John Winter's mood was of a contempt no less savage than he felt for the scruffy vandals of the R.A.F. Regiment.

Further on, after a diversionary piece about the state and appreciation or lack of it of the contemporary English literary scene, Henriques continues the description of the flight, or non-flight.

Evidently on the long haul from Hong Kong there had formed all kinds of friendships, cliques and cliques within cliques, from all of which Winter felt ostentatiously excluded. For Winter, it was just the kind of personal situation—that of the outcast and nonentity—which he most feared. Nobody here knew him or wanted to know him. Even if he did succeed in finding an associate for himself, it would only be one whom nobody else wanted.

172

Poor John! How he suffers! If he has arranged to dine at a restaurant with a good friend the good friend is always early to spare John the agony of sitting alone in a public place. Nor is "agony" an exaggeration. He suffers intensely from being alone, not because he wants company, but because lack of company must surely (he feels) make him conspicuous: conspicuously defective of the qualities that would provide him with company. This is probably much too simple an analysis of John's pain.

In the old days, before his withdrawal which culminated in his flight to the Aegean, John would have joined any company such as this in the Cypriot airport, as a personage. Faces would have turned towards him and turned away guiltily when he observed them. He would catch them out whispering about his identity. Perhaps he would then let them see by chance the printed label on his brief case—John Winter. The company would have opened out to let him into it . . .

People are very like pigs, and, if John had been a farmer, he might have seen some hope of relief. Pigs cannot abide a stranger to the herd and will savagely attack it. If the strange pig cannot escape and run away, it will quite possibly be killed. There is always a problem for the farmer who wants to add a new sow to his breeding herd, but there is always a sure solution. For, even more than pigs hate strangers they hate being driven where they do not want to go. (And they do not want to go anywhere unless it be for food.) Hence, when a farmer introduces his new pig to the herd, he should drive the herd somewhere, anywhere, across a field, through a gate, into or out of a pig-house, it does not matter where, so long as he drives them against their will. So resentful will the pigs be towards their human master that they will accept the newcomer as an ally rather than a stranger. And at Cyprus, the passengers of that Commonwealth Airways plane had suffered so much from the masters of their flight that they were just about ready to welcome John Winter into their company if he had not been so sure of their unfriendliness that he could not recognise this favourable situation.

His pain and discomfort at being a stranger in the herd were crippling. He could not even look at the faces of his fellow-passengers. He had been too diffident, too resentful, too angry—all these sentiments being aroused by his alone-ness—to review the individual components of what he felt to be a hostile assemblage.

173

Airborne at last over Cyprus, John Winter began to feel almost at ease. The stewardess had found him a gangway seat next to Mr Harris at the very back of the plane, and Harris had been asked to move the coat, hat, bag, books and papers which he had dumped on the seat to make it look occupied. He did it with a great deal of fuss and reluctance. "Be it on your own head, old boy," he said to Winter. "You won't get much peace next to me. Long years of sinful living in the East have gone to my bladder."

"Shall we change seats then?" John suggested.

"Not on your life, chum! I like looking out." Later he said: "It needs wile to get the best seat in the plane. A wily bird is Jasper Harris! I got the tip off a pilot years ago. 'You should see the statistics,' he told me. 'If anyone's saved at all, it's the chaps in the tail-end.' That's for me, I thought, and I've thought so ever since."

The loudspeaker hissed, crackled and eventually uttered: "This is your captain, Captain Fosdike, speaking. There is a change of plan. Our next stop will not be at Rome, as previously announced, but at Athens . . ." His further remarks about altitude, speed and time were mostly inaudible beneath the general laughter, jeers and catcalls, to which many passengers must have contributed, informing John Winter that this last annoyance had many antecedents.

"The sting of it is," said Harris to John, "that the bastard can't hear what we think of him. You can't answer back a loudspeaker." He drew a great breath and bellowed: "You, Captain Fosdike, you miserable, incompetent caricature of a pilot, can you hear me?" Most of the passengers turned round towards Harris, smiling, evidently applauding him. The priest smiled and winked. As a mutineer, at least, Harris was popular. "Fosdike, Fosdike, you footling little fox," Harris continued, "come out of your earth and hear what we think of you! Buy a book on flying and hang an L plate on our tail; leave those controls alone—they do better without you—and come here, *here*, man, and talk to us like a man . . ." But Harris had overworked his joke and lost his leadership. While he was bellowing, even he, whom nobody could have called sensitive, must have felt his supporters peeling off, one by one, as they found his abuse sounding less and less funny until it became distasteful and eventually repugnant. The bellow, unloved and unaccepted, cut short for lack of inspiration, seemed to

174

hang in the cabin like an offensive smell, and there was an unusual, uneasy quiet. "Pack of cowards, aren't they?" Harris said
noisily to John. As usual—John was thinking—he had got himself
paired with the man whom nobody else wanted.

"No!" said Harris, "I gather that nothing has gone right with
this trip ever since Hong Kong. Personally I only joined the plane
at Singapore, me and that smooth type, a doctor from Balik-
papan."

"Which is he?" John asked.

"Doc Hargreaves."

"Which?"

"The handsome gent, fast worker, dark, sardonic face. He'd got
the lovely Sally before ever the plane got off the Singapore runway. I've known him for years."

This, then, was the pair whom John had observed in reflection
at Cyprus. They were sitting together, not far up the cabin from
John Winter and on the opposite side of the gangway, so that he
could observe them in detail. The young doctor had the window
seat. He was attentive, protective, possessive, and the woman
sitting by the gangway was glorious, with long tawny hair flop-
ping on her shoulders as she turned or swung her head, movements made with great vitality, almost with enthusiasm.

"Succulent piece," said Harris. "I'd have gone for her myself
ten, twenty years ago when I was a man."

They had of course fastened their seat belts and extinguished
their cigarettes. The aircraft had lost height and had left the sea
behind when the engines uttered, or seemed to utter, an inappropriate growl, and the plane banked sharply. John opened
his eyes. The port wing was almost stroking a village built into a
hillside like a fortress. The plane then tilted quickly to starboard,
to let the other wing caress a terraced vineyard. Having shaken
clear of the imminent hills, the plane struggled back seawards
and then, regaining height, circled over the sea more casually,
sedately.

"For heaven's sake, what now?" Harris asked loudly.

The loudspeaker was active again: "There is no cause for
alarm . . ."

"Who was alarmed?" asked Harris.

"A spot of bother with our undercarriage. It's not locking
properly, I'm afraid. You may smoke and undo your seat belts. I

175

shall have to use up our fuel before . . ." The loudspeaker whistled, groaned and had evidently been switched off.

The conclusion, lost in the moan and crackle of the loudspeaker, was obvious. As it happened, John Winter had already experienced a belly-landing, with the fire-engines racing abreast of the plane down the runway and the ambulance following behind, and fourteen people taken off to hospital, bells clanging, some of them dead. Another belly-landing? John Winter was of course frightened: he could have closed his eyes to pray . . . he did close his eyes for "Our Father which art in Heaven hallowed be Thy name . . . Thy will be done . . ." But he had opened his eyes in interest—how were the others taking it?—excitement being stronger than fear at this moment, and this fear being such a little one, and so little lethal, by comparison with the dread terror which belonged to his depressions. The little fear of being killed, burnt in the conflagration, was even stimulating, even exhilarating, acting like a shock, a shock treatment, in a numbed personality.

With wonder John Winter found that at last, under the impetus of an immediate fear, he could examine himself. Nobody in the plane was showing enough fear as yet to be of much interest: since they probably had had no previous experience of a stuck undercarriage, they may have been unaware of the crisis. Anyway there was nothing to divert Winter's inward-seeking thoughts, which seemed suddenly to have been blessed with a new velocity. Almost as if he were drugged! His thoughts sped here and there like children in a strange garden: they found an exciting thicket of shrubs, played around it and abandoned it for a strip of lawn, a monkey-puzzle, a walk bordered with catmint . . . they found the dread fear of his depressions and examined it laughing.

Only a little frightened at the imminence of death, John Winter could take out from its hiding the monstrous fear of death which belonged to those depressions. It seemed to him to be a universal fear suffered by all men but a million times enlarged for John Winter's torture.

In the plane he now saw that the notice telling him to fasten his seat belt and stop smoking was lit up again and Captain Fosdike was talking breezily through the crackle and croak of the loudspeaker: ". . . some rather unpleasant evolutions . . . Please fasten your seat belts as tightly as you can . . . You'll have gathered that I believe in taking my passengers into my confidence. So I'll explain that I'm going to climb and dive, several times perhaps, to try to shake down our undercarriage. I should get out those brown paper bags, ladies and gentlemen . . . Nothing to be ashamed of . . . I myself shall be as sick as a cat, sick as a cat . . . But is a cat sick?" Fosdike was behaving a little strangely. "*Is* a cat sick?" he repeated. "I rather think . . . I rather think . . . Here we go, chaps!"

The plane climbed and dived, climbed and dived again. Evidently the evolution was unsuccessful. Everyone was sick, and the smell of vomit was suffocatingly evoking more nausea, but the plane continued its broad, hopeless circling within distant sight of the Greek mainland. Nothing could be more unpleasant. The stench made the plane seem inordinately warm and John was sweating heavily.

Why was he here? Why had he embarked on this journey, homing on his past triumphs and defeats, running after the little enticement held out by Goodman, instead of sticking it out and trying again in Nigros—or killing himself there? Having failed at Nigros, what reason had he to expect any recompense that would bring relief from a television camera in Bristol? Why had he succumbed so readily—indeed instantly—to this ridiculous invitation?

The aircraft banked steeply and bumped. Damn Fosdike!

Now that unpleasant circumstances had made John ask why he was there at all, why this journey, they revived the old question. What happened to him in front of a microphone or a television camera or—but to a lesser extent—any public audience? The truth was, he now suspected, that the stimulus of these media could often conjure up from John's complex and unhappy character a personality with whom he was scarcely acquainted. Of all the personalities which he comprised—for we are all of course many people in one body—this public personality was at once the least ignoble and the least familiar to himself. John Winter did not really know him at all; wished he knew him better; wished he could be him more often and without the external stimuli of public attention; wished he could be him now instead of being the man who was sick and afraid and wanting to pray but could not. The public John Winter could have prayed, for he had courage and did not disbelieve in God. Perhaps he had a positive belief in God? John Winter did not know him well enough to tell.

7

Paddington Station

Lamego alias Winter alias Henriques, is at the end of Winter's trip home, on the way to the broadcast at Bristol, trying to catch a train at Paddington. This piece was one of those intended at one time to be the start of the book.

Meego arrived at Paddington Station on the afternoon of 18 April 1957, the day before Good Friday; a man at war with pain—it would be more accurate to say squabbling with pain at that particular moment—in defence of his sense of urgency: "Go... go... go... Keep going" repeated and repeated in a machinery rhythm: a man depending on his sense of urgency for his life-long search, his pursuit of courage.

He had done half-a-dozen writing jobs in Israel. In Rome he had given a flashy little lecture to a pretentious audience. At Rome Airport they said there was fog over London, so that the B.E.A. plane which made the round trip from Heathrow to Athens, to Rome and back to Heathrow again had not yet reached Athens on its outward flight, so there was no guarantee that it would get to Rome any time in particular or to England in time for Meego to get to Broadcasting House, Bristol, for a job that same evening. So Meego took to Air France which at least took off from Rome, as Air France usually does, but got no further than Lyons, because France was fog-bound also, which meant a very sordid train journey from Lyons to Paris and a very lucky flight onwards from Le Bourget home: and all this with a slipped disc, and to what purpose except for the sake of dashing about for the sake of dashing about.

This programme broadcast from Bristol was a fairly new idea, and a bright one; it went out at eight o'clock every Thursday evening and was called *Mood of the Moment*. It consisted of an interview between a "celebrity" (a new one each week—judging from the number of celebrities we can produce, we ought to be the masters of the world) and Freddy Grisewood who, since he

178

conducts a programme called *Any Answers* at eight-thirty, is thus enabled to do two jobs, and earn two fees, on one visit.

In *Mood of the Moment* Freddie Grisewood has to extract from the "celebrity," in the course of conversation, some incident that had befallen him, or some notion or problem that had occurred to him, in the course of his journey to the studio. (Some touching little scene in which the celebrity saw an old lady bustled out of her seat by a couple of teddy-boys in the R.A.F., and helped back by a horse-tail-haired girl, which made the celebrity remember how, thirty years ago ... and so think ... and so on.) Since most of the celebrities had been writers or journalists of intelligence, or at least of perception and sensitivity, and all of them articulate, the programme had gone with a swing for its first ten weeks; and since Meego was a quite intelligent writer, and notoriously articulate before a microphone, and had moreover made a very long journey of several thousand miles to the studio, it looked like going with a swing this evening. It would depend, however, on Meego catching the 5 p.m. train to Bristol in the middle of a Bank Holiday crowd that evening. There was no reason why he should fail to do so. His plans had been made six weeks earlier, his railway ticket had been bought for him by the B.B.C., and his seat reserved in the corner of a first-class railway carriage facing forwards.

He had only to get to it.

It was not altogether easy. With the pain in his back, and the surgical corsets which he had got in Rome and which made him feel like a cripple, he was gripped by the herd that shuffled and shoved itself forwards, cudless cattle with nothing to chew on except discontent which was very well justified, because they had nothing to be contented about. Where the hell were they going? Getting away from over-grazed pastures, to other over-grazed pastures somewhere else, at somewhere-on-sea, visiting Uncle Alfred, or Mum and Dad, off to pleasure grounds, fun-fairs, amusement parks, holiday camps, laden down with what they had meant to leave behind but had decided to take at the last moment, blankly suffering, moist with sweat although it was quite chilly. "Where's Fred?" The woman with tousled hair and all those unnecessary chins—the whole woman was unnecessary—who sometimes drifted away but always seemed to return to an appointed station on Meego's right hand, kept on asking, not plaintively, not

179

addressing anybody in particular, but just uttering a crescendo, aggravating bellow like that of a cow with uterine itch—"Where's Fred?" And on the left hand there was a young man who was at least alive because he gripped a girl by both her upper arms and, thrusting her before him, sang into her ear—"Put us on a beach, somewhere out of reach, and it spells love."

It said on the wireless, so the taxi-driver said, that the crowds were record crowds in spite of the inflation, and because of the cost of living, so the taxi-driver said, British Railways had put on extra trains, but not enough, and the ungainly cow came barging again against Meego's rump, looking for Fred. From somewhere behind a voice like broken glass.

In this herd Meego had no status; did not even belong to it; had got there by accident. Nobody belonged to it, but it was nevertheless a herd. There was no cohesion except pressure behind and a railway carriage and ten inches of space in the corridor somewhere ahead. Talk about a good-humoured English crowd! This was nothing but a pain in the back and an amorphous mess of sub-humanity with a family element about it, such as a couple and two children, man and his girl, a woman and child, an oaf shouting to a lout—"Larry, Larry. Hey Larry!" Why this vulgarity, when Lawrence is an honourable name? Was there in every age, regardless of so-called classes and orders, this same touch of vulgarity which . . . As usual before an unscripted broadcast of some importance, Meego's mind was flexing itself angrily with words and phrases finding their place in a pattern of discontent.

"Moonlight upon it, oh for a sonnet, spells love . . . ."

There was a "they" at the back of all this. How dare they! How dare they eliminate human distinction by driving us in this fashion? How dare they run their railways in such a way that traffic collapsed when it exceeded half-capacity, while road traffic, having exceeded capacity a generation ago, had long agglutinated into miles, endless miles, of incoherent stoppage? That would do for tonight. Here was the mood of the moment. So they don't have enough trains, so that each shall be less unprofitable; they won't build us new roads, so that ours are the worst in the civilised world, and the highway a stinking crawl of cars and trucks as repugnant as the train to which they herd you, step by step, inch by sweaty inch, elbowing next-door ribs, next-door suitcase, string-bound bag banging by knee-cap, and somebody's breath gusting its halitosis into my face. Fine for tonight! Fred, where's Fred? Meego said: "I guess he's right here, Ma'am."

"Oh where, where?"

"Bumping into my bum."

"Thanks ever so ... Come here, you! Wait till I get my hands on him!"

To Meego she smiled and was at once pretty, almost radiant. Almost not over-chinned. He was all but saved. But here was the barrier. "Your ticket?"

A voice from the loudspeaker said: "There are plenty of trains for everyone—if I may have your attention for a moment. We are running as many relief trains as we can muster, just as quick as we can get you loaded and pulled out, just so quickly we can pull in another relief train from the sidings. We on British Railways are anxious to make your journey as pleasant as possible and we do appreciate ..."

"I asked you for your ticket." It was a very rude voice from a sour-faced ticket-collector.

From above: "If I may have your attention, please, for just one more moment ... For your own convenience, please, be very careful to get into a coach marked with your actual destination. If in doubt, consult the staff of British Railways who are on the platform for the express purpose of helping you."

"Your ticket!" Meego was shoved from behind and unbalanced into a step forward.

"Did you hear me?" A hand was put on his forearm. To be touched physically with inimical intent seemed to set up a chemical reaction in Meego's nervous system and enraged him.

"Where's Fred?" God Almighty, she can't have lost him again. "Starlight our gimmick, lends us a lyric, spells love ..."

Meego was looking for his ticket, searching in every pocket, and the pain in his back was bad. The crowd split around him, heaving and stumbling through the gate to the platform, unpent by the two collectors punching the green tickets to right and to left. "You are holding everyone up. Where's your ticket?"

"Can't you make an effort to be civil? All I want is a little civility. I've got a ticket."

"I've got to see it before you pass this barrier." Inside a B.B.C.

envelope Meego found the ticket clipped very efficiently to the piece of paper which was his seat reservation.

"Just as I thought," said the ticket-collector.

"What do you mean?"

"It's out of date."

Meego saw that the collector was right, right by a couple of days. The B.B.C. must have bought the ticket thirty-two days ago when they sent a girl along to reserve the seat while Meego, at that time, was still somewhere in the Negev, travelling by Jeep down to the Gulf of Akaba.

"Look," Meego said, "this ticket was got for me by the B.B.C."

"So what?" the ticket-collector asked.

"You can see the envelope," Meego said. "It's got my name on the one side and B.B.C. printed on the other."

"So what?"

"The B.B.C. must have made a mistake. All I can say is. . . ."

"I said—so what?"

"If you insist," Meego said, "I'll pay you for a new ticket and get the refund on this one."

"I can't take money here."

"I'll settle it on the train or at the other end."

"You'll not pass this barrier without a proper ticket. Those are my regulations."

"Your regulations!"

"That's what I said." He was a red, frog-faced man with, under each jawbone, a sack of flesh that filled and deflated itself like a pulse. Evidently from his accent he was one of the sturdier officials imported from the North country to stiffen the softer, kindlier and more lenient natives of the West. Like a true North-countryman he knew with pride how to be "awkward." Here were Meego and the ticket-collector, an island of awkwardness and angriness surrounded by the slow-moving crowd which seemed somehow to ignore them. Somehow Meego and the ticket-collector had shifted their ground a few paces to Meego's disadvantage, away from the barrier and on the wrong side of it. The smell of dispute must have drifted abroad, for the ticket-collector's place at the gate had been taken by a substitute and he himself had been reinforced by a tall, pale man with a little dark moustache who stood at his shoulder. This new man had a badge reading "Inspector" on his cap.

"This is ridiculous," Meego said.

It was the Inspector who now continued the argument, while the collector stood silently regarding Meego with bulging eyes like cooked sago pudding, and beneath the overhang of flesh about his jowl the two pouches inflated and deflated as he breathed through his open mouth.

"What's ridiculous?" the Inspector asked. He had pale grey eyes over which the lids drooped.

Very passionately Meego explained the whole thing, explained who he was, explained how the ticket had been bought for him, explained that he was in considerable pain from a slipped disc, added that he was perfectly willing to pay anybody for a new ticket so long as he could get quickly to his reserved seat and rest himself, and he sufficiently controlled himself, in a manner which was extraordinary for him, to apologise and to say that he was sorry.

"Being sorry, doesn't help, does it?"

Meego then began to pity himself. "I am in considerable pain," he said, "yet you are asking me to make my way through this crowd to the booking office and . . ."

"We're not asking. We're telling you."

"When I can perfectly well buy another ticket on the train, or at the other end, if you will let me through now."

The doors were banging; the engine was hissing; the train was clearly about to leave.

"Can you give me any reason why I should let you through without a proper ticket?"

"Several," Meego said. "It makes no difference to anyone whether or not I trade in this ticket and buy another for the same price. Secondly, I have a bad back, strapped up at this moment in a surgical belt; and, anyway, I haven't time to get through this crowd to the booking office and back in time to catch this train, which is the last train to get me to Bristol in time for a broadcast at eight o'clock, which is why the ticket was got for me by the B.B.C., here, see for yourself, and finally, here is my Press Card." Meego held out the dark red folder with the gold crest, provided by the Institute of Journalists, bearing his photograph and his signature. It was taken by a third man who had now joined the others, short and square and deadpan. This was now a quartet, this islet in the slow-moving river of the throng which split astride them. The deadpan man holding the Press Pass asked: "What's this got to do with us?"

"It provides you with a positive identification," Meego said.

Deadpan said: "We don't want a positive identification; we want a proper ticket." He had opened the pass, so Meego pointed to the print and read from it, "*This Pass is recognised by Police, Railway, and other Public Authorities*, which means you," Meego said.

"Never heard of it," said the pale-faced man.

"Never," said dead-pan.

The first Inspector, having closed his mouth, now seemed to be chewing something and stayed silent.

"I've got to catch this train," Meego said.

"Not without a proper ticket," said dead-pan.

Meego asked: "What's the reason for this obstructiveness?"

"Who's being obstructive? It's you being obstructive trying to travel without a proper ticket." They could hear the Guard's whistle from the platform answered by the train's siren and clanking start.

"By sheer bloody-minded obstruction you've made me miss my train, my last possible train . . ."

"We don't want that kind of language, mister. Who do you think you are?"

"You know exactly who I am. It's written on this Pass. It's written on this envelope. I am also a member of the public, and you are public servants."

"We are Railway Officials."

"The Railways are owned by the public."

"We know your sort. You're one of the sort that wishes they wasn't."

"I do now," Meego said. "You wouldn't have behaved in this ill-mannered, oafish fashion under the old Company."

"Are you being abusive?"

"Your job is to serve the public."

"Our job is to enforce the regulations."

"There's no point in arguing now," Meego said. "I shall of course complain."

"I should if I was you."

"What is your name?" Meego asked.

"I'm not giving you my name," said the third man.

"Nor me," said the second. And the first shook his head.

"You don't think we have to give our names to anyone who asks them?"

"We don't have to give our names."

"Not bloody likely." The first man, then, was still articulate.

"You can't touch us, mister."

"You can complain all you like, but you can't touch us."

"Who does he think he is? Asking for our names?"

On their uniform there was no number or mark to identify these inspectors—inspecting who, inspecting what?—from the scores at a London terminus. The three nameless faces loomed through the fog of Meego's rage, all three smiling.

"No names, no pack-drill," said one of them.

They were all laughing now, and now there seemed to be more of them, more and more Inspectors, as if the whole of British Railways was made up of Inspectors inspecting each other, all gathered like blow-flies to a killing, their cluster enclosing Meego with nameless laughter, ringing him with faces drawing ever closer, frog-faces, deadpan faces, degenerate faces, all nameless and laughing. Meego's eyes made a tour of them, searching for a trace of humanity to relieve the horrible viscosity of namelessness that had hold of him in its slimy grip of laughter: "Hasn't one of you got a name?" The reply was more laughter, as Meego heard himself saying: "You bastards, you nameless bastards!" It was the one word to snap the stem of their laughter.

"Who are you calling a bastard?"

"Who's a bastard?"

"Who are you calling out of his name?"

The tall, pale-faced man with the light grey, unfocused eyes and the little dark moustache came so close that he touched Meego. "Calling me out of my name, are you? Calling me out of my name!"

"What name? You haven't got a name," Meego said.

"My name's my own affair. You called me out of it. Called me a bastard; called me out of my name; called us bastards."

"So you are," Meego cried, "the whole nameless lot of you."

"Take care, mister! It's the way to get hurt."

"Hit me!" Meego said. "Go on, hit me! You'd do me a favour by hitting me. Then we'd get somewhere. We'd get into a Police Court. We'd get your names out of you."

185

"Think so?" asked deadpan.

"Think so?" the tall man asked in a soft voice. His pale grey eyes were still unfocused. "See this?" His clenched fist was held in front of Meego's face, just brushing his nose. "You'd never know what hit you, see? You'd wake up in hospital, and nobody wouldn't ever know what hit you. 'Cos you don't know our names, see? 'Cos nobody don't know our names, see?" The fist was waved gently round Meego's face until a twist of its wrist brought a knuckle against his cheek-bone, just cutting it, but painlessly, although he found afterwards that it had drawn blood. "See? See?"

"You'd better get out of it," a voice said behind Meego.

"You might want this again," said the deadpan as he pushed Meego's Press Pass into his pocket. "It might come in handy, seeing it's recognised by the Railway Authorities."

"Get out of it, see?"

When Meego told a friend about it, back in his club an hour later, he said: "I hadn't the courage, I just hadn't the guts to hit one of them in the face. Why, why, why?"

His friend got him another whisky and soda, but he could not stop him reproaching himself.

8

Hospital

Henriques spent much time in one hospital or another during the final ten years of his life. However he did not waste this experience, neither at the time when he became heavily engaged in fighting some bureaucratic battle or other for those in the wards less fortunate and eloquent than himself, nor in his writing.

He was a man who had to possess whatever it was that happened to come his way (in this instance it was his illness) as he possessed silver snuff boxes and pieces of jade, and because he possessed things he had to know about them, to read about them and to enquire about them, and this enquiring possessiveness when applied to his illness caused many complications.

I would have said that in no circumstances whatsoever would Laurence Lamego have gone into a public ward of a hospital as a State patient. First among the many and exacting demands made by his nature on a suffering world is that of privacy. This I understand and respect. Since I happen to know Laurence Lamego—who has always been known as Meego to me—better than anyone else in the world, although I do rather dislike him, I accept his declaration that he would accept any physical deprivation up to the limits of, say, starvation, exhaustion to its climax of unconsciousness and even severe pain, which he bears very badly, rather than the public exposure of those indignities which are inevitable in the diagnosis and cure of grave illness. Yet the irresistible logic of events following upon a haemorrhage in one of the best bedrooms of the Savoy Hotel at the moment when Meego was putting on his white tie and tail coat, reinforced with a long and congested bar of relatively undistinguished military medals, landed Meego within a few hours in circumstances which had cost the State a great deal of money, but to which he would have truthfully and infinitely preferred solitary confinement, provided it was genuinely solitary, in even the most primitive and severe of our unreformed penal institutions. While fixing those medals in the Savoy Hotel, Meego felt a sudden and very acute pain in his stomach. Before he could even tear off his stiff shirt and white waistcoat, and long before he could get through into the bathroom with its glamorous sunset view up the River Thames, he had begun to vomit. It lasted only a few seconds and it took the pain with it, leaving only a strange bruised feeling round his midriff, collecting from among his memories the after-effects of falling almost into a booby trap in Caltanisetto, Sicily, August 1943, in fact a part of those very events which he had been about to celebrate eighteen years later under Royal patronage.

Meego was not often sick. Moreover he was puzzled on this occasion not only by his customary abstinence, during periods of work, which had kept him from either food or drink all day, but also and more particularly by the fact that he had drunk no coffee since the previous night. Yet the stain which splashed across his white waistcoat resembled closely in colour and texture the grounds of coffee, so very closely indeed that it could scarcely be anything else. In five, ten or perhaps fifteen seconds Meego had drawn again from among his recollections a very similar mishap to a girl in a taxi. Long, long ago. Even before the war, even long before the war, and the girl was long dead. Consequently Meego got to the telephone and asked for the hotel doctor.

The young man came quickly and evidently knew his business. He seemed slightly hurt rather than surprised that Meego should pronounce his own diagnosis. He also showed enough sense and perception not to argue, nor even to offer much reassurance, but contented himself with a technical correction which, by its quick score of a badly-needed point, reduced his patient to manageable co-operation. "To be more precise," he told Meego, "it is haenatenesis: in other words, bleeding from the stomach."

"Let us not be pedantic," Meego answered. The girl in the taxi had suffered, so he had been told afterwards, from a haemorrhage. It had taken her more than a year to die from cancer of the stomach. Meego, always anxious to be heroic when it cost noth- ing, was reluctant to surrender his cancer. The young doctor was more than reluctant to admit it. "Slight bleeding of the stomach . . . due to any one of a score of conditions, many of which com- pletely trivial. Nevertheless . . ."

They compromised with a telephone call by the young doctor, during which Meego experienced a state of detachment, not un-

188

familiar, liberating the mind enough for him to find himself somehow lying on the bed composing a letter to *The Times* about
British Railways: the people called Inspectors, grossly unhelpful
to the public, inspecting apparently nobody, sporting waxed
moustaches, lacked identifying numbers and declined to give their
names: they were nameless little dictators. Meego, armed with
Press Pass which specifically stated that it was recognised by the
Railway Authorities and Police, had been treated as an ordinary
member of the public who rated no consideration. At his subsequent interview with the Stationmaster, this official had stated that
he could take no action whatsoever, since the offending Inspectors,
five in all, ringing themselves round Meego and even offering
him physical violence, could never be identified. What a subject!

By the time the letter was half composed, the doctor had made
half a dozen telephone calls which Meego had neglected to over-
hear. Anyway, the doctor knew his job so well that had Meego
been listening, his one side of the conversation would have con-
veyed little. He registered only that the young doctor wished him
to see a consultant, a certain Mr Merivale, an unequalled expert
in something or other—Meego failed to discover what. He was by
then disinterested.

It was the Assistant Manager of the Savoy Hotel who really
settled affairs, having known Meego at Scapa Flow and Sullom
Voe in the Shetlands during the early years of the war in his
Commando periods. Consequently, in his detachment, Meego
accepted the arrangements made for him.

The ambulance-men who very shortly arrived were as kind and
helpful as Quakers. Somehow they packed for Meego a small
suitcase containing what they said he would need. They got him
into pyjamas and tucked him up on a stretcher as if he had been a
child, and he noticed nothing until they drew up at St Matthew's
Hospital, an L.C.C. establishment which, unknown to Meego,
had formerly been called The Cancer Infirmary. This was the
place chosen by the hotel doctor because of a devoted confidence
in a certain consultant there, a Mr Thomas Bax. Meego was not to
know that it would be three days before he got a sight of Mr Bax.

It was at St Matthew's that the indignities began, since these
modern teaching hospitals remotely controlled by a strictly non-
political, strictly egalitarian-minded, committee of persons who
in the majority were socialists by inclination, and controlled

189

mainly for the benefit of the unskilled staff so that they consequently attracted nobody of much calibre. Although the Savoy
Hotel doctor had arranged affairs with this celebrated if unknown
Mr Thomas Bax, and due instructions had been transmitted to
the Registrar, the hour was doctors' dinner time, the place
appeared to be in a state of organised abandon, and Meego found
himself apparently clamped to a hospital stretcher—too small for
a man of over six foot, and too narrow for anyone—attended by
nobody, befriended only by a semi-conscious young adolescent
who proudly claimed to a fractured skull while "doing a ton" on a
motor-bicycle, but otherwise instilled with the feeling that his
only function was to justify the expenditure of State funds on a
posse of educationally sub-normal employees clustered around a
television set (the volume tuned to the maximum) issuing a programme entitled "Emergency Ward 10." Fortunately for Meego,
his distaste for these general circumstances provoked a second
haemorrhage or haenatenesis which came to the notice of a dear
little jet black girl in nurse's uniform whose huge eyes emitted
intense and tempered concern. Again there followed a period of
detachment during which Meego was apparently transferred to a
ward rocked by megaton reception of strange songs, later identified as rock-'n-roll, evidently of immense popularity, delivered by
persons of indeterminate sex. It was the man who had done a ton
with no greater damage to himself than a fractured skull who
helped the little black girl tuck Meego into bed. There were
apparently no other nurses, nor indeed any other staff in evidence,
since this dinner-hour of the doctors coincided with the tea-break
for such females, married women who had formerly endured
some kind of medical training, who did a few hours work on the
shift, principally from 6 p.m. until 10. A woman dressed in dark
blue, and addressed as "Sister" was heavily engaged filling in a
large book resembling a ledger. The records of this place were
going to be correct, if nothing else.

By midnight, when Meego should have made his speech to the
reunion of Special Service troops engaged in Sicily by the uneasy
Allies—this honour having been conferred on him by reason not
of his wartime achievements, but of his reputation—whereafter
he would have been greeted with the utmost cordiality by men
whose faces were long forgotten, was duly installed with his left
arm anchored to a blood-transfusion apparatus, his right hand

deprived of its essential cigarette, his indignation de-activated by a quarter of a grain of morphia, and his mind, which would normally have been untouched by this minimum dose of a drug to which he was only too accustomed, had yielded to exhaustion and the side-effects of exasperation to re-engage itself with the Editor of *The Times*.

The night passed peacefully enough, the scant staff failing to observe that for Meego it was sleepless. Every few hours they renewed his morphine injection, and occasionally somebody took his pulse and spared a glance for the robust if primitive apparatus of his blood drip. From his many and diverse experiences in hospital, since he is a man prone to physical accidents, he knew very well that a nurse should have visited him each quarter of an hour, but was glad to be spared these visitations and equally to conserve his legitimate protest for ammunition on a later occasion. Unconsciously he was preparing for battle. While determined to transfer himself into a private ward, he was no less bent on reforming an establishment which plainly needed the reincarnation of a militant Florence Nightingale. The expenditure of public money on this collection of Dickensian staff was insidiously firing his mind with indignations rendering his own dilemma almost irrelevant. With the belated and overdue dawn, no more punctual than British Railways, his circumstances and afflictions would doubtless monopolise the attentions of the senior medical staff, presumably diurnal since they had hitherto been conspicuously absent, no less than the gossip writers of the national press. In another hour they would be waking him up to wash him: pleasurably anticipated as a just cause for protest and thus reducing him to a deep sleep of no less than twenty minutes. It allowed the night nurse or Sister, whoever and wherever she might be, to record in her Report Book that he had spent "a good night."

This misled Sister Armstrong, who arrived like a calm typhoon at eight o'clock, into the mental classification of Meego as "comfortable," a patient due for initial assessment but otherwise needing no attention from her almost non-existent staff beyond the routine furbishing of one who had to be presented as clean, immaculate, comfortable and composed as a corpse after it had been processed by what is known in hospitals by the nurses as "last offices." Before she had realised that anything in the least unusual had been insinuated into her ward during the night, she

191

was involved in the bloody battle of the bed-pan. Being a woman of very great humanity and experience she accepted the compromise of a commode. Indeed, if Sister Armstrong had been supported by just a Staff Nurse endowed with the slight skill of a first-year probationer in a good teaching hospital, she would have got control of Meego by the sheer arrogance of her authority. But even a Sister Armstrong cannot personally tend the forty occupants of an over-crowded ward bedded four feet apart in conditions approved by an L.C.C. committee which had spared little time for the study of the Crimea. In fact Sister Armstrong was three parts a saint, having insisted on surrendering all the power, privilege, responsibility and repute of a Ward Sister in the eminent teaching hospital where she had qualified in order to serve in the medical slums of these L.C.C. institutions. While she had not yet acquired an indisputable halo, there was visible to some of her patients a prismatic phenomenon resembling an aura of selfless dedication and just plain love.

Although her hair was iron grey, Sister Armstrong somehow gave the impression that a girl was alive in her person, liberal with humour or even a kind of fun which seemed to assume as not worth mentioning the tender if firm competence and lavish experience of one who, from her adolescent years, had been a nurse by vocation. On her left breast there was pinned a dingy medal ribbon, long in need of renewal, much scarcer than the D.S.O. which it resembled and equalled in precedence, awarded for gallantry in action but so rarely that few if any hospital staff nowadays suspect its identity or respect its significance. Meego did. Consequently he, opening his eyes to the lady who stood tall and calm at the foot of his bed, was able to lead with the first remark that came into his head: "Good morning, Sister! It's nice to see you've been fighting." She smiled slowly, having been watching him already for the two or three seconds of silence which gave the illusion, rare and precious in hospital, of unhurried interest in his circumstances and himself. She came round the bed, standing beside him now, and her hand seemed to move with instinctive purpose rather than design as she touched the blood-transfusion apparatus and then a pillow, adding that fraction of extra comfort which amounts to comforting, until she was holding his wrist, but as if it were his hand, although she was of course feeling his pulse as she asked: "So you've been in the wars

192

yourself?" It was clever, he thought, since she was obviously fishing for information, as was her job, to assess a new charge, while answering him in kind yet surely without recognising his allusion to her strap of ribbon or guessing what he had meant.

"I've had it," he said with satisfaction. "Cancer."

"Fiddlesticks! It's much more likely to be a peptic ulcer."

"I'm not an overworked tycoon."

"How would you describe yourself, by your occupation? You said some very funny things to the Night Sister when she took your particulars. You called yourself a charlatan."

"Very accurate."

"And your next of kin, your wife, you gave her address as the Windward Islands?"

"Again, possibly not inaccurate. She ran off with an ornithologist on the way to the Antarctic."

"I'm so sorry."

"I'm not."

"Mr Lamego, you may be here for quite a time, you know. Is there not somebody whom we should inform?"

"It would be kind of you to tell my literary agent." He gave the name and address. "Otherwise, I would prefer to keep this to myself."

"Would I be wrong in addressing you as Colonel Lamego?" she asked. "Colonel Laurence Lamego?"

The question gave him great pleasure: after so many quick years but infinitely slow days of intermittent illness while his work declined and diminished, he had slid from the notoriety which is nowadays known as fame to the obscurity which was his due. "You have read my books?" he asked.

"On the wireless mostly I've heard you . . . I like what you say, very much, sometimes."

"Not very often nowadays. In the old days . . ."

She touched her grey hair. It was much the same colour as his own. Unable to stay with him any longer, for she was disastrously overworked in this place, she had to tell him that there seemed little chance of getting him into a private room in the immediate future. This evidently distressed him greatly, so that she became evasive. Not tomorrow, nor probably the next day, nor . . . The waiting list was long. Then she was gone, continuing on her round of the ward.